Sports Heroines
on Film

D1557475

Sports Heroines on Film

A Critical Study of Cinematic Women Athletes, Coaches and Owners

VIRIDIANA LIEBERMAN

McFarland & Company, Inc., Publishers

Jefferson, North Carolina

LIBRARY OF CONGRESS CATALOGUING-IN-PUBLICATION DATA

Lieberman, Viridiana, 1982–
    Sports heroines on film : a critical study of cinematic women
athletes, coaches and owners / Viridiana Lieberman.
        p.   cm.
    Includes bibliographical references and index.

    ISBN 978-0-7864-7661-9 (softcover : acid free paper) ∞
    ISBN 978-1-4766-1693-3 (ebook)

    1. Sports films—History and criticism.   2. Heroines in
motion pictures.   3. Women in motion pictures.   I. Title.
PN1995.9.S67L53 2015
791.43'6579—dc23   2014038969

BRITISH LIBRARY CATALOGUING DATA ARE AVAILABLE

© 2015 Viridiana Lieberman. All rights reserved

*No part of this book may be reproduced or transmitted in any form
or by any means, electronic or mechanical, including photocopying
or recording, or by any information storage and retrieval system,
without permission in writing from the publisher.*

On the cover: Michelle Rodriguez in *Girlfight* (2000), © Screen
Gems/Photofest

Printed in the United States of America

McFarland & Company, Inc., Publishers
    Box 611, Jefferson, North Carolina 28640
        www.mcfarlandpub.com

This book is dedicated
to all the fiction and nonfiction women
playing and working in sports.
May your stories forever be celebrated
for their athletic glory.

Table of Contents

Acknowledgments

Every sport requires the support of a team. Whether you are an individual athlete or amongst teammates, there is an important element of guidance to help you achieve success. This book is no different.

None of this would be possible without my trainer, Lindsey Averill, who taught me the skills to be victorious, challenged me with daily critical conversation and instilled the confidence necessary to play my best.

I'd like to thank my coaching staff: my head coach, Dr. Jane Caputi, for igniting the passion that inspired this book and educating the knowledge to complete it; and my assistant coaches, Dr. Christopher Robe and Dr. Christine Scodari, for expanding my experience in cinematic studies that has now fostered this work to be a direct stepping stone towards my future film projects.

It's important I give recognition to the arena I played in, the Center for Women, Gender and Sexuality Studies at Florida Atlantic University, a vital core of education, illumination and an invaluable contribution to humanity.

I cannot overlook my teammates, my friends, who always encouraged me to stay on course. A night at the bar required at least one round listening to me deconstruct our favorite films from our youth and today … and you always stuck around for another.

Thanks to my greatest fans, my parents, forever loyal and dedicated in their belief in me.

A special thanks goes to my M.V.P., my partner Danielle, for being my captain of encouragement, my superstar of support and allowing me to eat, sleep and breathe sports films far longer than the designated time for a game.

Finally, I would like to thank my hometown Boston, the birthplace of my love of sports.

Preface

First, let me share that I'm a fan of sports movies. I am not only a fan of sports movies; I'm an athlete as well. Sports movies are my pep talk to hit the field, a time capsule of camaraderie with teammates and, most of all, the oasis I turn to for inspiration. However, I've always found recurring plotline problems that frustrate me. Why is it that the love story always trumps the big game as the final shot of the film? Why does she have to sacrifice so much more than her male teammates do? Why does she need a beauty makeover to be better at her sport? These are the things that make my head drop as I exit the theater.

Although the visual confirmation and celebration of women in sports has grown in the media, even touching the mainstream here and there, the cinematic presence of female athletes is still minimal. There are few films centered on female athletes and even fewer that have drummed up enough attention to be categorized as "popular." With such a slender (pun very intended) amount of cinematic female athlete representations, those select precious few stand as much-needed role models for female athletes. It's important that we recognize the power of cinema as a resource of education and impact in society. With that in mind, it's also important that we continue an analytical dialogue to ensure that we are aware of what these films are educating in their gender representations.

There is a gap in theory about female characters in sports films. When I wrote my first paper in graduate school, I remember plopping down on a stool in shock that I couldn't find a book that solely focused on cinematic female athletes. There was a plethora of books on the subject of women in sports, but not on women's sports films. So, as a film lover and athlete, I quickly pledged to create this content. With a lack of specifically direct resources, I've founded much of my theory and research in cultural studies in sport, film theory and feminist theory. I've also utilized feminist analysis of other film genres, such as melodramas and romantic comedies that mirror the female character's struggles in sports films.

Having my book heavily driven by textual criticism, with attention to feminist readings of gender, I recognize the necessity of historical context. With this in mind, it was important that my analysis be sensitive to the corresponding progression of the women's movement and specifically the timeline of women's sports history. It's incredibly interesting how, depending on the year of release, these films play a hand in progress and/or repression in the ongoing struggle for women to be recognized as athletes and find their place in the sports world.

Although this book was inspired by cinematic female athletes, my research led me to important films that starred females as coaches and team owners as well. All of my research translated quite seamlessly to these primary positions in sports and I feel that this book would not be complete without also sharing the stories of these powerful cinematic sports heroines.

This book contributes content to a much-needed branch of sports textual analysis and feminist film theory. However, this book is only one step in the process of revealing both problematic and empowered choices in cinematic representations of female athletes. There is much more to be done. With my analysis predominantly residing in popular American films, there is a wealth of cinematic content from around the world and the independent film community that can extend the conversation. Furthermore, in-depth audience analysis could reveal the tools to create a truly empowered cinematic female athlete. I hope this book motivates critical conversation and inspires further research and analysis of women's sports films.

My dream is that this book will aid the creation of a cinematic female athlete that, without compromise, can excite a mass audience, give rise to a celebration of women in sports and instill the confidence in women, both young and old, to run onto the playing field.

Introduction

The ball is on the one-yard line. There are four seconds left in the game. The music cues as she turns in slow motion to signal the wide receiver. As the music crescendos, so does the suspense as the ball is set in motion. The audience is on the edge of their seats. She nestles the ball between her palms, placing her fingers directly on the stitches. A hand waves from the end zone and her eyes catch it. With one fluid movement her arm arcs over her body. The music drops, there is silence as the ball floats through the air. Just a moment later, hands reach up and grab it, cueing the music and sparking pandemonium as the team celebrates their victory. It's a scenario we've seen before, though usually it is only men playing these roles. We can fill the lead role with a woman because anything can happen in movies … right? Movies should create a space where we can watch our imagination come to life and suspend our disbelief. But in truth, there are societal influences that infiltrate her existence in this scenario and determine plot lines outside of winning "the big game."

The sports film is a popular genre. In some ways, these films are akin to highlight reels, conveying emotional climaxes in wins and losses, winners and losers, aggression and dominance. They are also the epitome of a kind of propaganda for male-dominant culture, packaged for entertainment purposes. One is hard-pressed to find many leading female roles directly connected to the sport in male-dominated sports storylines.[1] With an abundance of male-driven sports stories, Hollywood is reinforcing a continued focus to associate athleticism with men. The lack of female protagonists is symbolic of the very conflict these heroines face in their storylines: struggling to be recognized as an athlete, coach and franchise owner. The portrayal of women in these primary roles in sports films represents social attitudes and values and, when looked through time, also shows how the women's movement has been able to influence, or not influence, cinematic representations and, concomitantly, social understandings of women and athleticism.

It's important that we recognize the role that movies play in influencing cultural understanding. Cinema representations affect and reflect the reality of our everyday lives. When an audience views a film about a certain topic, that reconstruction will become part of their education on that topic.[2] For example, if someone were to view a film about Alaska, the images and characters would serve as insight into that state. This translates with sports films as they educate viewers on the rules of a sport and also the skills necessary to succeed on that playing field. The act of relating to, or escaping into, these cinematic atmospheres yields knowledge and creates a dialogue that the viewer will forever take with them and share in their thoughts. Movies are an influential medium in transmitting ideologies. In other words, if we think of movies as just fantasy and escapism, we are in danger of continuing to embed constricting and oppressive definitions of who we think we need to be, rather than embracing who we are. In light of this understanding that film exerts an influence over societal thinking, an exploration into the nature of female representation becomes necessary.

It's truly a disservice how few female-driven sports films there are. Our cinematic landscape is rich with the history of male athletes and the heroic wins of male-dominated sports. A majority of this book is focused on women playing and working in male-dominated sports because while traditionally feminine sports—such as figure skating and gymnastics—require diligence, training, skill and talent, their focus remains encapsulated in the ideologies of feminine gender construction. In other words, these sports encourage practices relegated to the sphere of femininity—for example, gracefulness and beauty. Storylines that feature female athletes practicing and working in traditionally male sports are focused on the perpetuation of hegemonic masculinity as the standard. These male-sanctioned domains exploit an ideology that encourages domination and brute force. These storylines celebrate forms of masculinity that females must emulate or submit to and reveal our societal roots in sports ideology.

In order to examine how the portrayal of women athletes, coaches and owners in sports films represents certain social attitudes and values, we need to take a look at some key historical and conceptual ideas, including a brief history of women in sports, and some basic concepts from both gender and film theory.

The Starting Line

Although women were actively playing sports for centuries, women's sports programs didn't begin until the early 1900s when women's colleges built curricula for physical education. As these programs grew and expanded in popularity, there were competitions among female teams. However, the sports these women played were limited by gender constructions, with the most "aggressive" sports still contained and modified for a more acceptable (read: feminine) style of play. One example of this was disallowing guarding, a forceful but strategic blocking motion, in women's basketball. There were further allowances in women's sports such as in 1902 when the playing of best-of-five sets standard in tennis was reduced to a best-of-three for fear of women's overexertion.[3]

Beyond the regulation of which sports women played and how, the main issue early on was with women's athletic attire: "modesty versus immodesty."[4] Women were offered access to sports yet had to wear clothing that was not suitable for movement and flexibility. Most notably, long dresses or some variation of a long skirt stood as a universal uniform. Ultimately, their outfits did not relate to function. That was a battle that was won slowly over time. Even today, it can be hard to find access to certain protective pads for high-impact sports and a continuing pressure to wear some variation of a skirt in tennis. Perhaps part of the expectation that female athletes wear feminine clothing was in reaction to the fact that simply by playing sports women were challenging their role in western society.

One of the most prominent eras of progress in women's sport was the early 1940s, during World War II, when the first women's baseball league, the All-American Girls Professional Baseball League (AAGPBL), was established. With many ballplayers at war, there was a void that allowed the league to be formed to continue the sport of baseball. The league did not last long, only running from 1943 to 1954. Although its short lifespan was due to a lack of spectator interest, once all-male baseball returned, the lasting impression of the AAGPBL continued to present the possibility of sports as a job and opportunity for women.

The 1970s were the next prominent decade for female advancement in athletics. Not only did we watch Billie Jean King defeat Bobby Riggs in "The Battle of the Sexes" tennis match in 1973, we watched as the country took notice and acknowledged a right for women's access to sports. This was a flourishing time for the women's movement that resulted in the most politically supportive and influential advance in women's sports: the 1972 passage of Title IX. Title IX was the first federal law to prohibit sex discrimination in any educational institution receiving federal aid. Having the law on their side, women's athletic programs not only sprang up but also were afforded the funds to compete properly, with the correct equipment and travel benefits to reach out to teams across the country.

It should be noted that although Title IX is still active and has enabled exponential growth in women's sport, schools still try to cut corners. There are now debates over what "counts" as a sport. Colleges favor one female sport over another (e.g., basketball over volleyball) and recent controversies have arisen over what qualifies as a sport, such as the question of cheerleading. Most schools find their priority in profit-driven mainstream sports such as football and basketball. Although there is both men's and women's basketball, this co-ed equality does not adhere to football. Football has overshadowed and challenged many women's sports programs. Even with a law in place to protect this encroachment, sports as a business is still pushing against women's involvement.

Furthermore, it's important to recognize that although Title XI opened the doors for many female athletes, it closed doors for many female coaches and women in other positions in sports programs. When Title IX was put in action, a lot of female sports programs were folded into male programs yet the females who ran those women's sports programs previously did not transfer into these new hierarchies. As female athletes became more accepted, they were simply integrated into a male-dominated sports system continuing to promote the idea that an expertise in sports still remained with men. Although limited, there are currently female coaches on every level of play through college but it's worth noting that of the 122 teams playing in the four major American male professional leagues (football, baseball, hockey and basketball), there are zero female head coaches, assistant coaches and assistant to the assistant coaches.

However it cannot be denied that the access, and therefore advancements, because of Title IX propelled us to our most recent progressive moments in women's sports. The most impactful is arguably in 1999 when the U.S. women's national soccer team won the World Cup. In soccer, a sport highly popular everywhere *but* in the United States, the U.S. team prevailed and inspired the world to watch, including the U.S. It was a moment when the whole world turned its eyes to support women's sport.

There are also individual athletes who have attained mainstream fame in such sports as tennis, with the Williams sisters, and IndyCar (and now NASCAR) racing, with Danica Patrick. In 2013, Patrick made headline news by becoming the first woman to win the pole at the Daytona 500. As a coach, Patricia Sue "Pat" Summitt broke the record for wins among both men's and women's NCAA Division 1 basketball in 2005. She continued coaching and adding to that record until 2012. There have also been female athletes famously breaking through previously male-sanctioned sports leagues: In 1992 Manon Rhéaume became the first female to play in an exhibition game in the National Hockey League; in 1999 Katie Hnida became the first woman to score in Division I Football; and in 2003 Annika Sorenstam became the first woman to compete in a PGA Tour event. The struggle now is spectator interest and with that, sports as business. Female sports leagues are fighting for screen time on television and female athletes are seeking recognition that does not require marketing based on a beauty standard. It cannot be denied that women's sports are always progressing, but it also cannot be denied that female athletes require a continued effort to project constructed feminine values rather than be celebrated purely on their athletic success. Further, the televised and marketed priority of male-driven sports continue to place sports within the male domain and undermine female athleticism.

This timeline will play a relevant role in my discussion of women in primary sports roles in film. Each prominent decade is synonymous with their growth in appearance. However, along with an increasing accessibility to certain sports, there is a continued negotiation to balance traditional gender constructions. The more un-feminine a sport is played, the more a female involved must mediate her femininity.

Throws Like a Girl

The challenge of an equal playing field has been, and always will be, gender power dynamics. The gender power structure, reflecting dominant male ideology, begins at a young age in sport. For example, girls and boys are split in ice hockey at the Pee Wee level once checking (a defensive body hit) is introduced. They are split, supposedly because of their differing bodies and the inherent skills of those bodies, but the actions that are then designated for each gender go on to actually build different skills, strategy and strength. In short, the sex segregation builds and produces different bodies that actually reflect the prejudices of gender ideology.

Sports send both genders into very different conceptual as well as bodily directions. While sports play an important role in a boy's initiation into manhood, girls find their rite of passage through activities based on appearance such as learning to use makeup. Young girls compete on the runway of pageants while boys are encouraged to build strength and size on the playing field.[5] These foundational beginnings have affected our evolution as two genders. We are not simply constructing ideas of how we must act, but our physical nature is changing.

Watching sports plays an equally instrumental part in a young male's initiation into manhood. There is a ritual element to witnessing a game, memorizing statistics and the daily investment in a team. Therefore we cannot only interpret sports as gendered masculine, but the implications of viewing sports as equally masculine-identified. This can be directly related to the action of watching a film. Cinema similarly recreates the ritual element of watching an event on screen. Cinematic devices of sound, music and shot selection only enhance a spectator's experience of that filmic representation. Everything is heightened. Furthermore, movies are presented as equal access to a spectator of either gender. In a self-contained sports film, we are taught the rules and handed our team and players to root for, thus negating the necessity of a previous sports education. However, rather than creating an experience where either gender may exit the theater feeling they can equally connect to the sports world, by predominantly centering sports storylines on male heroes and male-dominated sports, sports films are continuing a masculine-identified viewing experience.

Throughout the history of sports, competition has become embraced for actions of aggression and dominance rather than skill and strategy. It is important to observe that women do in fact have certain physical strengths that differ from men (such as endurance), but male-dominated sports stress male traits (such as size) as part of a universal model of excellence.[6] We witness just as many highlight reels of brutal hits and violent fights as we do of game-winning goals. Therefore, if hegemonic notions of masculinity are grounded in notions of superiority and dominance, sports of all kinds could be categorized as gendered masculine. This creates a space where women are either simply excluded from playing sports or forced to emulate actions designated for men. Either way, being "feminine" is thought to naturally reside outside of sports.

Competition is anchored in encouragement of the very actions women are taught are un-womanly, such as aggression and a self-centered orientation. Women, more than men, are supposed to act cordial and sportsmanlike (read: polite). The media blitz surrounding Tonya Harding's involvement in the attack against her competitor Nancy Kerrigan during a practice session for the 1994 U.S. Figure Skating Championship is a clear example of this. The tension between femininity and athleticism defined Harding. Prior to the event in 1994, the press regularly displayed Kerrigan as the elegant lady and Harding as the "tough cookie."[7] Tonya was known for executing difficult tricks and power throughout her routine, a more athletic style than grace.[8] The attention, and then criticism, of these athletic (and therefore masculine) characteristics in Harding prior to accusations of her involvement in the assault on Kerrigan exemplifies the struggle for many female athletes: Femininity and athleticism are mutually exclusive concepts that must both be navigated.

This is the framework that sets the backdrop for sports films. These "reel" female athletes must work their way through a male-defined atmosphere. Their actions are always set in comparison to their male counterparts. This is translatable to our cinematic coaches and franchise owners. Their success is measured by how well they can mimic masculine coded skills and still return to a comfortable, feminine, secondary role. Men's character, for example, can be loyalty to their team. Women's character must also mean loyalty to men.

Controlling the Time of Possession

Psychoanalytic feminist film theory is anchored by the investigation of a gendered gaze. The gaze is the audience perspective while watching a film. This can involve the framing of a shot or the story in its entirety. The action of owning the gaze is dominant, and since dominance is connected to masculinity, the gaze can be thought to be masculine. Known as the "male gaze," this is visually translated when women are placed as an object or spectacle, to be looked at, presented for the male spectator and literally translated when a male character is introduced to view her in that way within the story.[9] With sports films as an active agent of masculinity, one could think that by entering the masculine domain of sports, these female athletes would challenge the male gaze. It's shocking how female-centered sports films so obviously, and abruptly, make an effort to maintain the male gaze and continue to place these cinematic female athletes as objects and/or secondary. Most commonly, the gender infringement caused by an athletic heroine is reconciled by a male figure (be it lover, coach or father) who steps in to guide her, save her and to give permission for her entrance into sports, thereby re-establishing male ownership of the gaze. Additionally, the more a cinematic female athlete asserts her agency, the more her path to re-correct a secondary and subordinate female role becomes a primary focus in the story.

With the male gaze in mind, it's important that we recognize how cinematic portrayals of women and men reveal actions of performance within gender. Sports, defined as the male domain, puts cinematic female athletes, coaches and franchise owners in masculine territory. Should a woman stand in these perceived masculine roles, we watch her turn from a kind, attractive, nurturing woman to an aggressive, cold, manipulating competitor. However, she is *not* seen as a competitor, she is seen as an incomplete woman. Therefore, our cinematic female athletes must embody incompleteness, a lack of or a need for a male counterpart to restore their femininity. They must inhabit a space as secondary, subordinate to men.

With a pressure to place women in this subordinate space, there is no understanding that a woman can be "normally" masculine. This real world issue is constantly reflected in our cinematic landscapes. There are two forms of "punishment" for a female athlete who dominates in her sport: questioning her biological sex and questioning her sexuality. When women grow too tall, too strong or even too highly skilled at a sport, their biological sex comes into question. There is a history of demanding sex tests of female athletes who have high-quality performance.[10] These tests are medical examinations to confirm that a woman is a biological woman by her organs and chromosomes. If she proves to be a woman, the other option is to question her sexuality. In sports there is a stereotypic, homophobic and gender-policing understanding of female athletes as all being lesbians.[11] Access and success on a male-sanctioned playing field is somehow thought to shift a female athlete's sexual desire. The stigma and eroticism that surrounds lesbians effectively creates a "go to" for the unfamiliar reality of female athletes. This is yet another strategic attack against female empowerment. Female strength in the male domain is a threat to gender norms.

These tensions are easily alleviated in sports films by imposing a heterosexual relationship on the heroine. Rather than being celebrated for her athleticism or knowledge of the sport, the cinematic sports heroine is then celebrated for her ability to reside in reference to a male character as a daughter, girlfriend or wife.[12] In such films as *Pat and Mike* (1952), *Coach* (1978), *A League of Their Own* (1992) and *Little Giants* (1994), a romantic relationship is introduced to remind the viewer that the female athlete is in fact heterosexual, recognizably feminine and therefore safe. Other films such as *Million Dollar Baby* (2004) and *Whip It* (2009) offer platonic male characters who grant the female athletes permission to compete in their sports, thereby still defining women as secondary, in need of invitation. In other words, a male must be introduced to re-assimilate the cinematic sports heroine and effectively persuade the audience to not be threatened by her "alternative" gender representation. This is where we find ourselves in the current struggle with the film portrayals of sports heroines. If we cannot even imagine, create fictional plotlines, where a woman can fully function as an athlete, coach and franchise owner without the necessary support of a male character, then we are simply stunting female empowerment in these films.

Chapter 1 focuses on films about female athletes in individual sports: *National Velvet* (1944), *Pat and Mike* (1952), *Million Dollar Baby* (2004) and *Girlfight* (2000). As individual athletes, these female athletes are solely defined by their coaches, lovers, family, friends and themselves. In *National Velvet, Pat and Mike* and *Million Dollar Baby,* it is what happens "off the field" that leads to these female athletes' demise (literally or metaphorically) as they are assimilated back into the patriarchal order. The stronger a female character gets, the more the plot necessitates a return to patriarchal balance. As discussed before, a staple in this re-assimilation technique is imposing a heterosexual relationship. Through a cycle of conflict and resolution driven by "needs and responsibilities" of the female protagonist's role in the family structure, these athletic female heroes have no choice but to accept their rightful place as primarily wife or mother or suffer a worse fate, death, such as in *Million Dollar Baby*. In a more positive stance, *Girlfight* actually refuses this presentation of hegemonic gender roles, with a story that awards the female athlete empowerment and a career in her sport.

Chapter 2 explores films that center on female athletes on female teams: *A League of Their Own* (1992) and *Whip It* (2009) with reference to *Bend It Like Beckham* (2002). In *A League of Their Own,* one female character is presented as the ultimate (constructed) standard of the feminine ideal woman and her struggles and eventual re-assimilation into patriarchy stands as a role model for her teammates and the audience. She is presented as the only one who is really complete, leaving the rest of her teammates symbolizing lack. Her placement as celebrated hero promotes dated ideas of femininity. In *Whip It* and *Bend It Like Beckham,* we acknowledge the power in placing a father figure at the climax of a story who permits the female athlete to play in her chosen sport *only* after she has fully surrendered to her place in the feminine domain (in these cases, desiring to be a beauty queen or needing to please her sister). The choice to play is taken out of the hands of these female athletes and we witness another missed opportunity in presenting female empowerment.

Chapter 3 critiques films that place individual female athletes on male teams: *The Bad News Bears* (1976) with reference to its remake *Bad*

News Bears (2005), *Little Giants* (1994), *D2: The Mighty Ducks* (1994) with reference to *The Mighty Ducks* (1992) and *The Longshots* (2008). All of these films are based on a misfit team formula: A team comprised of players who lack playing ability compensates by rebelling against societal norms using humor. The boys on these teams are clumsy, weak and slow. This is their conflict. This lack of athleticism as boys makes them outsiders, and thus the misfit team. As a designated outsider of a male sport simply by her gender, a female teammate becomes the ultimate symbol of the misfit team. However, the female athletes in these films are skilled, fast and strong. In most cases, they are more talented than every boy in the league. Therefore, these films place the female athlete's ultimate conflict as her struggle to fulfill a female gender–constructed role such as girlfriend, daughter or niece. Furthermore, in an effort to contain her talent, by confirming her as an exception to the masculine standard of the sport, an equally (or more highly) skilled male athlete is introduced to the team to balance her strength and/or stand as the re-assimilating relationship for her acceptance from the audience. Finally, if none of these conflicts or resolutions are present, such as in *D2: The Mighty Ducks,* the female athlete's celebrated moment to perform her athletic talent is redirected and credited to instructions given by her male coach, stripping her of the opportunity to be acknowledged for her own skill.

Chapter 4 discusses popular films centering on established female sports: *The Cutting Edge* (1992), *Wimbledon* (2004), *Love & Basketball* (2000), *Blue Crush* (2002), *Personal Best* (1982) and *Stick It* (2006). In varying degrees, each of these films allows us to accept, and even celebrate, the competitive spirit within cinematic female athletes. Perhaps this is because these films are already set in sports that have professional women's leagues so we are already familiar with these forms of female athleticism. However, even though there are progressive choices within these storylines, we still continue to watch the same patterns of sacrifice. *The Cutting Edge* shows us a strong female athlete who reveals that her conflict has less to do with competing and more to do with pleasing her father and connecting with her love interest. Although *Wimbledon, Love & Basketball* and *Blue Crush* exhibit heroines who negotiate their desire to win with their ability to be desired, these three films afford us a progressive step toward an empowering final impression for women's sports.

With a love interest not present, *Stick It* gives us a cinematic female athlete who is celebrated and validated for her toughness throughout the film with no need to submit to romantic attraction. While we cannot overlook that her happy ending is heavily reliant on her connection to a father figure, *Stick It* begins laying the groundwork of accepting competitive values in femininity.

Chapter 5 considers films about both men and women dressing in drag in order to play as an equal among the opposite sex: *Ladybugs* (1992) with reference to *Juwanna Mann* (2002) and *She's the Man* (2006) with reference to *Motocrossed* (2001). Both the male athlete in *Ladybugs* and the female athlete in *She's the Man* open an important conversation about the performativity in gender through their physical makeovers and exaggerated acting. Unfortunately, both of these cinematic athlete heroes do not open a conversation about the perceived innate male dominance in sports. In *Ladybugs,* we watch a male athlete who dresses in drag on a female team. The female team is so terrible that he is given credit for their every advancement. Rather than showcase any skill, each female athlete on the team is a female construction punchline (e.g., one female player can't concentrate on the ball unless it's covered with sparkly butterfly stickers). Although *She's the Man* is based on Shakespearean romantic entanglements, having the cinematic female athlete choose to dress in drag inspired by, and placed in, the venue of sports grants us some very empowering visuals of a female athlete among male teammates. Unfortunately, we also watch her compromise her athletic image by entertaining antiquated notions of femininity (becoming a debutante). Both of these films create an opportunity to showcase athletic ability free of preconceived gender-defining values amongst teammates, but fail to take advantage, simply furthering oppressive ideas in athletic difference. *Juwanna Mann* and *Motocrossed* provide us with challenging portrayals for both gender presentations. Although these two films were not particularly popular, it's important we acknowledge their positive plot choices to promote gender equality in sports.

Chapter 6 examines films portraying females as coaches: *Coach* (1978), *Wildcats* (1986), *Eddie* (1996) and *The Mighty Macs* (2009). Without the conversation of physical capability, these coaches should thrive from their knowledge of their sport and their ability to train and lead their teams. However, the position of coach carries with it the burden of many layers of relations with players. Being a coach is not just setting up practice drills or calling plays; the coach must also create trust, earn respect and take responsibility for every player under their guidance. This complicated and powerful role creates complicated and powerful cinematic gestures towards the heroines in this chapter. Each cinematic female coach faces different battles and different outcomes, all while presenting a lot of the patterns that our cinematic female athletes face such as a romantic relationship or simply displacing her motivation from a purely sports-driven goal. These female coaches have the skills and the knowledge to lead their teams to victory if their teams can succumb to the idea that their coach is female before the season ends.

Chapter 7 evaluates films that place a female as the team and franchise owner: *Slap Shot* (1977), *Major League* (1989), *Any Given Sunday* (1999) and *Secretariat* (2010). The position of owner is the highest and most powerful position in a sports organization. The owner hires, fires and ultimately holds the fate of everyone involved in that team. Because professional sports rely on funding, the owner is seen more as a business associate than having any connection to the field of play. With this in mind, the owner's strategy relies on seeing everything as an investment; anyone who isn't benefiting that investment, or could perhaps return more by leaving, is a choice the owner has the power to make on her or his own. It's all about money. This is where the position of owner can quickly become the villain. If the core value in a team is money rather than the legacy or pride of the game, it's easy for fans of that team to turn on the owner. What we learn in the cinematic landscape is that the best way to distract from the dark reality of this position is to have it embodied in a woman. Her disconnect from the sport and the "old boy's club" that built it, immediately places her as the outsider. No matter how smart or financially strategic she may be, she is placed in opposition to the hopes and dreams of her players. As we will see, this allows for some truly harsh cinematic treatment of these heroines.

Within these chapters I create a concise evaluation of these plotlines as texts, these characters as examples and the scripted choices made that ultimately decide what these woman represent and/or are allowed to represent. I conclude by exploring the prospect that the portrayals of cinematic sports heroines can be a source for social transformation. Sports are a tangible playing field for gender equality. The problem is that sports have literally become a "battlefield" that supports the understanding that aggression is rewarded in men and punished in women. As women break this mentality, men become more and more threatened. With threat comes the negative connotation that has imprisoned women's independence from the start. The question isn't if women can occupy these roles, it's if we can imagine them outside our embedded patriarchal culture.

1

Dismount

The Façade of Female Empowerment

Women's roles as athletes in film should embody empowerment and influence a vision of equality. They compete among men and even against men and succeed. The problem is, winning isn't enough. These cinematic female athletes must negotiate more than just a sports victory to have a happy ending; they have to embody a social definition of female. This definition is grounded in the constructions of family, specifically their ability to be a daughter, wife and mother. This carries heavy significance in the cinematic female athlete's struggle to participate in these previously male-sanctioned sports and ultimately dictates the outcome of her story.

In *National Velvet,* directed by Clarence Brown in 1944, 12-year-old Velvet Brown (Elizabeth Taylor) wins the Grand National, the most prestigious horse race in the world. This was the first major film awarding a female a powerful stance among men in the sporting world. Her mother, Mrs. Brown (Anne Revere), is also portrayed as strong in that she was the first woman to swim the English Channel. At first glance, this film appears to be the starting line for respectable portrayals of women. However, on closer inspection, this film becomes the origins of a cinematic genre that places women's athletic aspirations as secondary to fulfilling a women's subordinate role in patriarchy. *National Velvet* was the beginning of an unfortunate false front for women's empowerment as athletes in sports films. By looking at *National Velvet* and *Pat and Mike,* followed by the recent film *Million Dollar Baby,* we'll evaluate the messages that are relayed by these strong female athletes and how their stories' conclusions serve to continue patriarchal ideology. We will conclude by evaluating *Girlfight*, an arguably empowering alternative to these unhappy outcomes for female athletes.

The Dark Horse

In order to properly analyze *National Velvet*, we need to revisit the era of World War II. With men off at war, America relied on women to take their place in the workforce. The media's main efforts, also more generally, were to get women into the factories to build supplies for the war. Although there was a strong push for women to work, there was also the start of a controlled effort to keep them "womanly." From the start of the war, there was concern that women would not easily return to their domestic duties after gaining access to previously masculine-sanctioned work. Therefore, the media both sent a message for women to leave the home and work but made clear that this was only for the duration of the war.[1] However, once the invitation was given, it was not easy to give back. When the soldiers returned from war, there was a struggle with and against women who wanted to continue working outside of the home. *National Velvet*'s release toward the end of World War II was no coincidence. I believe it was scripted within the efforts to return these female workers to the home. The film's theme resonates as: You can have this moment, but then it needs to pass and you need to return to your rightful place as wife and mother. With this historical influence as a foundation, we watch the formula built for cinematic female athletes. In many of the films discussed in this book, it is clear that female athletes can recognize their skill and talent, but they must also recognize their place in taking on the roles assigned to them by patriarchal ideology.

It is unfortunate that our first celebrated cinematic female athlete comes in the form of a child. Placing Velvet as the main character in *National Velvet* only amplifies the notion that competing at a high level with men is a young girl's dream. The effort of female athletes, metaphorically, is infantilized by Velvet's age. Because she is a child, any female independence she exhibits must be placed with childish things. Velvet lacks agency because she is a child, which minimizes accomplishments and ambition. Further, establishing this first female athlete in a younger age profile continues the tradition of athletics as an acceptable venue for girls only when they are young. Once they grow up, this phase ends and they move on to their subordinate responsibilities as a woman.[2] *National Velvet* becomes a cinematic transmitter of this unfortunate message.

Velvet loves horses. We watch her pretend to ride a horse everywhere she goes and she even practices these motions in her bed at night. She admits, "Every day I pray to God to give me horses, wonderful horses. To let me be the best rider in England." When Velvet first meets the horse that will soon be hers, it is love at first sight. She names him "The Pie." After the horse runs rampant, damaging much of Velvet's town, the owner organizes a raffle with the outlaw gelding as the prize. In an act of fate, Velvet wins The Pie. Now as his owner, Velvet has the right to ride him all over town. She also has the right to enter him into the Grand National. Velvet would have never known about the Grand National if it weren't for her friend and soon-to-be trainer Mi Taylor (Mickey Rooney).

Mi is the first person we see in the film. He walks along the road, marked as a nomad by his backpack. Once he is introduced into Velvet's life, we learn that Mi is the son of Velvet's mother's old swimming coach. We also learn that he is a thief. He uses his relation to Mrs. Brown's coach to get into their house so he can steal money. It is Velvet's innocence and passion for her horse that slowly work to transition him to a caring and supportive trainer. Mi used to be a jockey but, after a bad fall, he now fears riding. Mi knows everything about horses and what it takes to race in the Grand National. When Velvet goes behind his back and enters The Pie in the race, it is not intended that she will ride. She will be the owner and she wants Mi to be the trainer. They will find a jockey together. What's most interesting about Mi's character is that among the many moments he could have stolen Velvet's glory, he doesn't. Most notably, when they decide the jockey they've paid for isn't worthy of their horse, he opts to ride in the race himself. As he rushes in to tell Velvet, he finds her sleeping dressed in a jockey helmet and silks. When he wakes her up to ask what she's doing, she announces that she will ride. Mi does not challenge her choice. He even helps cut off her hair and masquerade her as a boy through the entire registration process. He recognizes her passion and he acknowledges that she deserves this. Mi, like his father, has helped a female athlete achieve her aspiration.

If this were the story, there would be little to argue against. However, as Velvet is a child, Mi is not her parent. Although Mi is instrumental to Velvet racing, he does not have the final say in Velvet's dream. Velvet's mother Mrs. Brown ultimately grants Velvet permission to race The Pie in the Grand National. Mrs. Brown becomes a weapon for the film's miseducation. As the first woman to swim the English Channel, she stands as a role model to both Velvet and the audience. Now, years later, we see that Mrs. Brown is a strong independent woman running her household. It is clear that Mr. Brown (Donald Crisp) carries little power, as she treats him like another one of their children and repeatedly overturns his requests, including Velvet's opportunity to ride. Although we are entranced by Mrs. Brown's outward wisdom and calm but fierce confidence, this is where she becomes dangerous. Within that attractive role model exterior also come the messages and directions for assimilation: You can be strong and independent but only when you have the other requirement of life's happiness, a family.

Seeing as it's Mrs. Brown who grants Velvet the opportunity to ride, it is also Mrs. Brown who states the rules. In the most "educational" scene, Mrs. Brown leads Velvet to the attic to a trunk filled with the relics from her famous swim. She not only gives Velvet permission to follow her dream, but also her swimming prize money to use. This is Velvet and the spectator's initiation into patriarchal gender constructions. This is the birth of a conflict and resolution for female athletes in films. The conversation is as follows:

> VELVET: Often I just sit and wonder about you. I wonder what you're thinking. You don't think like us, Mother. You think back here [*motions to the back of her head*].
> MRS. BROWN: I've seen you do the same. We're alike. I, too, believe that everyone should have a chance at a breathtaking piece of folly, once in his life. I was 20 when they said a woman couldn't swim the Channel. You're 12. You think a horse of yours can win the Grand National. Your dream has come early. But remember, Velvet, it'll have to last you all the rest of your life...
> VELVET: We'll win for you, Mother!
> MRS. BROWN: Win or lose, it's the same. It's how you take it that counts and knowing when to let go. Knowing when it's over and time to go to the next thing.
> VELVET: The next thing?
> MRS. BROWN: Things come suitable to the time, Velvet. Enjoy each thing,

forget it and go to the next. There's a time for everything. A time for having a horse in the Grand National, being in love, having children. Yes, even for dying. All in proper order at the proper time…
VELVET: But who is going to tell Father?
MRS. BROWN: I'll do the telling. I don't think your father believes in the importance of folly.

So although there is an acknowledgment that every woman deserves her time, it can only be once and it will have to last her the rest of her life. A woman must carry the ability to recognize when her adventure is over. Apparently the term "folly" encompasses a woman's accomplishment in men's sports.

Velvet wins the race. However, after she crosses the finish line she faints, disqualifying her from an officially sanctioned victory. This is irrelevant as the country celebrates her as a national hero. At the end of the film, Velvet is inundated with offers to go to Hollywood with The Pie. Her father sees dollar signs; her mother simply sits back to see if Velvet has learned her lesson. She has. Instead of going to Hollywood to act in movies with The Pie, she chooses to stay at home because it's best for her horse. She fears that The Pie wouldn't understand the media circus. She tearfully admits, "I'd sooner have that horse happy than go to Heaven." At this moment, her undying love of her horse represents her ability to be a mother. If the message isn't clear enough, the audience shares one last moment with Mrs. Brown as she explains how, unlike Velvet, Mi's future is wide open:

MRS BROWN: Remember the night we talked in the attic? Remember how we said things come suitable to the time, all in proper order? Tonight I was proud of you. When we asked you about the telegrams, you knew the race was over and it was time to go onto the next thing. Would you not allow the same for Mi Taylor? It's time for him to leave Velvet and make his way in the world; or would you say, "Don't go, Mi, because I'll be unhappy"? The world's opened up for him again, Velvet. He'd shut himself away from it, before he was angry with it. But that's over. I think he'll come back.
VELVET: That's what he said, Mother. He said, "Only way to come back is to go."

Her last statement is paramount to the female athlete. For Mi, "the only way to come back is to go"; this was simply another experience in Mi's life, and his opportunities are endless. We began the film with Mi walking along the road to this story, now we leave with the image of him walking to the next. For Velvet it's the opposite, "the only way to go is to come back"; Velvet has experienced her singular opportunity but now she must return to her path toward becoming a mother.

National Velvet forwards the idea that the female athlete is an item of "folly." A woman's time of athletic success expires, not because of age or injury, but because she must recognize the patriarchal world she needs to be a part of and then assimilate into the acceptable behaviors that are acceptable to the female role. This need for female assimilation is a direct result of the country's fear that a woman's *traditional* place in the home would evaporate following the movement of women into the work force during and after World War II. One might even argue that Anne Revere's 1945 Oscar win for her portrayal of Mrs. Brown reaffirmed and validated a national desperation to affirm the reality or "truth" of her character's position. In other words, honoring Revere underscored Mrs. Brown's message: Women were allowed a little playtime, but eventually there were more pressing things to do, mainly creating and maintaining a family.

Pat and Mike, an arguably empowering female athlete portrayal, was released in 1952.[3] This film exhibits an adult female character who is a strong and confident athlete. There is still a necessity to introduce a male partner for her happy ending; however, she continues on to a career in sports. Her journey is daring in a time where women were being urged into the home. We will briefly touch on the plot to illustrate this.

Patricia "Pat" Pemberton (Katharine Hepburn) sets out to be a professional athlete to prove to herself and her fiancé Collier Weld (William Ching) that she is more than a "little woman." Pat teams up with a manager, Mike Conovan (Spencer Tracy), who leads her to a successful career in golf and tennis. Her conflict stems from her inability to play well while Weld is present. At one point when asked, "What's your handicap?" she plainly replies, "My fella." He is to blame for every one of her championship losses. After she quits her job as a physical education teacher and loses her first golf championship (due to her fiancé's attendance), she decides to put the engagement on hold to prove to herself and everyone else that she can be a successful athlete.

As the film progresses, Mike enables Pat much like Mi did with Velvet. It's a positive role and Mike treats Pat as equal to any other athlete he trains. A love connection does arise between them, but it is not fully realized until later in the film when Mike is put in danger. Two of his investor-goons corner him in a parking lot and Pat comes to protect him. She fights the two men off while Mike just stands by helplessly and watches. This action effectively challenges his manhood. Moments later, his embarrassment continues to be dragged out at a police station where they re-enact her actions to further illustrate his inability to defend himself. This leads Mike to admit he has turned Pat into a "great big Mrs. Frankenstein." He says, "I just don't like the combination. I like everything to be 5–0, 5–0, I like a 'he' to be a 'he' and a 'she' to be a 'she.'" This comes after an entire film of him training and interacting with her as a respected athlete. Apparently "50–50" is only available as long as other gender pretenses apply. It's as though someone waved the "wrap it up" card and Mike had to get his act together before she got out of hand.

After Weld catches Mike leaving her room (he went in to close her window), he assumes that they are having an affair. He storms into her room and begins to become aggressive with her. Having just watched Pat take down Mike's investor-goons, we know she is completely capable of handling this situation. However, instead of defending herself and fighting, she shouts for Mike to help her. Although Mike is powerless and unhelpful again, Weld leaves. Pat strategically chooses this damsel in distress act to re-instill Mike's manhood, and seduce him into recognizing their romantic relationship stating, "I need someone to look after me." She must enact the role of weakness in order to achieve her desired partner.

The entire film hinges on her consciously and subconsciously displaying weakness. First she exhibits weakness for her fiancé, losing her athletic skill when he is around. Then she has to intentionally exhibit weakness to keep Mike by her side. In the final shot of the film we watch Pat as she orders Mike around the golf course and he happily obliges because she is now his in every way. While this still enacts the formulaic need for a male partner for a happy ending, the ending does enable us to watch Pat continue in her athletic career.

Regarding this new conclusion, it cannot be overlooked that the director of *Pat and Mike* is George Cukor, a gay man, commonly referred to as a "women's director" by many critics. This references the fact that his films were predominantly for female audiences. In his book *George Cukor,* Carlos Clarens reveals:

> The heroines of Cukor are never the sweet comforting creatures of Victorian fiction, whose final goal and fate is an epilogue of empty, safe respectability, the cosy glow of some perpetual twilight, so often transposed to the screen in an equivalent series of happy endings and fade-out kisses.[4]

As we've viewed with Pat, her happy ending includes a continued athletic career. In addition, Cukor's choice to film Pat and her athletic play from full body wide angles allows us to admire her playing ability as athletically skillful rather than closeups that would detract from this skill, instead evoking a male gaze of objectification. This will be relevant to remember when we evaluate *Personal Best* later in the book.

Although Pat's weakness is embodied in her fiancé, Cukor incites a new view of relationships through Pat and Mike that can translate to empowerment. Clarens writes, "As a rule, Cukor finds his own special tone in a refreshing camaraderie between the sexes, in the crisp give-and-take of married couples, or in a growing bond of mutual respect."[5] Through a majority of the film, Pat and Mike's partnership comes from a place of joint respect. She respects him as a coach just as he respects her as an athlete. It certainly helps that the character of Pat is played by Katharine Hepburn; "like Garbo and Deitrich before her, she appears gifted with the two sexes of the spirit, Michelet's *sine qua non* for the true artistic temperament; a child of the century, bewildered and steadfast, all humanity and no gender."[6] Hepburn's androgynous effect and Cukor's direction make the character of Pat stand as a new embodiment of the cinematic female athlete.

With *National Velvet* and *Pat and Mike* introducing the mandate that the female athlete needs also to be a mother or wife, *Million Dollar Baby* and *Girlfight* represent a modernized struggle where the lines are not so clearly drawn.

The Glass Jaw

Million Dollar Baby and *Girlfight* are stories set in the world of boxing. Boxing is a sport of pure violence. It is the ultimate combat, therefore male, sport. These films present a new female athlete like we've never seen before, a female athlete who uses the violence of her sport to find her identity.[7] However, with such an extreme sport come extreme challenges for our cinematic female athletes. First, we'll address *Million Dollar Baby,* directed by Clint Eastwood in 2004, a troubling film that literally sacrifices its female athlete for a celebration of the father figure. Then we'll look at *Girlfight,* directed by Karyn Kusama in 2000, a film that carries a conclusion that is arguably one of the most empowering of all the films discussed in this book.

Although *Million Dollar Baby* has a prominent female athlete in the story, the film is centered on Frankie Dunn (Eastwood), a successful boxing trainer and manager. We meet Frankie later in life, when he is respected for his classic knowledge and values but outdated in his business method. He puts off progress for boxers because he's overprotective. Boxers want money. Frankie wants pride. Frankie is the ultimate patriarch.

Frankie is introduced as complex and distant from those around him. This is due to an unexplained long-time estrangement from his daughter. The only person he has a relationship with these days is an old boxer, Eddie Scrap-Iron Dupris (Morgan Freeman). In the height of Eddie's career, Frankie watched him pushed to the limit of losing an eye. Eddie stands as a reminder to Frankie to avoid risks and protect his fighters. Eddie is also our narrator and represents our closest link to the inner workings of Frankie. When Maggie Fitzgerald (Hillary Swank) enters the story, Eddie knows that this is just what Frankie needs.

We first meet Maggie as she is admiring Frankie's work, managing his boxer in the ring. When she approaches him about working together, he's quick to say, "I don't train girls" and later refers to training girls as "the latest freak show out there." Even when she assures him that people think she's tough, he simply responds, "Girlie, tough ain't enough." So we begin watching her prove she's more than just tough, she's perseverant. Day after day she shows up to the gym, to the displeasure of Frankie.

Maggie's introduction, via the narrator, states, "She came from southwestern Missouri, the hills outside the scratch-ass Ozark town of Theodosia, set in the cedars and oak trees somewhere between nowhere and goodbye. She grew up knowing one thing: She was trash." When Frankie finally takes notice of her, she tells him:

> MAGGIE: My brother's in prison, my sister cheats on welfare by pretending one of her kids is still alive, my daddy's dead, and my mama weighs 312 pounds. If I was thinking straight, I'd go back home, find a used trailer,

buy a deep fryer and some Oreos. The problem is, this is the only thing I ever felt good doing. If I'm too old for this, then I got nothing.

This is our female hero. This is where she begins. We are to believe, much like she does, that Frankie is the person who can help her rise above all of this. So here we begin her journey to becoming a celebrated boxer. This is also where we quickly learn Frankie's number one rule: protect yourself at all times. This is repeated frequently throughout the film. It is eventually credited as the gift that could have saved her life. That will be addressed later.

This film presents damaging female representations. The only female representation we see are animalistic female boxers, sexualized women presenting the round numbers in the ring, uneducated and vulnerable Maggie and her irresponsible mother Earline Fitzgerald (Margo Martindale). There are no empowered females to be found. What's worse is that Maggie's mother is the only other female character awarded any major presence in the film. Her introduction comes when Maggie buys her a house and her only response is "Government's gonna find out about this, they're gonna stop my welfare." This is her mother. This is the life Maggie ran from yet throughout the film, she is consumed by the need for her mother and her family to love her. Meeting her family only makes viewers more grateful that Frankie is in her life.

As we watch Maggie's boxing career progress, we repeatedly watch her knock out her opponents with one quick punch. With this, Frankie is forced to do the one thing we know he fears most: take a risk. With a lack of challenging opponents, he moves her up in weight class. This sets her up to fight Billie "The Blue Bear" Osterman (Lucia Rijker) for the WBA welterweight title. As the narrator tells us, "Billie was a former prostitute out of East Berlin. Had a reputation for being the dirtiest fighter in the ranks. Didn't seem to matter to her that something like that could kill a person." Maggie was invited to fight her earlier in the film, but Billie's reputation was too much of a risk for Frankie. Now Frankie's worst fear is about to be realized.

The championship match begins and Maggie is winning. Billie begins breaking the rules to try and keep up. After being absolutely dominating in the third round, the bell rings and Maggie celebrates. She lets her guard down. She does not protect herself. Billie throws an illegal punch that sends Maggie falling. The stool where she sits between rounds is not in its usual position and her fall is broken by its edge. The crowd goes quiet. She lies there motionless. The next time we see her, she is hooked up to a life support machine in a hospital. The final 40 minutes of the film are dedicated to watching Maggie confined to a bed. If this film was about her, this would stand as the resolution of her storyline; the fight of her life ends her. However, this story is about Frankie and thus we now follow him as he, along with the audience, is slowly tortured as it becomes clear her physical state will never improve.

Frankie never leaves her bedside and never stops pursuing all options to help her. He is the only one who refuses to accept her reality. She knows she is never going to recover. Her family knows this too. When her family comes to visit, her mother commits the disgusting act of shoving a pen into Maggie's mouth for her to sign her boxing assets over to her. Maggie refuses, spitting the pen out. This is also where we begin to exonerate Frankie from putting her on this deathbed. Even in her debilitated state, she musters up the energy to admit she didn't protect herself, and no matter how many times Frankie told her, now she's paying for that. All of this leads up to Maggie's final request.

Earlier in the film, we shared a moment with Maggie while she admired the innocent and unconditional love between a little girl and her dog. This prompted her to tell Frankie the story of her dad's dog Axel. She stated, "Axel's hindquarters were so bad he had to drag himself room to room by his front legs…. But one morning [my father] got up, carried Axel to his rig and the two of them went off into the woods, singing and howling. But it wasn't until he got home that night alone that I saw the shovel in the back of the truck." Now, on her deathbed, all she has to ask is "remember what my daddy did for Axel?" and her request is clear. Upon Frankie's refusal, she replies with the following:

> MAGGIE: I can't be like this, Frankie. Not after what I've done. I seen the world. People chanted my name. Well, not my name, some damn name you gave me. But they were chanting for me. I was in magazines. You think I ever dreamed that'd happen? I was born at two pounds, one and a half ounces. Daddy used to tell me I fought to get into this world and I'd fight my way out. That's all I wanna do, Frankie. I just don't wanna fight you to do it. I got what I needed. I got it all. Don't let them keep taking it away from me. Don't let me lie here till I can't hear those people chanting no more.

She has no identity outside of boxing.

After watching Maggie try to end her own life by biting her tongue repeatedly, Frankie finally decides to grant her wish. But not before being relieved to do so by the one person who knows him best, Eddie. As Frankie gathers the medicines to make her passing painless, Eddie comes in for one final vote of confidence that this is the right decision. As Frankie breaks down and admits, "I killed her," Eddie says:

> EDDIE: Maggie walked through that door with nothing but guts. No chance in the world of being what she needed to be. A year and a half later, she's fighting for the championship of the world. You did that. People die every day, Frankie. Mopping floors, washing dishes. And you know what their last thought is? "I never got my shot." Because of you, Maggie got her shot. If she dies today, you know what her last thought will be? "I think I did all right."

That's success for Maggie: a life that is "all right." On the surface, her story appears to be driven by her choices. She finds Frankie, she chooses Frankie, she follows Frankie and she asks Frankie to let her go. But this moment is not for her. It is to release Frankie from his guilt and responsibility for her death. It is to celebrate *his* accomplishment. Maggie is defined by the favor Frankie granted her: purpose. In their final moment together before he assists in her passing, he shares that "Mo Cuishle," the name he gave her that she heard chanted from the crowds, means "My darling, my blood." Her purpose was to be the daughter he had lost so long ago, illustrating that he could redeem himself by being the father he always wanted to be. This stands as the most damaging example of a female eliciting change in a male character's masculinity. Yes, she finally receives the loyal and familial love she's always wanted, but she gets this at the tragic conclusion of her life. He continues on.

At the end of the film it is revealed that the entire narration was Eddie's letter to Frankie's daughter in an effort to mend their relationship. Throughout the film we've watched Frankie receiving the letters he wrote her, all with "Return to sender" on them. Now Eddie has written one of his own, the story of Maggie. This letter would have been far more empowering if it shared the story about an incredible woman Frankie trained rather than proving what kind of man he was for training her. This takes her place away as a role model and places the inspirational power solely with him, the patriarch. This film is about his legacy, not hers. At the end of the film, Eddie concludes:

EDDIE: Frankie didn't leave a note, and nobody knew where he went. I'd hoped he'd gone to find you and ask you one more time to forgive him. But maybe he didn't have anything left in his heart. I just hope he found some place where he could find a little peace. A place set in the cedars and oak trees. Somewhere between nowhere and goodbye. But that's probably wishful thinking. No matter where he is, I thought you should know what kind of man your father really was.

The last image of Frankie we see is of him sitting alone in a diner. Earlier in the film Maggie shares that she used to take her father to this diner. Frankie, perceived as an honorable father now, sits in this diner.

But feminist viewers like myself cannot get lost in sympathy for him. We cannot overlook the film's overriding necessity to exonerate Frankie for Maggie's death. We have been constantly reminded that if she had listened to his mantra "above all, always protect yourself" she might have survived this story. We are still reminded that even a strong, determined female character such as Maggie, is still in need of protection. *Million Dollar Baby* is a celebration of and redemption of the patriarch, the father figure. We may have met a strong, passionately driven female athlete but in the end she dies for it. Further, she is punished for never posing as an object of the gaze by any male character and never being actively viewed as trying to take that position. Maggie could have proposed a new space, unidentified by objectification. However, the film sends the message that this is not a space that can be survived.

Taking Cukor's directing influence into account was imperative to the empowerment allotted to *Pat and Mike*. Perhaps no director has more of an agenda approaching his female athlete story than Clint Eastwood with *Million Dollar Baby*. It's no surprise that Eastwood chose this story to produce, direct and star in. In *Persistence of Double Vision: Essays on Clint Eastwood,* William Beard writes: "The Eastwood persona represents probably the strongest icon of heroic masculinity in popular cinema over the past quarter-century."[8] In other words, Eastwood has created himself to be an icon of hegemonic masculinity. Beard argues:

Eastwood is unique in his dual position as overpowering cinematic persona-icon and creative filmmaker; as gigantic reflector, perpetuator, and even producer of mainstream cultural and ideological values; and as idiosyncratic, complex manipulator of the narrative environment(s) he has inhabited.[9]

This is important to take into consideration with *Million Dollar Baby.* Through this film, Eastwood has produced and perpetuated mainstream cultural and ideological values of a woman's place as secondary and in need of protection. These values are directly designated as the tensions against Maggie. Eastwood's character of Frankie takes center stage as yet another figure of "heroic masculinity." Frankie has been vindicated as a man, by surviving and by supposedly doing right by his surrogate daughter (unlike his actual daughter).

Eastwood's success has allowed him complete creative control in the Hollywood system. Studios fully entrust him because his name allows little financial risk. According to Robert E. Kasis and Kathie Coblentz in their book *Clint Eastwood Interviews,* "Eastwood seems likely to keep selecting his projects on the basis of the only criterion he has cited repeatedly to interviewers: The story is something he himself would want to see on the screen."[10] So what kind of female characters has he said he would want to see? In an interview in 1988, Eastwood admitted that he is a fan of strong female characters because he grew up on films where women had very important roles in stories. He states, "Clark Gable's role in *It Happened One Night* was only good because he had Claudette Colbert's to play off of. Those movies are more true to life than many films now where you have the guys sort of motivating most of the stories and the women in secondary positions."[11] In a 1992 interview he continued, "A male character loses a lot of his interest if all he has opposite him is a decorative partner." Maggie is anything but a "decorative partner."[12] However she is definitely relegated to the secondary position. Eastwood's vision of power for a female character is limited to her effect on the male lead. In *Million Dollar Baby* we watch Maggie go so far as dying for Frankie to be redeemed.

In 2005, the Academy of Motion Picture Arts and Sciences awarded *Million Dollar Baby* four Academy Awards: Best Director, Best Actress, Best Supporting Actor and Best Picture. With so much recognition, it also became a target for criticism. Many complained about its sentimentalism and lack of recognition for life as a quadriplegic. What's missing is any critical recognition of how the character of Maggie was treated. Centering the film on Frankie takes everything away from our female athlete, including her life.

I am grateful to now transition to *Girlfight,* which has some of the same plot points as *Million Dollar Baby* but awards its female athlete the lead role and a far more empowering conclusion. Directed by Karyn Kusama in 2000, it deliberately puts forth a feminist theme. Like Maggie, teenager Diana Guzman (Michelle Rodriguez) finds her identity in the world of boxing. What differs from *Million Dollar Baby* is that Diana is not under the control of anyone. Yes she has to convince her trainer to take her on, but once she is fighting, she continues to make her own decisions in and outside of the ring. She is also allowed a successful romantic relationship. Moreover, the conclusion to Diana's story leaves us with true empowerment for this female athlete. We will address all of these points in the following analysis.

Girlfight is unique in its awareness, and rebellion, of the female social construction. This is introduced immediately. Less than three minutes into the film, we watch Diana pummel a girl, who she later describes as "always with that mirror of hers. Let me get made up just perfect so I can suck your dick which is all I'm good for anyway." Diana is fully aware of the façade of currency in beauty and subordination. After having her mother commit suicide in response to her father's abuse, Diana recognizes and adamantly rebels against any "ladylike" decorum that may have contributed to her mother's defeat.[13]

When Diana punches a male boxer and he says he forgives her because she "never learned how to be a lady," it is suggested that Diana's demeanor and actions are not innate, they are "learned." This could also lend to the fact that Diana is being raised solely by her abusive father. However, it is quite clear that Diana wants nothing to do with her father and what he represents. Diana is one of the strongest, and far more rebellious, cinematic female athletes we will discuss in this book. She challenges the very core of female construction. For the purposes of comparing *Girlfight* with *Million Dollar Baby,* we will focus on similar plot points and how they differ to challenge Maggie's infantilized role and her ultimate demise.

With *Million Dollar Baby* centered on Maggie's relationship with her trainer, we'll first address the relationship with Diana and her trainer, Hector Soto (Jaime Tirelli). Diana is initiated into boxing through her brother, Tiny (Ray Santiago). He wants to be an artist, but is forced into boxing lessons by their father who thinks art is a waste of time. Additionally, their father wants Tiny to learn to be a man and toughen up. The first time Diana enters the gym, she is introduced to a new world, a world that fits her. She recognizes that boxing is not a world where you prove your worth in physical appearance or your ability to be subordinate; your worth is in your ability to physically dominate your opponent. It is an absolute; you either win or you lose. This isn't a sport that forces you to rely on anyone else. As she puts it, "It's like you're all you've got. You're all alone in there."

Much like Frankie, this gym's trainer Hector is passionate about the fundamentals and is known to pick caution over big money in the progress of his fighters. Similarly, he won't let a girl in without friction. He tells Diana she can train, but she can't fight because "girls don't have the same power as boys." However, unlike Frankie, Hector surrenders quickly to the idea of her fighting as long as she can pay him. Throughout the film, Hector is only her trainer. He teaches her the methods to become a successful boxer. That's it. He's the only person she listens to and respects because he is her key to this new world. She is not his surrogate daughter; he treats her like any other boxer. He doesn't expect or pressure her to be anything else.

Next, we'll address Diana's family. Diana's father, Sandro (Paul Calderaon), is an abuser. Her mother committed suicide in response to this abuse, which left Diana to protect her brother and herself. Unlike Maggie who is an independent adult, Diana is a teenager still confined to the guardianship of her father. However, unlike Maggie's undying desire to be accepted by her family, Diana is just trying to survive until she can get out.

In one of the film's climactic scenes, Diana stands up to her father. He doesn't want her to box and when he tries to assert his authority, she calls him out on his treatment of her mother: "The only thing you had the heart to love, you practically beat into the grave." She continues, "You just had to push her, didn't you, Dad? ... Until she'd rather die than answer to you, huh?" This prompts him to hit her and thus she begins to box against him and wins. While choking him, she exclaims:

> DIANA: I could snap your neck right now if I felt like it. I could kill you if I felt like it. Mom begged. Did you stop when she said "Please"? ... You belong to me now. How does it feel to see so much of yourself so close? How does it feel?

In this action, Diana creates an interesting dynamic for her father. She shows him what it feels like to be abused. As Leslie Heywood and Shari

L. Dworkin articulate so well in their book *Built to Win: The Female Athlete as Cultural Icon:*

> By physically overpowering him, by being as threatening as he ever was, Diana holds a mirror up to her father where he can see what abuse looks and feels like, where he can experience first-hand the devastation of "belonging" to someone else, having yourself erased in this way.[14]

This film addresses Diana's family as a source for her rebellion. She confronts and changes this abusive dynamic herself. This is a far cry from spitting out a pen on your deathbed, the only agency that was ultimately allowed to Maggie.

Finally, let's look at the story element withheld from Maggie: a romantic relationship. Diana's love interest, Adrian (Santiago Douglas), is also a boxer. For Adrian, boxing is a ticket to a better life and keeps him out of trouble. Although this declaration of her heterosexuality could arguably have been introduced to ease the audience's acceptance of her masculine appearance and actions, the film continues to challenge their dynamic as a couple that exists beyond the heterosexual norm. During their relationship, Adrian is sensitive, supportive and likes her for who she is. He likes that she doesn't surrender to what girls are supposed to be. He even admits, "I feel pretty fucking small around you."

In the most interesting turn of events, the climax of *Girlfight* is a boxing match between Diana and Adrian. As Hector reads:

> HECTOR: A gender-blind amateur boxing proposal is a statewide initiative that responds to the ongoing demands for officially sanctioned amateur matches while also addressing the expanding presence of females in the sport. Male and female amateurs within the same weight class are allowed to compete with each other in the ring.

After watching Diana dominate in her short but quick career as a boxer, she is matched with Adrian for New York's first gender-blind amateur featherweight championship. The stakes are high. Beyond the fate of their relationship, this is a major step towards going pro for either of them. She wants to fight, he doesn't. He threatens to sabotage his weight, saying, "I haven't trained all this time to be stuck in the ring with a girl." This enrages her as she replies, "You're afraid I might win... You're gonna play it all manly and protective on me now... All I know is, if you don't fight me in this match, you're less of a man than you think you are." Diana's priority is the fight, not her boyfriend. Additionally, she has no mercy for his pride. Adrian does decide to fight, and he gives it his best effort. In the end, Diana wins.

What sets this movie apart is its conclusion. After winning the fight, we share a quiet moment where Diana is alone. She sits in a locker room on the verge of tears, torn between celebrating and being devastated at the realization she can't have Adrian *and* be a boxing champion. But she's wrong. A few days after the fight, while we watch her clearing out the maintenance closet she's been using as a locker to make it a more permanent space for her career, Adrian shows up. The following conversation takes place:

ADRIAN: I gave everything I had.
DIANA: Me too.
ADRIAN: Boxing, going pro ... I wanted it to be my ticket out. But I gave you an opening. It was stupid.
DIANA: But that's what happens. You just take advantage.
ADRIAN: Yeah. So, now I lose your respect, huh?
DIANA: No.
ADRIAN: After the other night? Come on.
DIANA: Adrian, you boxed with me like I was any other guy. You threw down and you showed me respect. Don't you see what that means?
ADRIAN: That life with you is war.
DIANA: Maybe. Maybe life's just war, period.
ADRIAN: You said it. My life's been a mess since I met you ... So, you gonna dump me now?
DIANA: Probably.
ADRIAN: Promise?

And with that, they kiss. Her happy ending is based on choices she actively makes. She chose to box Adrian and, after beating him, it is her decision to stay with him.

Girlfight introduces a new heterosexual dynamic. Firstly, Diana and Adrian's relationship is established with the knowledge that Diana is more physically dominant. Secondly, both Diana and Adrian have equally shared emotional moments of strength and vulnerability. Their relationship is built on a new understanding of two individuals rather than any innate gender definitions.[15]

The characters in *Girlfight* expose and challenge our assumptions about gender.[16] Unlike *Million Dollar Baby, Girlfight* presents us with a female athlete who represents more than her ability to compete; she illustrates what competing can represent. Equality isn't only about watching women win. Women need to witness stories where these female athletes take control of their own careers and can do it all, through *their* choices. Watching women learn their strengths and utilize their agency as individuals will eliminate the myth of passive femininity.[17]

No one can be defined without being in a fixed state. Women must break free of the definitions of patriarchy. A woman does not need a partner, a family or a championship cup. These should be a matter of "want" for her. Velvet wants to ride, so she should ride until she wants something else, not because her time is limited according to her mother's schedule of life. Pat can continue playing, with Mike as her manager, whether she is in a relationship with him or not. Maggie should not have to die in order for Frankie to be redeemed. But Diana will continue boxing whether Adrian desires her or not. These women's careers are not and should not be contingent on patriarchal values.

These films should not encourage a battle of who is better in sports, men or women. They should expose the equal but different strengths of females and males. As Hector admits in *Girlfight:*

> HECTOR: Remember when I told you that girls can't be boxers? … Girls—excuse me, *women*—have a lower center of gravity. Maybe they're more grounded once they build strength. It makes 'em a different kind of boxer… The way to prove it is to get more women in that ring.

The way to celebrate women's strengths as athletes is to see more on the screen. We need more stories about Diana Guzman and fewer stories about a female's athletic accomplishment categorized as folly.

2

Hitting Foul

Missed Opportunities in
A League of Their Own *and* Whip It

To play as a team requires the ability to work together, trust each other and encourage each other to compete against your opponent. Since the social construction of being feminine doesn't particularly support women being competitive or simply displaying as much aggression as needed to compete, female teams create a safe space where a group of women can work together and keep that judgment at bay.[1] However, this idea is not displayed in cinematic portrayals of female teams. Instead, we watch a group of women whose diversity evolves into a comparison, allowing one player to emerge as the ultimate woman. It does not require a suspension of disbelief to have a story display one player emerging as the top talent; however, what characteristics that player displays (other than athletic skill) can be a defining message to an audience. We are continuing to see cinematic female athletes who fail to rise above their patriarchal subordinate status because these films utilize a team collaboration to present a comparison signifying what women are "supposed" to be rather than a collaboration allowing these women to simply work together.

Both *A League of Their Own* and *Whip It* represent storylines that set up an empowered horizon and goal for female athletes, yet fail to allow their heroines to claim it. In *A League of Their Own,* the heroine's primary goal is not to be an athlete, but to be a conventional wife and mother. *Whip It,* which is supposed to be thematically centered on a female athlete actively choosing her identity, features a heroine who chooses an identity of subordination and constructed femininity. Both these films offer the façade of empowerment by featuring dynamic female athletes, but in actuality they reaffirm stereotypes of subordinated women and gender power dynamics.

A League of Her Own

A League of Their Own, directed by Penny Marshall in 1992, is based on the first year of the All American Girls Professional Baseball League (AAGPBL). Before I continue with an analysis of the film, it is important to reflect on the actual history of the league to better understand conflicting choices in its adaptation to film.

In 1943 the first and, to this day, the only women's professional baseball league was established, the AAGPBL. Its creation was attributed to the loss of male ballplayers to World War II, greatly diminishing the sport and business of baseball. This was also the time of Rosie the Riveter where women were encouraged to leave the home and work. Women were given an outlet to push themselves and see what they were truly capable of, and America's favorite pastime, baseball, was one such outlet. This opportunity for female athletes was unprecedented considering baseball was a previously definitive male sport. However, this wasn't simply about allowing females to play ball, this was also a controlled effort to contain and control the image of women. These female athletes were exclusively chosen for their ability to broadcast a "safe" feminine representation.[2] Although this opportunity was only allotted to women who fit this bill, it cannot be denied that the very existence of the league propelled and inspired women to demand broader opportunities in work and sports.

Forty-nine years later, in 1992, *A League of Their Own* was released, earning over $100 million at the box office. Although a financial success, most critics were not fans; they accused the film of having a condescending attitude toward women, playing to easy laughs and they questioned if there was any real baseball played.[3] *A League of Their Own* veered far away from the reality of the empowering impact the AAGPBL had for its players. The critics revealed the very problem with the film— not in their direct reviews, but in *how* they reviewed it. In reality, the few hundred women who played in the AAGPBL were given access to a previously male-defined source of confidence, which then instilled them with the ambition to pick professions previously out of reach, such as teachers, doctors and lawyers.[4] *A League of Their Own* does not illustrate this; instead, it embraces and encourages the very negative stereotypes of women that kept them from envisioning these possibilities.

A League of Their Own was inspired by *A League of Their Own: The Documentary*. The producers of that documentary, Kim Wilson and Kelly Candaele, are also credited as the storywriters on *A League of Their Own*. Since the film's plot is supposedly based on such expertise, the changes and choices within the plotline are all the more distressing. At first glance, there are a few obvious differences: Instead of being founded by a chewing gum mogul, the fictional league is funded by a candy bar bigwig. Although the players share the first or last names of actual players, none of the characters fully embody the storylines of any real members of the AAGPBL. The team names are accurate. The Racine Bells were the first champions and there are many signifiers consistently setting the atmosphere of the 1940s such as the clothing, music and news footage. Beyond that, the storylines are fictional and thus can be analyzed as conscious choices adapted for Hollywood. These choices can be held accountable for their plot decisions, which characters are endorsed and how they are treated. The film may take place in the 1940s but it was made for the 1990s and could have presented new modes of empowerment birthed from that experience by presenting the true stories about these diverse and talented women who opened a gateway of opportunity in careers on and off the field.

The film follows Dottie Henson (Geena Davis) and her sister Kit (Lori Petty) as they join the Rockford Peaches, one of the founding teams of the league. They meet a slew of characters including the loud-mouthed comic duo Mae Mordabito (Madonna) and Doris Murphy (Rosie O'Donnell); Marla Hooch (Megan Cavanagh), a socially awkward, tomboyish woman who is an unbelievable hitter; Evelyn Gardner (Bitty Schram), an overly sensitive mother who brings her nightmarish son on the team's road trips; and their manager Jimmy Dugan (Tom Hanks), a drunk, washed-up famous ballplayer who doesn't believe women can play baseball. The film awards all of these players redeeming story arcs. Mae and Doris go from being nobodies working in Doris' father's dance-hall to building a fan base and an identity in the league. The team helps Marla find her femininity and therefore she finds love and gets married.

Evelyn becomes the signifier of Jimmy's growth as their manager by teaching him patience in dealing with her emotions. By the end of the film, Jimmy turns down an opportunity to coach men, instead deciding to continue with the Rockford Peaches.

Throughout the film, the Rockford Peaches quickly become the star of the league thanks to Dottie's talent, skill and beauty. However, this doesn't bode well for Kit, who desperately wants to escape out of her sister's shadow. This causes enough conflict that Kit eventually is traded to another team. The climax takes place in the league's championship where the Rockford Peaches face off against Kit's new team, the Racine Bells. The final game-winning play is centered on Dottie and Kit. As Dottie is a catcher and Kit is the runner coming into home to score, it is up to Dottie to tag Kit and hang on to the ball to win the game. However, Dottie doesn't hang on to the ball and therefore Kit wins. This is done in an ambiguous fashion, allowing the viewer to question if Dottie dropped the ball on purpose to benefit her sister. However, before we can establish that argument and what it represents, we must take a deeper look into the film's other representations that make Dottie's choice to drop the ball ultimately oppressive.

In order to fully understand Dottie's character and the film's representations of women, it's necessary to analyze how the league itself contributes to gender norms. *A League of Their Own* establishes the inception of the AAGPBL with an original newsreel celebrating famous male ballplayers who joined the military and additional news footage, manipulated to include our fictional characters, showing how AAGPBL players were marketed to the masses. These news flashes continually appear with messages that allow the audience to ascertain these players' femininity. With such marketing slogans as "trading oven mitts for baseball mitts" or pulls such as "catch a foul, get a kiss," there was an obvious fear that women would lose their place in the home and their femininity because of their access to baseball, a treasured masculine domain. The league manager proclaims, "Every girl in this league is going to be a lady." This includes charm school, wearing makeup and having to play in dresses. In the film, these elements are confronted with humor. Although the girls scoff at their uniforms and appear aware of the ridiculousness that these are "necessary" to play baseball and still be a woman, the sequence of charm school blurs the lines of judgment and entertainment.

We witness a montage of women balancing books on their head for posture, drinking tea with delicate hands and learning how to sit with their legs crossed "because a lady reveals nothing." Among these moments, we see humorous displays of players' "feminine" inadequacy, such as Doris who wolfs down her snack accompanying the tea with less than delicate hands. However, these comical gestures seem innocent until we see Marla, the non-stereotypical woman, as the butt of the joke. We had been introduced to Marla while a scout was viewing her hit homerun after homerun. Her father admitted to raising her like a son and stated, "If she were a boy, I'd be talking to the Yankees." No matter how many homeruns she hit, the scout wasn't interested. It was quickly clear that talent alone does not carry value of success in this story. She must be pretty too. Marla's failure to carry the "currency" of beauty is presented as her problem, despite her expert play.[5]

As the charm school instructor makes her way down the row nit-picking each player's "problem" areas according to the beauty standard, she stops in front of Marla and simply states, "A lot of night games." Later there is a sequence of recreated newsreel footage introducing the star players while exhibiting their talents and their beauty. Marla is presented once again as a punchline. Through an extreme wide shot, too far to see any detail of her face, she stands motionless and the announcer simply states, "What a hitter." Rather than celebrating Marla's difference or fighting back to illustrate the problems in this blatant beauty myth judgment, the audience is brought in for the joke and laughs with the 1940s, emulating the very problems this film should criticize.

As mentioned before, there are other characters that are highlighted for their alternative attitude and manners such as Mae, a perceived promiscuous, tough-talking blonde who offers her breasts for PR to be used by the league, and her best friend Doris, a fast-talking, brash, over-weight brunette, about whom one player states, "She reminds me of my husband." At one point Doris shares that she met Mae at her father's dancehall (insinuated as a strip club), stating, "She was one of the dancers, I was a bouncer." Doris and Mae are introduced together and never leave each other's side. They bicker and support each other like a classic comic duo and, for all intents and purposes, a lesbian couple.

There is a literal display of this one night when the team sneaks out to a bar to rebel against the league manager's orders, "no smoking, drinking or men." In this scene we watch Mae put on display, allowing the audience to learn Doris's position in reference to her: Doris admires Mae as she dances, then Doris joins in with a male partner and we watch them both simultaneously dance in a wide shot. However, in a choreographed moment, it is quickly apparent that this could represent them dancing with each other. Just as Mae slides between her male dance partner's legs and over his back, we watch Doris do the same only *she* slides *her* male partner between *her* legs and over *her* back. As Mae continues to dance between male partners, she is flung into Doris's arms and passed back into the dancing men. At the conclusion of the song, she falls into Doris's arms and embraces her in excitement.

Later, in the bar, we have our first opportunity to see Mae physically with a man. After her introduction and continued reminders of her promiscuity, this first time should appear characteristic yet she awkwardly chugs a mug of alcohol while the man, whose lap she sits on, comically tries to interest her but ultimately fails. It is only after she finishes every last drop of the drink that she kisses him. Additionally, in this moment, Doris stays by her side, sitting across the table through the entire sequence. Their connection goes beyond a recognizable female friendship and mimics more of a romantic relationship. Doris protects, promotes and admires Mae, and Mae always comes back to Doris as such.

The film partakes in a continued desire to re-affirm every player's heterosexuality, no matter how masculine she may appear or whatever coded lesbian references appear. Mae has no problem having men at her disposal, but the film awards Doris two twin stereotypically nerdy guys who follow her and inundate her with flowers and encouraging praise. There is no sexual attraction evidenced by Doris, but these men treat her far better than her husband, of whom she says, "He's stupid, he's out of work, and he treats me bad." In this moment, Doris also admits that all of the other boys "made me feel like I was wrong, you know? Like I was sort of a weird girl or a strange girl, or not even a girl just because I could play. I believed them too but not any more, you know? I mean, look at it, there's a lot of us. I think we're all all right." After saying this, she tears up the photo of her husband and tosses it out of the bus window. This signifies her empowerment because she recognizes her difference as a strength and not a curse. However, the film's continual need to keep her fulfilled with her male twin's admiration reinforces her place on the heteronormative spectrum. As the newsreels affirming femininity appear to want to distance the league from suspicions of lesbianism, so does the film.

Queer readings of film narratives expose an important understanding that the complexity in sexuality, and therefore gender definitions, has always been present in popular culture texts. There is a positive effect for queer viewers who can find points of identification within a text that otherwise is drearily heteronormative.[6] But there is also a positive effect when straight audiences recognize and connect to queer realities while interpreting queer storylines. They can find their own queer relation to the text, recognizing that labels such as homosexuality, gay or lesbian are not the constricting and discriminated classification heteronormative culture has deemed them to be. There is a range of queerness that many, queer and straight, find themselves connecting with in their own way. However, the necessity of a queer reading in itself reflects the constant need to veil ideas of sexuality under the hegemonic heterocentric storylines. Simply alluding to a homosexual relationship between Mae and Doris is not enough. Queer-identifying audiences have had to embrace a "we'll take what we can get" approach in mainstream cinema. This is not acceptable. By 1992, homosexuality had entered mainstream conversation and it should have been acknowledged, without disguise, in the narrative. Further, by acknowledging the relationship between Doris and Mae amongst other players who were not gay could have enforced the notion that sports does not ensure a women's homosexuality.

Adding to the film's heteronormative spectrum, Marla, presented farthest from the feminine norm, gains her acceptance after the girls give her a dress "and a lot of liquor" and she drunkenly sings to an admiring man in the bar. This stands as her initiation to recognizable womanhood. This man later becomes her husband as she passes under an arch of her fellow players' baseball bats at her wedding ceremony. Elated, she exclaims, "I'm so happy!" At least, from a feminist point of view, she adds, "I'll be back next season." But the ending is definitely pushing her not toward rebellion but toward conformity: By entering a traditional marriage, our most "confused" female representation has been redeemed.

Beyond the re-establishment of the heterosexual norm, the film also mocks women by mocking conventional femininity and the emotionality that is associated with it (in contrast to supposedly emotionally more contained masculinity). Evelyn, mother of the cartoonish annoying child who is brought on road trips, is mocked for crying when their manager, Jimmy Dugan, yells at her, making the now classic statement, "There's no crying in baseball!" Showing weakness is not acceptable in sports and certainly not competitive according to this conventional view.[7] Jimmy represents this form of masculinity. In this scene, he explains that his coach used to make him feel worthless and that's just a part of the game. This scene only exists to endorse the skill of denying emotion and attaching that skill to male dominance. In addition, this later stands as the signal that Jimmy has changed his ways and cares when Evelyn performs the same mistake. Instead of screaming at her, although looking like he's going to burst, he instructs her to work on that for next season. In this sequence of events, there is only criticism of her emotional display, not sympathy. He must change, not her, because she can't help or control her sensitivity as a woman. One umpire even states, "Treat each of these girls as you would your mother," signaling that they should be treated differently in this sport then men. This supports a false argument that sports cannot be equal between men and women. Rather than challenge the system, these characters, such as Evelyn, Doris, Mae and Marla, simply continue their role in supporting the celebration of what they are not, which turns out to be the main character, Dottie Henson.

Dottie is strong, talented, tough and, most importantly, beautiful. One newsreel even states that she "plays like Gehrig and looks like Garbo." While the media nicknames Mae "All the Way Mae," a double entendre referring to her off-the-field sexual behavior as well as her ability to steal bases, Dottie is simply named the "Queen of Diamonds." Dottie quickly becomes the standard for the ideal "lady," against which the other women are compared and to which they fall short. In a *New York Times* article, the adviser on the film, Pepper Davis, stated that the character of Dottie Henson was made up of six AAGPBL players.[8] One of the prominent ballplayers who formed her character was Dorothy Kamenshek; known as the best player in the history of the AAGBL. She played first base for the Rockford Peaches for nine full seasons, injuring her back in 1949, but continued to play with a brace, and retired in 1952 to pursue a career in physical therapy. Kamenshek reflects the stories of many of the ballplayers who played in the league. As opposed to Dottie, the real players played for many seasons. Many played until the league was disbanded, and those who left the league left for job opportunities or because of playing injuries. Therefore, the choices made for the fictitious Dottie Henson's goals and conclusion are relevant observations of creative intent.

The film opens in present day where we watch a significantly older Dottie caressing pictures of her husband and the family that she's built. Right off the bat (pun intended), we are assured that, despite her participation in such a masculine sport, she has succeeded in raising a family and being a mother. This is our lead character, and this is her accomplishment before we even see a playing mitt. Dottie is hesitantly packing for an AAGPBL reunion. She doesn't want to go because she doesn't think anyone will remember her and playing "was never anything important, it was just something I did." Right away we are faced with Dottie representing weakness and a constant self-defeating need to avoid recognizing the importance of what she did or her talent. This is the beginning of a distressing construction of admirable femininity as self-abnegation in our hero. She projects an image of a woman who needs to nurture and mother, and considers her athletic desires secondary, despite her first-place talent and skill.

When we first meet the younger ballplayer Dottie, she doesn't want to play. She finds other things more important in life, such as the farm, waiting for her husband to return from war and starting a family. She states, "I'm married, I'm happy, let's not confuse things." Her younger sister Kit pushes her to go because Kit won't be accepted unless Dottie goes. Dottie accepts because she is responsible for her sister's entrance to the league. This is not to say that she is not competitive, peeking through a window as Kit desperately begs the scout to take her, but the manner in which she joins allows her the opportunity to remind the viewer that she does in fact find raising a family more important. Since Kit is her family too, then she is accepting out of responsibility to Kit, not herself. This continues throughout the film, leading to important choices that define her character beyond the role of a captain or older sister and highlighting her role of mother.

This becomes Dottie's foundation as a character. Through her story we witness a constant push to recognize her ability to nurture. By placing Dottie as the captain of the team, star of the league and empathic motherly hero of the film, the audience is immersed in a dated social conditioning, continuing ideas that women are inherently more sensitive to others.[9] This story takes place in a time period where women have the opportunity to leave the home and take over previously masculine domains, including baseball. This film should celebrate that gateway, not promote that era's obsolete and oppressive gender ideology.

Dottie's relationship to her sister Kit dictates when and how Dottie distances herself from her desired role of wife and mother. Whenever she gains momentum as the star player and chooses to embrace it, her sister steps in as a reminder of that over-step, and Dottie retreats to her secondary subordinated nature. This plays an important role in a scene late in the film when the team is about to win a playoff game, but Kit has exhausted her pitching talent. She has never been pulled from a game, but when Jimmy asks Dottie what she thinks, Dottie finally chooses the game over her sister and sharply says "She's done, she's throwing grapefruits up there." For the first time, Dottie fully surrenders to her competitive spirit. As a result, her actions commence immediate punishment for deviation from an antiquated construction of femininity.

Immediately following Dottie's disregard for her sister, the film forces us to recognize that playing in the league is not Dottie's prescribed role; she is a wife, sister and mother. This is accomplished in a number of ways. First, in a miscommunication where Dottie offers herself up to be traded to alleviate Kit's frustration, the league trades Kit instead. When Kit comes to attack Dottie, Dottie exclaims, "I'm so sick of being blamed for everything that's bothering you. I got you into this league, God damn it, I didn't even want to be here." Second, the reality of the war sets in with the reminder that these women, including Dottie, have husbands fighting. Instead of seeing Dottie play in another game, we cut directly after to watch her crying for fear of losing her husband, which immediately cues his entrance. It is clear that Dottie will not hesitate to abandon her baseball career for her original goal of being a wife.

It is important to reference Dottie's relationship with Jimmy up until this point. Audiences may have expected a romantic relationship to blossom between these two. Although Dottie and Jimmy have had a

45

special connection throughout the film, Jimmy never stands as a threat to Dottie's marriage. Dottie cares for Jimmy as she cares for the other girls. She helps him quit drinking and encourages him to be the man he wants to be. He is another person Dottie takes responsibility for.

It should be noted that the change in Jimmy's character could, in itself, question ideas of masculinity. He begins as a man who has lost his masculinity due to the loss of his ability to play baseball and to fight in the war because of a bad knee. Jimmy deals with the loss of these two masculine outlets by drinking and wasting away. What problematizes a positive reading of Jimmy's change throughout the film is that his change is perceived as one that can only live in the company of females. His choice to continue coaching women's baseball demonstrates a valiant dedication to their athleticism but it also leaves a message that he cannot go back. He doesn't return to male baseball where he could have the opportunity to instruct and exhibit a change in how masculinity is defined there. He embraces new ideas of coaching sports, but only while hidden behind the very female players who inspired it.

Even though Dottie leaves the team as they head into the championship, she chooses to come back for the final game. This sets the scene for her ultimate sacrifice. This championship sequence illustrates further that she is always perceived as a woman who cares for, and sacrifices for, others. At the film's climactic moment, we are set in a situation where the game comes down to one play. This play is ultimately placed between Dottie and Kit at home plate. The consequences are simple for the audience: If Dottie hangs on to the ball, she wins, if she doesn't, Kit wins. Dottie does not hang on to the ball. This moment is played in an ambiguous fashion so that one can question if Dottie purposely let go of the ball to benefit her sister. I argue she did.

Throughout the film, Dottie's competitive spirit occasionally appears. At one point she boldly states, "I was fine until that scout came into our barn. Besides, I'm no quitter." Even if she appears to innocently fall into the maternal and coaching roles she plays within the team, we glimpse an underlying conflict as she sometimes shows real enjoyment in being the star. She performs feats of athleticism, such as catching the ball while in a split, and we witness her matching Jimmy's masculine ballplayer demeanor in chewing and spitting. Most influentially, she makes the choice to cut her sister from the game rather than let her play.

The fallout from this crucial moment leads the viewer to question if Kit really won at that moment. More to my point here, it shows that her "femininity" is not the full measure of her character. Nonetheless, the film shows it as right that she squelches that part of her character.

There are a few moments in particular that bolster my argument that she purposely sacrificed the win in order to benefit her sister. One moment takes place in a montage earlier in the film where we witness her complete this very play against an opposing player. But the paramount moment takes place directly before Dottie and Kit come head to head. Up until this point it has been made abundantly clear that Kit feels invisible when Dottie is around. She has never had her own moment of glory. Once this final championship game is tied up due to Kit's problematic pitching, Kit sits in the dugout crying. There is a very specific moment we are meant to share with Dottie as she sees this. Without this last trigger for Dottie's care, Kit's victory might have been accepted as hers alone.

The scenario is set and we watch Kit hit her game-winning ball. With each base she passes, the film slows down her action and raises the score. The crowd goes wild, the dugouts are screaming. We see a moment of Dottie's surprise and then she watches as her sister rounds the bases. There is a cacophony of sound. As Kit rams into Dottie, we witness every second of this hit, from three different angles, as they fall to the ground. To conclude the sequence, we see a closeup of Dottie's hand as she lets the ball loose. Through the entire hit, Dottie held the ball; once her hand comes to rest on the ground she releases it. If the previous story and visual elements I've discussed aren't enough to convince an audience that Dottie chose to let the ball go, we watch as Jimmy stands on the edge of the dugout defeated and Dottie stands by his side smiling, admiring her gift as Kit is carried off the field by her celebrating team. By sacrificing her win for her younger sister's happiness, our heroine's femininity is now redeemed.

This is the constructed fear of females in sports. Detractors always say that women will let their emotions get in the way, that emotions such as mercy and sympathy have no place in competition. The goal is to win. Femininity equals sacrifice. The goal in sports is to dominate. Dottie as our main character embodies all these stereotypes. She does little for herself. She tries to get traded for Kit, leaves for her husband

and ultimately loses the game on purpose. Dottie's character is perceived as the strongest character because she gives up the most. This is a profoundly unfeminist portrayal.

The reality of the AAGPBL is that these female athletes earned their place on the field. Hall of Fame ballplayer Max Carey once said, "They were more serious than the skirts they were required to wear, more intelligent than the various board directors who would not let them become managers."[10] In 1954, the league was disbanded due to a lack of spectator interest, but the landscape of female athletics was forever changed. The AAGPBL was an influential gateway for women to access independence and confidence to challenge their restriction to the home. Although this is referenced in conversation in the film, it is unfair how little this is portrayed. The most prominent player who reflected this was Kit, who ultimately moves to Racine and works to continue playing. This could signify an empowering choice and perhaps prefigures the next generation, but Kit is not the hero of this story. Additionally, even though Kit follows her own path, in the pseudo–present-day sequence at the conclusion of the film she enters with a flock of grandchildren. Once again, sexist viewers are reminded not to fret, for she became a mother too.

The song that opens the film is "Now and Forever" by Carole King. Although a love song, within the context of the film the celebrated "moment" refers to the rise of the AAGPBL. Harkening back to Mrs. Brown in *National Velvet,* this implies that the moment has passed. There was a window of opportunity for these women and the "lucky ones" reaped the benefit. The truth, however, is that that moment was a giant step for women's empowerment. Even with the troubled actions of objectifying that were deemed necessary to build the AAGPBL, women played and they played well. The game gave them hope that there were endless options for women. Unfortunately, *A League of Their Own* fails to explore those options. This film reasserts stereotypes, gender power dynamics and social constructions. It's an example of Hollywood's choices to disempower women, even those women who historically proved themselves to be powerful. One of the most empowering moments in history is then represented in a loosely based adaptation that re-defines and returns women to their constructed roles and stereotypes.

The choices made in *A League of Their Own* present the power of projecting patriarchal ideologies through the story of a female athlete hero, Dottie, who chooses to forgo her career. What happens to a story when the power to choose is no longer given to the female athlete? In recent films about female teams, such as *Whip It* and *Bend It Like Beckham,* the lead heroines would not even play in their championships without the permission and approval of their fathers. This stands as a new form of subjugation.

Being His *Own Hero*

Although *Whip It* is a story placed within an all-female sport, the sport of roller derby itself is definitive of hegemonic masculinity. The sport is known, and advertised, for its violence, much like male-defined sports such as football and wrestling.[11] The sport consists of two teams of "blockers" who whiz around a small track with individual team members, "jammers," trying to pass them. The strategy is very physical play where success is contingent on your toughness to both give and take a hit. Roller derby is definitely a contact sport and female participation in contact sports such as this immediately challenge a female gender construction.

Roller derby is certainly a product of third-wave feminism. Although the sport has been around since the 1930s, and was originally co-ed, the interest level waned and it didn't really pick up again until 2001 in Austin, Texas. The sport was reborn as an all-female league with a new dramatic element bringing aggression with sexuality and drama through players enacting characters they create.[12] Dressed in torn T-shirts, lingerie and makeup that borders on war paint while violently knocking each other down, these female athletes boldly challenge traditional femininity to the extreme. They can be sexually objectified in their attire, yet their actions are singularly dominant and aggressive. While other female athletes opt to present themselves in conventionally sexually objectified ways in the media outside of their sport to balance the assumed masculinity from playing, it could be argued that roller derby athletes control their objectification by displaying sexual agency as they actively play.[13] However, this is problematic. By binding their sport with elements of objectification, the sport continues (and celebrates) the tradition of a need to be objectified. We must ask: Do viewers really understand that this is ironic? Or do they simply see it as another form of objectification?

These are all elements we watch in *Whip It*. These teams are comprised of women who range in sexuality and style, and never question the fact that the popularity of the sport is, in part, linked to their being sexually objectified. In *A League of Their Own*, female players wore the modified uniforms and played their sex roles so they could have the opportunity to play a traditionally male sport. In roller derby, these women choose the uniforms they want and create their derby personas as a part of their sport. With these thoughts in mind, it's important to recognize *Whip It* as a tension between both feminism and anti-feminism.

Whip It, directed by Drew Barrymore in 2009, is based on Shauna Cross's 2007 book *Derby Girls*, a fictionalized account of her experience competing in roller derby. Cross also wrote the adaptation for the screen. The film is about Bliss (Ellen Page), a 17-year-old girl from the small town of Bodeen, Texas. Desperate to get out, she knows she is better than her peers who spend their time playing the traditional high school power structured role of drinking and wasting away. When the film opens, she is desperately trying to wash out blue hair dye but is unsuccessful and therefore loses a beauty pageant. Right away we recognize that Bliss has no desire to be or be around pageant girls. It is established that she takes part in pageants to please her mother Brooke (Marcia Gay Harden).

Whip It has flashes of clearly feminist intentions. Remembering that initiation into adulthood for women lies in image-related forums such as pageants, whereas men's is in sports, *Whip It* exhibits a literal translation of these ideas. Only in this film, the pageants represent an initiation into a dated sexist femininity-based construction and the sport is presented to challenge that and introduce a new kind of femininity. Another feminist highlight takes place in an early scene at the diner where Bliss works. She is confronted by a group of her peers who ask, "So are you like alternative now?" and Bliss responds, "Alternative to what?" A statement like this blatantly challenges the existence of a standard. The idea of a universal standard, or norm, is the antithesis of the sport Bliss is going to find herself in.

However, this film does present conventional stereotypes of men within the character of Bliss's father Earl (Daniel Stern). Earl is a diehard sports fan who, with a family only comprised of women, finds his link to masculinity in watching sports. However, throughout the film it is revealed that he feels a need to hide his obsession with sports from his wife, comically portrayed as an affair. In a scene where Bliss catches Earl watching football in his van parked in an abandoned parking lot, she asks, "Why do you feel like you have to lie to her?" He responds, "You gotta pick your battle with your mother because she is a fighter." This is one of many moments that the film vilifies her mother for being a fighter, most notably when she is placed as the parent against Bliss competing in roller derby.

We meet Earl as he watches a football game in his garage. As Bliss, her sister and mother arrive home, they hand Earl her sister's pageant trophy and rush inside. Earl stands there as a football knocks him in the head, re-directing his attention to the father and son next door passing the ball. They give him a wave, a taunt reminding him what he does not have (masculinity) as his activities are being circumscribed by his wife. Earl then returns to his female-populated home. This happens again later in the film when Bliss returns from her first match and Earl watches his neighbor hammer in two signs supporting his sons as football players. This reoccurring interaction plays an important role in the film because these moments expose why Earl supports Bliss' new athletic passion in such a masculine sport. It is not purely for Bliss' happiness that he gives permission for her to compete; it bolsters his manhood to have a pseudo-son. This is even more problematic when Earl is placed as the only reason Bliss gets to compete in the championship. She doesn't initially choose to compete but he swoops in and saves the day, giving her permission and encouraging her to follow this path. We will revisit this later.

It isn't until a trip to Austin with her mother and sister that Bliss is introduced to roller derby. She is in a store buying a pair of military boots when she first sees a group of roller derby girls. She goes to her first match and she recognizes that this sport may be an outlet that fits her. After the match when she nervously tells her soon-to-be mentor Maggie Mayhem (Kristen Wiig), "I just want to tell you all, that you are my new heroes," Maggie responds, "Well, put some skates on, be your own hero." This is the film's motto. It's even printed on the DVD jacket.

From this point on, the idea and the attitude of these derby girls exude this message: "Be your own hero." This is a driving force for Bliss. She breaks out her old skates, goes to tryouts and makes the team.

Bliss is non-confrontational at the start of the film and she learns how to be aggressive, earning her the name Babe Ruthless. With this new "confidence," Bliss stands up to her nemesis at school by pushing her over the stairwell in a celebrated moment. This equates confidence with dominance. This is a problematic idea of empowerment. It precipitates the hegemonic masculine idea of violence equating to confidence and therefore empowerment. Bliss is now empowered through violence.[14] Bliss's violent revenge at school is symbolic of an earned toughness, perceived empowerment, from roller derby.

This education comes from the diverse, but equally aggressive female athletes in the league. Each team in the league has a clever theme and her team is named the Hurl Scouts. Her teammates have such names as Maggie Mayhem, Smashley Simpson (Drew Barrymore), Bloody Holly (Zoe Bell) and Rosa Sparks (Eve). Her best friend refers to her teammates as "a gang of roller-skating she-males." These are all different women who are tough in individual ways. At a party after Bliss's first match Smashley Simpson and Bloody Holly compare bruises on their outer thighs. Framed between their thighs are two men sitting on a couch in shock and awe. Traditionally this framing would attract, but instead the women's bruises add a sense of dominance and aggressive rebellion to the previously only objectified landscape of the female body. These derby girls create new role models for Bliss and the audience.

One of these role models is Bliss' mentor Maggie Mayhem, a single mother who skips the parties so she can take care of her son. Bliss' villainess rival is Iron Maven (Juliette Lewis), the league's star, who later reveals, "I'm 36. Guess when I started skating? I was 31 'cause it took me that long to find one thing that I was really good at. And you know what? I worked my ass off to get it." These athletes are portrayed as real women and a new breed of role models. This is all the more reason for the viewer to root for Bliss to follow her own path.

There are featured male characters other than Earl in the film: All of the coaches are male, the announcer is male and Bliss' boss is male. But these are all alternative representations of masculinity. These men embrace the alternative style of clothing the women wear and they are far overshadowed in toughness and aggression by the women around them. They present vulnerability and show their emotions. For example, the Hurl Scouts' coach Razor (Andrew Wilson) is constantly trying to have the team follow his plays. When they continue to dismiss them, he literally throws childish tantrums. The announcer and organizer, "Hot Tub" Johnny Rocket (Jimmy Fallon), strives to be cool but consistently comes off as a young boy desperately wanting acceptance to this "cool club." There is even a cutaway where we are introduced to Smashley's fiancé while she continually beats him on the ground; Bloody Holly explains, "He loves it." Added to this group of male characters is Bliss' love interest Oliver (Landon Pigg). As clichéd as it initially appears, her relationship with this musician turns into a uniquely empowering conclusion. This relationship carries weight in that she gives him her virginity but upon finding she can't trust him to be there for her, she breaks up with him. This takes place right before the championship. This love interest is not necessary for Bliss' story to have a happy ending. In fact, the very act of breaking up with him is an important step toward her happy ending.

With all of these characters and story elements set to challenge traditional gender constructions, it really comes down to the second turning point of the film to strip away Bliss' empowered conclusion. Throughout the film, Bliss' struggle with her mother is based on two different ideologies. This is summarized in an argument where her mother exclaims, "What do you think that the world thinks of those girls with all their tattoos? Do you think they have an easy time finding a job? Or getting a loan application? Or going to a decent college? Or finding a husband? No, you just limit your choices." Bliss replies, "You really need to stop shoving your psychotic idea of '50s womanhood down my throat." Her mother is clearly projecting her own desires and insecurities on her daughter.

The only time Bliss and her mother genuinely connect is after Bliss gets the impression her boyfriend is cheating. Romantic relationships are thus presented as the common language of mothers and daughters. Immediately after this reconciliation, Bliss offers to do the Blue Bonnet Pageant. Her mother blatantly says, "Don't do it for me." We are fully aware that this is exactly why Bliss is doing the pageant, yet Bliss lies, "Fine, I'll do it for myself." A flicker of hope passes in her mother's eyes.

Not too long after, Bliss learns that the pageant is on the same day as the championship. Desperate for her mother's approval, she chooses the pageant. This counts as two chances where Bliss could have taken a stand, could have followed in her teammates' footsteps to be and do what she wants. She can't do this for herself, but at this juncture in steps Earl.

After everything appears to have returned to normal and Bliss has chosen to regress to who she was at the beginning, Earl is there to save the day. One evening he searches the roller derby website and sees his daughter, poster girl Babe Ruthless, in action. His daughter has transformed into a contact sport athlete. He then goes to the roller derby locker room and gathers her team and brings them to the pageant to release her so she can compete in the championship. Even though Earl admits, "I cannot take losing the chance for our kid to be happy," this does not read as an act of recognition of Bliss' passion for the sport; it presents the idea that Earl has found his "son" and effectively, then, his manhood. This is signified at the conclusion of the film when he stands in his front yard nailing his *own* sign with Bliss' name and number. A gentle head nod to the neighbor and the message is clear.

Taking this decision away from Bliss negates an empowered outcome to her story arc. Although Bliss ultimately gets what she wants, it is hampered by her inability to make this happen herself. Further, if this film had feminist intentions, it would have been more admirable if her mother had been the one to offer her this invitation. Her mother had offered her the chance *not* to do the pageant. Bliss' choice to do the pageant truly was hers. Therefore, her father isn't saving her from her mother; he is saving her from herself. This is in direct violation of the film's motto "Be your own hero."

The final conclusion with Bliss's mother is when she finds Bliss's script she wrote for the pageant. In it Bliss states she admires her mother most, and "knowing my mother is proud of me, means more than any crown." This upmost dedication to please her mother is not reflected in the conclusion of the film, which does not celebrate mothers but actually celebrates fathers. It is not her mother who grants her what she truly desires, it is her father who hands her the skates. Thus the film hands the power and appreciation to her father and makes Bliss' success contingent upon her father's approval and assistance.

The act of "permission" to follow her athletic aspirations by a father figure is also mimicked in another film, *Bend It Like Beckham,* directed by Gurinder Chadha in 2002. Here our hero is Jess (Parminder Nagra), an Indian teenager who lives in London and dreams of playing soccer. Her desire to be an athlete puts her into conflict with her Indian culture. This forces a choice of family versus sports. Much as in *Whip It,* the scenario that sets the climax of the film is a double booking: Her sister's wedding and the championship game fall on the same day. She chooses her sister's wedding. The film endorses this choice and rewards her with her father sending her off to the game. Just as in *Whip It,* Jess's father appears to give permission only once she has completely regressed to her original place as sister and daughter in the family. Only then does he hand her permission to leave the wedding and follow her dream. Effectively this dismisses an empowerment that would have happened only if she had made that decision herself.

Returning to *Whip It,* it is relevant to note that Bliss' team does not win the championship. In fact, Maven, her competitive rival, wins. In that moment there is a respect afforded to Maven's earlier message: With hard work and dedication, success will be awarded in due time. Bliss receives only what she absolutely needs in the conclusion of the film: the recognition of what completes and inspires her. With her father handing her access, it is commendable that the film does not then also hand her the win.

Both *A League of Their Own* and *Whip It* initially introduce empowering backdrops for female athletes. However, they fail in presenting fully empowering female heroines. Whether it be exploiting the idea of a woman's need to nurture or taking away a girl's power of choice, these films fail to provide the progress they are trying to promote. For *A League of Their Own,* regressive stereotypes rule. For *Whip It,* the message to choose your own identity gets lost in a "happy ending" as a father stands up and "re-masculates" himself by countering the mother's wishes and sending his daughter on an athletic quest. Although there are problems with the ultimate conclusion of these films, audiences are still bearing witness to a spectrum of gender representations, including some unconventional ones. We watch a broad range of female bodies, styles and action types. The expansive field of female athletes portrayed offers an appreciation of the differences between one woman and the next rather than the simplistic difference between men and women.

Perhaps the answer really does lie in *Whip It*'s motto, "Be your own hero." This enforces individuality and the empowerment of self, which is fundamental in creating a positive representation and speaks eloquently to the liberatory potential of female athletic competition.

3

M.V.P.

The Most Vulnerable Player in Children's Sports Films

It's a fact that sports are sex-segregated. In almost every sport that men and women play, they are divided into separate teams and leagues. This has built a social framework so far buried in history that this split now seems natural. The result is an assumption that should women compete with men, women would suffer injuries both physically and, due to the inevitable abuse, mentally. This helps fortify men's place as primary and dominant in the sports world. Since the basis of sports is founded on constructions of masculinity, society overlooks the athletic ability of any particular girl or woman who seeks to "play with the boys" and instead denies her access due to her sex categorization of girl and woman.[1] These generalizations continuously build the gender power order. If all men are perceived to be stronger, then all women must be weaker.

Sports are a boy's initiation into manhood. For boys, you played sports and "fit in" or you didn't and were labeled an outcast. These "outcasts" are used as the basis for the convention of the misfit team in children's sports films. These teams are comprised of players who do not have the skill or talent to keep up with their peers. Some do not even have the desire to play, but they are trying to fit into society; often, their parents pressure them to participate. To enhance the outsider mark placed on such a second tier team, girls are presented alongside these less athletic boys.

The female athlete is the ultimate signal of a misfit team. A number of Hollywood films speak to this phenomenon. What's most interesting in these films is that the girl is often perceived as the most talented and skilled player. Her handicap is not her lack of ability; it is her gender. This becomes the conflict. Effectively, this also marries her success with her ability to re-assimilate into a recognizable female and feminine role.

To illustrate this, we'll take a look at the 1976 film *The Bad News Bears* and its 2005 remake, plus two Disney films released in 1994, *Little Giants* and *D2: The Mighty Ducks* with reference to *The Mighty Ducks* (1992). These films all exhibit a need to regulate their talented female athletes. She can't just be an athlete; she must be a non-threatening girl too. Each of these films demonstrates actions to contain and control the image of their female athletes. This is done in three ways: by introducing an equally skilled male player to balance her impact; by providing a love interest; and finally, if all else is absent, crediting her moment of success to the male hero. It must also be noted that there is a blatant absence of a mother figure in all of these films. This places all decisions and influences with the father or a father figure presented as a coach or manager. We will finish the chapter looking at *The Longshots* (2008), a film based on the true story of the first girl to play in Pop Warner football, but dedicates all of its screen time to her uncle who coaches her. With sports understood as a male's rite of passage, these films' skilled female athletes are poised to break the mold, fighting and earning their place on the field. However, we cannot turn a blind eye to additional story elements that reintegrate the audience into a sex-segregated social framework.

The Cut Off Man

The Bad News Bears, directed by Michael Ritchie, was one of the most successful films released in 1976. On the surface, it appears to be about a misfit underdog Little League team. In actuality, it represents a new perspective on the overly competitive nature of youth sports. *The Bad News Bears* differs from other misfit films in its direct rebellion against the classic underdog story of celebrating good character by granting the misfit team a winning conclusion despite their lack of skill.[2] In fact, this film celebrates bad character, enabling the film's conclusion to find success in *not* winning.

With this in mind, the female athlete would be assumed to have access to the same rebellions. However, this is not the case. Her terrain in the plot is driven by her desire for the coach to be the father figure he once was for her. She becomes the source of emotional complexity, a conventionally feminine role. It is also relevant to remember that the 1970s were an active time for the women's movement in sports, most notably in 1972 when Title IX was put into action. Females had gained equal access to collegiate sports and thus the presence of female athletes was growing. In a most odd turn of events, the flaws in presenting genuine female empowerment in the original *The Bad News Bears* actually pale in comparison to those in the 2005 remake, *Bad News Bears*. With so much progress made since the inception of Title IX, by attempting to stay close to the original film, the remake actively pushes back the image of the female athlete to a past era.

Let's first look at the original film. *The Bad News Bears* is the story of a group of misfit kids playing baseball in a league that is overly competitive. A father, whose kid has been rejected, assembles the team. He also argues for the rest of these "undesirables" to have an opportunity to play in the league. He reaches out to Coach Morris Buttermaker (Walter Matthau), a drunk, broke, washed-up professional ballplayer, to coach the team. The first thirty minutes of the film revolve around Buttermaker resisting his new job by continually drinking, making fun of the kids and forfeiting a game. He even uses the kids to work his pool cleaning service. When put in a position to find a sponsor for their uniforms, he chooses Chico's Bail Bonds. However, he isn't the only character with shock value; the kids swear, are violent and smoke. After watching the kids get ridiculed, the father who hired Buttermaker pulls the plug and disbands the team. This is the moment where Buttermaker reaches out to Amanda (Tatum O'Neal), the daughter of his ex-girlfriend. Earlier in the film, he mentioned that he taught a nine-year-old girl how to throw a curve ball, and it was "the most tantalizing knuckler you ever saw in your life. I mean, this thing was a thing of beauty. Came up to the plate and disappeared, it was like a ball of melted ice cream." Now he turns to her to save the team.

We are introduced to a now 11-year-old Amanda while she is running her business of hustling maps and directing tourists to stars' houses. She is smart-talking and snarky. Immediately we see that *she* is in the power position. Wiser than her years, she is portrayed more like his ex, rather than the daughter of his ex. She calls him out on his shortcomings, rips cigars out of his mouth and eventually will prompt his ability to care. However, when he comes to recruit her she doesn't want to play at first, stating, "You almost ruined me with that sports stuff." On a second attempt she tells him she's "through with all that tomboy stuff" and she's saving up for braces and ballet lessons because she's going to be a model. Buttermaker lures her in with a business proposition: In exchange for his paying for ballet lessons, she will play.

The issues with Amanda's representation are not due to an over-whelming friction from her fellow teammates. Beyond the initial out-bursts in her introduction to the team, the league and the Bears show little resistance to her presence. *The Bad News Bears* presents a team where Amanda becomes just another talented player who proves her worth through her skill. However, Amanda's worth to the team is quickly diluted as another male member is recruited. After her first game where we admire her as a pitching star, we are quickly introduced to Kelly Leak (Jackie Earle Haley), a rebellious young boy who previously has been shown wreaking havoc on the playing fields with his motorcycle. He smokes, is rumored to be a loan shark and is also presented as the best player in the area. Introducing such a talented male athlete so close to Amanda's introduction exposes an underlying fear implicit in the nar-rative of having the best player in the league be a girl. Kelly creates a balance so that Amanda's talents can't threaten the masculine institution of baseball.

In order to recruit Kelly, Buttermaker sends Amanda to convince him. Rather than winning a bet with Kelly to have him on the team, she loses, thus owing him a date. Now Kelly's introduction has a two-fold effect on diminishing Amanda's impact as an athlete. First, we have just watched a female enter a field and upstage all the male athletes by herself. By introducing a talented male figure, her power is diminished and her effect is softened. Second, her "proper" femininity is restored as this boy becomes a romantic interest for her, restoring her status as the object of a male gaze.[3] Kelly initiates Amanda into a desired heterosexual feminine role. He now actively holds the gaze on to Amanda, mitigating the over-bearing power she was exhibiting. When he joins the team, she asks, "What are you doing here?" He responds, "Some asshole changed my mind." In this sea of offensive material, her smile signals our recognition that this was a romantic gesture. She soon is riding on the back of this rebel's motorcycle and asking, "Can't this thing go any faster?" Clearly, she knows her place in falling for, and reforming, the "bad boy."

This is also the transition for Buttermaker to become a father. Instead of bickering like a couple, Amanda begins to settle into the role of a daughter. Upon learning that Amanda must go on a date with Kelly, Buttermaker becomes paternal and protective of her asking, "What if he tries something?" She responds, "I'll handle it." This sparks a new vulnerability in their relationship. As the film progresses we watch Amanda yearn more for Buttermaker's attention and show weakness at his avoidance. Her character becomes redefined as a girlfriend and a daughter. She transforms from a tough-talking equal to these recognizable (and regrettable) female constructions. While her teammates continue their vulgarity and continue to improve their play, Amanda is relegated to a place of symbolic relationship to these two male characters. It is important to note, none of the boy players engage in relationships with girls or connect with Buttermaker in the same way.

With Kelly enlisted, the Bears begin to win. We also watch Amanda begin her ballet lessons. The Bears have a shot at the playoffs and the film's attention turns to Kelly's character for skill and growth as he redeems himself and becomes a good kid, standing up for his teammates and caring about the game. Meanwhile, Amanda is reduced to a girl wanting Buttermaker to be the father she never had. In a pivotal scene Amanda admits to Buttermaker that she invited her mom to the championship in an obvious attempt to reunite them. This desperate plea for his attention and affection inflames Buttermaker, who tosses his beer at her, exclaiming, "Goddamn it! Can't you get it through your thick head that I don't want your company? If I did, I would have looked you up two years ago. I wouldn't have waited two goddamn years." Amanda leaves and we watch them both cry in separate spaces. With this show of emotion, the film has found its heart. Buttermaker has broken through his inability to care about anyone other than himself because he recognizes Amanda as a daughter, and as a figure with whom he should connect. Here again, like in *A League of Their Own,* we see the necessity of a female's active assistance in releasing a male from the restrictions of his masculinity. Buttermaker can now be a respectable coach and father, within the offensive language and style of the film that is.

The Bad News Bears ends with Buttermaker acknowledging the problems of overly competitive pressure in the league and generously lets the less skilled players have their turn on the field, which causes the team to lose the championship. However, the real damage is that done to Amanda's empowerment. From the beginning of the film, she is used either as a weapon to win the game or the daughter who breaks him. She is never simply a player on the team. Her gender requires her to be different and therefore differently handled. In the end, she is reincorporated into a conventionally feminine role.

Released 29 years later, the remake *Bad News Bears*, directed by Richard Linklater in 2005, exhibits a need to increase the level of offensive material and with that, increase the problems with the handling of Amanda's character. A few examples of the updated offensive humor are that the team has a handicapped boy restricted to his wheelchair, signifying what we are supposed to see as an absurdity as he becomes the ultimate misfit. Buttermaker (Billy Bob Thornton) is now in the business of killing rats and thus subjects his team to chemicals when he uses them to do his job. Their uniforms now are sponsored by "Bo-Peep's Gentlemen's Club." Buttermaker even attempts to enlist a little person to pose as a player in an effort to cheat and win.

In perhaps the most offensive move, changes were made that are more dismissive of strong female representation. Instead of a worried father starting the team, it's a litigious mother, Liz Whitewood (Marcia Gay Harden), who has stopped the league from playing until they allow a team for her son and the other players. Later in the film she even sleeps with Buttermaker to fulfill a desire she's always had for the "bad boy, the sexy scumbag, the serial killer who gets married in prison." She continues, "I have never felt like that until I met you." With these attempts at shock value, it's interesting that the remake actively chooses to tone down Amanda (Sammi Kane Kraft) by raising her vulnerability.

The same plot points take place for her as in the original; however, her interactions with Buttermaker are far more as a daughter and less challenging. When they first meet while she is working, this time selling faux vintage clothing at a flea market, we detect the vulnerability of both. Buttermaker appears far more genuine, showing pain when she mentions her mother. Instead of bypassing the impact her mother had on him, he tries to explain how adults grow apart. This version of Buttermaker and Amanda's relationship has less fast-talking wit and more emotional depth. With this version of the character, Amanda just comes off as an awkward, insolent youth rather than strong. Amanda is seen continuously begging for his attention and desperately fighting for recognition that they once had a relationship. This is directly addressed at the end of the film, when he remembers a key detail to a story they share, indicating that she does in fact matter to him. He even chaperones her date with Kelly (Jeffrey Davies).

Amanda's relationship with Kelly is far more developed throughout the remake as well. She is repeatedly seen by his side and even shares a kiss with him at the end of the film. By emphasizing Amanda's vulnerability as a daughter and a girlfriend, the remake has taken the plot choices of the original film and elevated this need to identify Amanda as a girl.

In 1976, *The Bad News Bears* came at a time where female athletes were breaking barriers utilizing Title IX to claim their rightful access to athletics. The 2005 remake takes place where there is an established presence of female athletes. The regressive nature of the remake reflects the idea that Title IX has now evolved to impact a different gender conversation. The problem is no longer having equal numbers of teams or leagues for men and women; it is continuing the impression that they must still play separately.[4] With athletics still being determined by sex-segregation, female athletes remain identifiable as different and thus differently handled. This expands in the cinematic form by continuing to usher in stories where Amanda continues to be relegated to a separate sphere governed by her relationships with patriarchal men.

With this in mind, we move on to analyze *Little Giants,* a story about a girl who outshines the boys around her but, like Amanda, her character is not defined by her talent and skill.

The Assist

The Bad News Bears is the forerunner to misfit underdog stories. Two films that followed suit were produced and distributed by Disney in 1994, *Little Giants* and *D2: The Mighty Ducks.* Disney would never produce a film using the risqué and offensive humor of *The Bad News Bears*; the studio's image is defined as safe and wholesome family entertainment, "safe" as in conservative and "wholesome" as in patriarchal and heterosexual.[5] Disney veils these themes and presents them to the masses as innocent and pleasurable entertainment. This also sets a very different method in categorizing a misfit and an outsider.

The female athlete characters in the films evaluated in this chapter already present a challenge in their participation in conservatively defined male sports. In *Little Giants*, the strength of the female athlete is countered by a traditional story of her first crush on a boy. Although I will briefly examine the original film *The Mighty Ducks*, it is in the sequel *D2: The Mighty Ducks* that we are introduced to a female athlete who is defined only by her skill. However, the audience is not fully allowed to respect her talent as an athlete because the climax of her story, or rather the moment when she should shine as the key to the team's victory, fails to be attributed to her skill. Instead, her ability to block the final goal is in direct response to the instructions of her male coach. These female athletes will present further examples of the need to establish recognizable, conventionally gendered roles. The mothers of these female athletes are absent in all of these films, thus their fates lie in the control of their fathers or male coaches and managers. With these films centered on kids and teenagers, the exclusivity of a father figure establishes a patriarchal foundation.

Directed by Duwayne Dunham, *Little Giants* is about a team of misfits fighting for their chance to play football. In actuality, the film stands as a story of two adult brothers fighting to prove their worth to the town and each other. One brother, Kevin O'Shea (Ed O'Neill), is the All American football star, while the other, Danny (Rick Moranis), is the so-called geek. The teams they coach reflect that backstory. Our hero is Danny's daughter Becky "Icebox" O'Shea (Shawna Waldron). In the opening of the film we watch her trying out for Kevin's Pee Wee football team. As Kevin is the town's celebrity, it is clear that Kevin's football team is the one to be on.

We first lay eyes on Becky as she knocks down a boy larger than her and whips off her helmet to reveal that she is in fact a girl, a common gesture in films.[6] Becky's introductory hit allows the audience to see her as just another football player before initiating any subtext of her gender.[6] However, this introduction is only for the audience and not the characters in Becky's cinematic world. Becky plays better than a majority of the boys in the tryout, yet her own uncle won't choose her for his team. Even with praise for her coming from everyone around him, Kevin still refuses to have a girl. His wife Karen (Mary Ellen Trainor) challenges him sarcastically, stating, "Girls can run countries, they can sit on the Supreme Court, they can discover radium, but they can't play Pee Wee football?" Kevin's only response is to offer cheerleading. Kevin is represented as the absolute football player, patriarch and example of hegemonic masculinity.

Football has become the ultimate standard for hegemonic masculinity. To be a true "American man," a connection (be it player or fan) to football is required.[7] *Little Giants* shows hints of parodying this idea, such as a father, Mike Hammersmith (Brian Haley), who admits he's been cultivating his son Spike (Sam Horrigan), grooming him for the game, and even admits "Every night, before he goes to bed, I massage his hamstrings with evaporated milk." Another takes place as each brother preps his teams running out of the tunnel to the championship. Kevin, our "manliest" coach, shouts, "It's not just a football" and his team replies, "It's our lives!" while Danny says to his team, "This is just a football, just air and pig intestines." However, the film still places Kevin as the standard to be reached. The film opens with Kevin's name on the town's water tower as the celebrated football hero. After his team loses to Danny's, the film ends showing the water tower now reading "The O'Shea Brothers." The goal is not to look past the celebration of Kevin's talent and fame; it's to be a part of it. Kevin never changes; he is simply forced to deal with the consequences of losing to his brother: a technicality of the water tower. In addition, when Danny and Kevin meet at the end of the game, Kevin states, "If I wasn't tough on you when we were kids, you never would've beat me today." Danny lets this comment slide and immediately proposes that they merge the teams and coach together. Kevin never confirms his interest in this idea, simply stating, "Let me think about it." There is no complete transition for Kevin and therefore his masculinity lives on in the hegemonically constructed definition.

In order to play, Becky gets her father to start his own team. This is reminiscent of *The Bad News Bears* only in this film the caring father, not the dissolute one, is the coach. In opposition to *The Bad News Bears*, the rebellious humor afforded to these Disney players is infantile and harmless. With the Bears, there were moments where we were laughing *with* their commentary on Buttermaker and social prejudices. We simply laugh *at* the Giants and their inadequacies. There is no offensive language, just displays of farting and blowing snot on each other. They practice in unmatched antiquated football gear. One even plays in a Darth Vader helmet. They present a highlight reel of PG–rated humor and are celebrated as helpless kids.

The Giants mirror a lot of the characters from *The Bad News Bears*. From the nerdy mathematician to a snotty-nosed quiet scrawny boy, many of these players are directly mimicking Bears characters. Most notably, just like Amanda, our female athlete Becky is initially the most talented player on the team … until shortly thereafter when a male athlete, Junior Floyd (Devon Sawa), is recruited. Junior is a talented, attractive quarterback and Becky is immediately enamored with him. The first moment she sees him, she argues with herself: "What a hunk. Wait a minute. What am I saying? I'm the Icebox. The Icebox doesn't like boys … except for that one." This is the defining moment where the film's focus on Becky's talent subsides. Her purpose turns from wanting the opportunity to play into attracting Junior's attention. This is also a clearly intentional moment to establish her as heterosexual. Her story is not about recognition of her as an athlete; rather, it becomes her desire to be recognized as a woman, that is, a heterosexual object.

Throughout the film Becky battles with her gendered identity. She dresses like a tomboy and bullies the boys. They literally go running whenever she steps up. Now with Junior around, her demeanor changes. Junior has entered the story to redeem her by initiating her desire to be desired, i.e., objectified.[8] This begins as she panders to Junior in practice. The film's score assists in this transition: The music changes to a seductive sax every time she and Junior share a moment. Now she is vulnerable and begins to recognize how far removed she has become from the girls around her. This opens her to the prospect of leaving football and joining a more "acceptable" place on the football field: cheerleading on the sidelines.

After watching Junior flirt with a cheerleader, the message is clear: Becky needs to be more like that cheerleader to win his attention. We immediately transition to a scene where we watch Becky applying makeup. Junior has not simply activated her desire to be desired; he has literally re-instated the power of the male gaze. Becky's storyline is now driven by her ability to encompass an identity of "to-be-looked-at-ness."[9] This sequence of events leads us to a scene she shares with her uncle Kevin in a diner. Here is the moment where Becky's guard goes down. She admits, "I thought I wanted to play, but now there's all this other stuff." This is separating sports from her ability to become a "girl." Sports are male, and she wants to be female. Kevin responds, "You wanna find a boy, you gotta figure out how boys think. And if this boy's a quarterback, he's probably gonna want some cute girl, not some teammate." Girls cannot be both. Therefore, Becky's goal is now pointed toward being attractive, not being the dominating football player she always wanted to be.[10] The scene concludes with Becky asking her uncle, "Do you think I'm pretty?" He responds, "No, I think you're beautiful." Whether this is a strategic move to remove her from the game or an actual nurturing moment from Kevin, it symbolically releases her to begin constructing a more "acceptable" female image. The ultimate patriarch, who helped inspire her path to football, has now inspired her to move on.

Between this moment and the championship, we watch Becky completely surrender to the concept that she can't have both Junior and football. For confirmation, Becky fearlessly states to Junior, "I bet if I was like those cheerleaders, you'd wanna learn [to kiss] with me." He responds, "But you're not. You're different. You're cool. You're the Icebox. I mean, come on, you're probably the only girl I've met that can beat up my dad." The dominating ability to beat up his dad is not currency for physical attraction. So the night before the big game, Becky turns to cheerleading.

There she stands, awkwardly, on the sidelines. With every play she seems more and more eager to run into the game. She misses the embarrassing defeat of the first half, the inspirational bond inspired at halftime and shares no part of the team's turnaround, scoring their first touchdown in the second half. It isn't until Junior is targeted and taken out of the game by a brutal late hit that she drops the pom-poms and joins the game. There she stands, with her bottom half dressed in a cheerleading uniform, her top half sporting a football jersey. This is an interesting turn of events. This image inspires a literal representation of two conflicting identities: constructed femininity and symbolic masculinity.

Further, she settles the score with Junior's attacker. This symbolic integration could be confirmed in the film's conclusion with Icebox winning both the game and the guy. However in the midst of their celebration when the Giants win the game, Junior and Becky only share a brief moment looking at each other. This could be read as a spark of romantic interest, but there is no guarantee he's changed his mind. Effectively, she can't have both.

On the DVD release of *Little Giants,* the director's commentary revealed that Becky's character wasn't in the original script idea, but when defining these "other" kids, she came to the forefront because she is a girl. This confirms the girl as the ultimate signal of the misfit team. In fact, when the character of Becky was added, she was described as physically "big, rough and tumble." I would not describe the actress Shawna Waldron as such. Yes, this film offers an empowered action when she abandons cheerleading to do what she loves, play football. However, there is still an emphasis that she must negotiate both to be happy. *Little Giants* may pose as a film that argues that all kids should get an opportunity to play sports; however, with regards to gender, this argument falls short. Becky represents how the female athlete has to gain access to additional fields, traditionally feminine fields and not sports, to define her "win."

The other 1994 Disney film about a misfit team, *D2: The Mighty Ducks,* took a different route with its female characters, allowing one in particular to appear quite empowered as an equal on the ice. This film is a sequel to 1992's *The Mighty Ducks.* While we're focusing on the sequel, I think it would be beneficial to briefly touch on the original film.

The Mighty Ducks, directed by Stephen Herek, is the story of a misfit youth hockey team that serves as community service, and punishment, for a DUI committed by a conceited lawyer, Gordon Bombay (Emilio Estevez). The team is a collection of undesirable and unskilled hockey players. Again, these are characters derived from those in *The Bad News Bears,* but with PG humor. For example, the boys admire a *Sports Illustrated* swimsuit edition, they rollerblade through a mall and they quack at their teacher. It just so happens that their rival team, the Hawks, is the same team, with the same coach, that Gordon played for in his youth. He is haunted by a missed championship goal and now has a team, once he comes around to appreciate them, to redeem him. The Hawks present a sterilized standard image of white and male with overtones of a militaristic master race. They play dirty and they are definitely presented as the villains. The Ducks are ethnically diverse and as they introduce themselves to Gordon, we learn that there is already a girl on the team, Connie (Marguerite Moreau).

With such a celebration of diversity you would think that Connie would have equal reign of the ice. Unfortunately her screen time is minimal. Although Connie plays, and even scores once, her image is continuously promoted as the girlfriend of one of the other players. There is a distinct intention to consistently place her by his side, holding his hand and kissing him at the championship. None of the other boys have girlfriends, but our one female athlete has to be one. Connie has the impact of an extra in this film. The idea of a female player blending into the background could be good, showing that they are just a part of the team; however, she has little to no presence athletically. The film's other female athlete Tami (Jane Plank) is introduced later. Tami and her brother are figure skaters when they are recruited to the team. After Tami is enlisted, we watch her far more than Connie. This purpose is quickly realized in the championship game when Tami is brought in to distract the opponent with her figure skating, thus allowing her a moment to score. She does not score playing hockey, she scores with her ability to be expressive and distracting. Her character is a symbol of hegemonic femininity, and Connie's ability to play hockey in the background does not mitigate that message. Tami's spotlight continues when a Hawk hits her, prompting a Duck to flip him over the railing. His form of defending her honor re-instills a gender power dynamic: She needs to be protected.

After this lackluster presence of female athletes in the original film, the sequel *D2: The Mighty Ducks* explores a female character, Julie "The Cat" Gaffney (Colombe Jacobsen-Derstine), who is introduced solely as a world-class hockey player. She has no love interests other than her love for the game. She presents the most empowered and equally placed female athlete of all the films discussed in this chapter but still becomes the victim of a move to re-establish a gender power dynamic.

D2: The Mighty Ducks, directed by Sam Weisman in 1994, takes the team from the original film and sends them to represent the U.S. in the

Junior Goodwill Games. Tami is no longer on the team. And while the original female on the team, Connie, is a player in this film too, she continues to be presented as the girlfriend, or the female to be protected by her teammates on the ice. We first meet Julie when the team's corporate sponsor, Hendrix Hockey, brings five of the country's top players to improve the team. Each player is introduced with their skill and an attached description of what makes them different. One player can skate like the wind but can't stop. Another can stick handle like a magician but tends to show off too much. One is purely an enforcer on the ice, working to violently clear opponents out of the way. There is also a male figure skater who had been overlooked, but has now transitioned to playing hockey well. Of these five players, Julie is the only one introduced purely for her hockey talent. In her introduction it is plainly stated that she won the State Championship for Maine three years in a row. Goldberg (Shaun Weiss), the original goalie, is presented as utterly lacking in comparison to her skill. However, throughout the film Julie is restricted to the bench as Goldberg is named the starter and continues to play.

After the team wins their first couple of games in the tournament, Julie approaches Gordon and asks for more playing time. Gordon says that he has to stick with Goldberg while they're winning. This prompts her to say, "I understand. But I left my team in Maine to show the world what I can do." Gordon responds, "Just give it time. You will show the world. I promise." After this conversation, there are only two moments where Julie is called into a game. The first occurs during their initial game against the Iceland Vikings.

Iceland mirrors their rival, the Hawks, from the first film in every way. They are white, militaristic and even wear similar uniforms. In this game, Team USA is losing badly enough that Gordon pulls Goldberg and puts Julie in. As Julie skates out to the goal, she overhears taunts from the Iceland players. First they say "Send in a woman to do a man's job?" and then "Don't break a nail." Julie responds by asking these players to help with her pads, immediately turning them into foolish seduced boys. While they are lured in by her advance, she knees them in the groin. She is then immediately kicked out of the game. We have yet to see her play. Additionally, we are faced with another situation where a female athlete attains dominance by mimicking a standard of hegemonic masculinity. Rather than proving her worth in skill, Julie's actions present the flawed understanding of empowerment through aggressive violence.

The second and final time we watch Julie play is in the climax of the film. This is the defining moment for her character. Again the team is facing off with Iceland; this time it is for the gold medal. The game is tied at the end of regulation, sending it to a shootout. Each team sends out their best players for a one-on-one goal attempt, goalie versus player. After a series of goals go each way, it comes down to one last showdown. Coach Bombay walks up to Julie:

> BOMBAY: Julie, you got the fast glove. I know this kid's move. Triple Deke, glove side. Anticipate it and you got him.
> JULIE: What if he goes stick side?
> BOMBAY: He's fancy. He'll go glove. Don't hesitate. Let's go.

We then watch this exact scenario play out. Julie skates to the goal, counts the very moves Bombay instructed, catches the shot right where Gordon told her and they win the big game. Simply affording her the winning save is not empowering. This was not an exhibition of her skill. Had the puck actually gone "stick side" and she corrected to save it, we would have witnessed the talent that won her this spot on the team. Instead we simply watch her ability to obey an instruction. It should be noted that one of Goldberg's saves in the shootout *is* a glove save. We haven't previously watched her play to establish she has a fast glove, but we've established Goldberg has one. This negates our acknowledgment of her skill. It effectively stands as a celebration of Gordon's ability to know the game and their opponent. Throughout this film we had the opportunity to be introduced to a female athlete not scripted as a love interest or as someone in need of being recognizably feminine. Unfortunately, the film comes up with a new way to control her, stripping her of empowerment at a decisive moment in her career when her skill is backgrounded and instead all credit is given to the strategic wisdom of a male hero.

The Mighty Ducks, unlike *Little Giants,* had the opportunity to present female athletes who played amongst their male teammates on an equal level. However, all these films undercut the empowering aspects of female athleticism by finding ways to put them back down into recognizably feminine positions. Whether it was protecting Tami or instructing a skill Julie already has, the male characters in these storylines represent patriarchal control. In *Little Giants,* Becky the Icebox is defined by her desire to be a girl. Her love of playing is overshadowed by her need to be desired by Junior.

In Disney's landscape of stereotyped princesses and princes, these female athletes have to struggle and negotiate a territory not so simply defined. They must find their connection to a traditional feminine space within the masculine landscape of sports. These are popular films and their promotion of ultimately disempowered female athletes is detrimental to the advancement of women and leveling the playing field of sports. It cannot be overlooked that the Walt Disney Company started an actual NHL team, the Mighty Ducks of Anaheim, named and directly marketed in connection to the original film *The Mighty Ducks.* Even though it was inspired by this underdog tale, there has yet to be a woman on that team.

The Longshots (2008) does not share the popularity of the *Bad News Bears, Little Giants* and the *Mighty Ducks* series but scenes that were omitted from the film are worth mentioning. In this new age of DVD special features, we are permitted to watch deleted scenes and in the case of *The Longshots,* those deleted scenes could have helped its heroine be the rule rather than the exception in female athletic capability.

The Trick Play

The Longshots, directed by Fred Durst, is based on the real-life story of quarterback Jasmine Plummer (played by Keke Palmer), the first girl to play in Pop Warner football history. She leads her struggling small-town team to the Super Bowl and, although they lose, the film aims to represent a core belief that girls can play football too. On the contrary, it is quite apparent as the film opens and develops that this story is not about Jasmine but about her uncle Curtis (Ice Cube). Much as we watched Frankie in *Million Dollar Baby* use Maggie to vindicate him as a father, Curtis uses Jasmine to rise up from his deadbeat state to become a respected coach and resident of the town. Jasmine is merely a subplot in this story of Curtis's comeback.

Curtis is introduced as an incomplete man. He looks disheveled, he doesn't work and he spends his days drinking at a park with other men who appear to also be in despair. He watches the peewee football team practice and we learn that he had quite the reign as a football champ in his youth. What stopped him was an injury and once he lost his ability to play, he lost his will to do much else. We are reminded of this by the football he carries everywhere he goes. Jasmine is introduced as an outsider whose only enjoyment comes from reading books. She wants to be a model when she grows up. When her mother has to pick up extra shifts at work, Curtis (the brother of Jasmine's father who deserted her) takes on babysitting duties.

At first Jasmine and Curtis don't get along. They don't understand each other and certainly don't show any desire to change that. One afternoon the local reverend and Curtis are tossing the football around at the park. When the reverend overthrows the ball, Curtis demands that Jasmine put down her book and throw the ball back. This is the moment where Curtis is handed a glimpse of her potential as a football player and begins his quest to inspire her to play.

The first problematic layer of this film is that Curtis simply projects his own desire to play onto her. This film isn't about him unlocking an athletic desire within Jasmine, one that she never knew she had because of gender difference; it is clear that Jasmine is taking part in this out of appreciation for having a father figure in her life. She recognizes this connection to Curtis as he trains in something *he* loves and dedicates his passion and time to her. There is never a point where it seems that her desire is specifically about football. Jasmine recognizes that her football skill may be her ticket "in" for both a father figure and to finally have friends. As Jasmine improves as a football player, Curtis progressively cleans his life up. Perhaps the ultimate confirmation of Curtis's rebirth of a man is when Jasmine chooses him over her own father, who shows up near the end of the film after hearing about her success. Her father is a no-show at the championship game and when she returns home and he tries to apologize, she rejects him and stands beside Curtis. Instead of focusing on Jasmine's journey as a female athlete finding her place on the field, the film focuses far more on Curtis's life off of it.

The bonding between Curtis and Jasmine is mainly dedicated to improving his life. He offers her fashion magazines in exchange for trying out for the football team; she instead proposes that she'll try out if he asks her teacher on a date. Her actions are always pointed at his benefit and not hers. Throughout the film we follow Curtis as he turns into a respected man for himself and a leader to help clean up his town. Although Jasmine gains the acceptance of her teammates, those peers are boys. The girls at her school continue to taunt her. The transition from her nose in a book to a celebrated quarterback only enhances her "outsider" label to them. Before Jasmine tries out for the team, Curtis instructs, "When you try out for the team, all this 'I'm a girl' stuff, you throw that out the window. 'Cause when you hit the field, you're not a girl. You're a football player." This is how she earns respect from her team, by being an athlete. Moments like these affirm that gender in sports can, and should, be separate. However, having this film so heavily set in Curtis's comeback, it consistently feels as though these positive messages are more set to benefit his image as a coach and a man, than for her progress as a player. This is confirmed while before the championship game, the film cuts to a locker room scene with Curtis (he's now the coach due to the former coach suffering a heart attack), not her or the team. After a moment alone, he marches into the room with the team and proceeds to give his pep talk. This wasn't really a film about the first female player in Pop Warner football; it's the story of a man and his town, who find their identity through the attention brought by her.

The DVD extra features reveal how little of the film is based on true events. Through multiple interviews, the creators and actors repeatedly frame the story as loosely based on the truth because they didn't know much about Jasmine other than her accomplishment. Director Durst says, "As for her story, the real Jasmine Plumber and everything it means for this film, I just hope she enjoys it and can accept that movies are a little bit more heightened reality then reality is. You know, she is like 'That didn't happen to me, I didn't go to that school.' It became a personal experience for myself in thinking [about] how I would react and live and tell this story opposed to what the real facts were with Jasmine Plumber." With this in mind, the choice to focus the film on Curtis rather than Jasmine was a creative choice, which in turn continues to promote a male's connection to football rather than the female who conquered it. What is most troublesome is that the DVD interviews reveal the message of the film not to be that girls can play football or even that girls can accomplish anything, it is, as Ice Cube states, "that one person can make a difference." That one person in this film is

Jasmine and the difference she makes is not in the sports world as much as in Curtis's life.

Two scenes cut from the film can now be seen on the DVD. They spread a supportive message of female strength and ongoing participation in sports. The first involves Jasmine and her mother Claire (Tasha Smith) in the backyard:

> CLAIRE: So I wonder where you get it from.
> JASMINE: What?
> CLAIRE: That spunk of yours.
> JASMINE: I got it from you.
> CLAIRE: Honey, I couldn't stand out there and let people tackle me like that. I don't have *that* kind of courage.
> JASMINE: Momma, you stayed here and raised me all by yourself, stopped the bank from taking the house. I don't know anybody as brave as you.

This scene promotes and appreciates different examples of courage and bravery. Courage doesn't come from withstanding aggression or violence, courage comes from overcoming odds and still standing strong for what you need and what you believe in. Beyond the power of this conversation, it is *who* is having it that makes this scene so important. Had this scene remained in the film, we would have watched a source of education and power placed in her mother. By eliminating this content, her mother is simply absent and Curtis stands as the sole educator, receiving all the credit for Jasmine's growth. Claire is the one who supports Jasmine, literally and figuratively. Once again, the power and credit is afforded to a patriarchal center, a father figure.

The second deleted scene takes place the following football season. Curtis is speaking to a group of athletes at tryouts and as he calls out players to ask what position they play, we see and hear girls who are in the mix. These female athletes represent a range of different ideas of "femininity" and body types. After seeing these girls as they pitch their playing positions, Curtis confidently responds, "Yeah. We're gonna be all right this year." This female diversity and desire of athletic involvement is a priceless addition to any film. If this was made to promote female empowerment in sports, there is no way this scene would be omitted. It's wonderful that the production team acknowledges that these scenes should be available for audiences to see, but it's disappointing to place them as an afterthought. The truth is, by placing these scenes on the DVD there is confirmation that these conversations and visuals were not the priority when it came to the story and theme of the film. The draw of this film is the idea of a girl playing football, but the outcome is that her athletic abilities are only allowed in parallel with, and to benefit, male achievement. Having these scenes sitting on the DVD, of second tier importance, reminds us that women still can't make the cut in their own stories.

As I repeat many times in this book, the visual representation of a female playing sports is always empowering. I can't deny that Curtis says and performs actions that are both supportive and profound toward the acceptance of females in male-dominated sports. But it's unfortunate that the story of the first girl to play Pop Warner football became a story about a man finding himself. This is her accomplishment and although she had help, and we should certainly acknowledge that help, she deserves more than a supporting role in her own story.

The Longshots reminds us of the impact of a mentor. In all of the films mentioned in this chapter, mothers and women are primarily absent in the female athlete's journeys. Whether it is a father or coach, the male has the primary knowledge. By that same token, the recurring theme of placing men as mentors reinforces the recurring message that men have to initiate women into sports. What we lack in sports films is a female mentor, coach and/or mother to the girl hero. Furthermore, with thoughts of Amanda in *The Bad News Bears* and Becky in *Little Giants,* it is clear that even with a growing acceptance of women in sports, there is an even more important emphasis to have these girls stay "girls" in the conventional sense. The athletic prowess of a girl should not be the quality that makes her a "misfit." The world of sports does not need to be redefined to include women; it needs to be redefined to include athletes, regardless of their sex and regardless of their gender presentation.

4

Love-Love

*Struggling to Make a Point
in Her Own Sport*

If all sports were solely based on strategy, endurance and athletic prowess, we would not see such a difference in women and men's participation from one sport to another. Instead we are faced with a sporting world that caters to gender ideology. On one end of the spectrum, we have combative sports and on the other, sports that are expressive. Although I have established the foundational ideas of sports (i.e., dominance and competition) as masculine, there are sports that advertise values within the feminine construction. Take a moment and imagine if you could assign a gender to each sport. Which sports would be female? Which sports would be male? Why?

Sports that are more socially acceptable for women, such as figure skating and gymnastics, are categorically expressive sports, while sports more socially acceptable for men, such as football and hockey, are categorically instrumental.[1] One section relies on a mastery of style, grace and presentation and the other relies on domination, size and violence. Furthermore, expressive sports are judged in a subjective manner rather than the absolute score of an instrumental sport. In football, you either get into the end zone or you don't. In figure skating, you may have landed a double axel, but how well did you keep your composure? There are sports that don't fall within an expressive or instrumental definition (i.e., soccer, basketball and tennis); however, there are different rules (and a sizable difference in popularity) between women and men's leagues that continue the gender divide.

In movies, we watch an exaggeration of these ideas. While most male-driven sports movies, based in the world of instrumental sports, carry subplots of love stories and other life trials, the central plot is still based on winning the big game. Many female-driven sports movies, based in the world of expressive sports, displace sport as the central conflict and instead frame her journey within a love story. Love as the sphere of desirability places the goal for the woman as to be desired or, at the very least, win the guy rather than win the game. There is also an action of taming a "shrewish" female athlete. She begins the story so tough, competitive and driven that she has lost her "feminine" qualities of nurturing, warmth and support. As the story progresses, her hetero-sexual love interest assists her in reconnecting with those values. This is not just conditional to expressive sports; we watch this played out in any movie based on a sport (be it tennis, basketball and track) that has an established female presence.

Placing a movie in a sport that is socially acceptable for women eliminates the need for conflict over her playing her sport. This should finally allow the story to center on her competing, rather than focusing the plot on notions of femininity. However, the pressure to embrace feminine values continues for cinematic female athletes, even in their own sports. We can explore these ideas in *The Cutting Edge* and *Wimbledon.* Even though *Love & Basketball* and *Blue Crush* are also centered on a love story, it is important that we celebrate their concluding images that are ultimately empowering. It's necessary to recognize that although *Personal Best* explored a visual range of female athleticism, it also promoted weakness as a feminine value. Finally, it is beneficial to take a look at *Stick It,* a story centered on rejecting gymnastics' restricting and subjective style of judging and also a story that revolves around a relationship with a male figure, in this case a father figure. These films continue a tradition of endorsing male characters to drive the story. Based in sports that are established and accepted for women, they should center on a cinematic female athlete's competition—not her ability to be a love interest or a daughter.

Kiss and Cry

The Cutting Edge, directed by Paul Michael Glaser in 1992, is the story of Olympic hockey player Doug Dorsey (D.B. Sweeney) and

Olympic figure skater Kate Moseley (Moira Kelly) joining together to make their gold medal dreams come true. Masters of their craft, both have personal hurdles they need to overcome in order to succeed. In the classic style of love stories, they each carry what the other needs to be complete. Kate is a phenomenal skater, who is uptight. Doug is a hockey prodigy who lives freely, driven by passion. However they both have a difficult attitude. Kate's competitive spirit has stripped her of trust and kindness, leaving her ambition to appear as spoiled, mean-spirited and cold. Doug's passion can be read as arrogant and irresponsible. These dueling characteristics are the overriding conflict keeping these two athletes from becoming a team and lovers.

Although not a box office hit, *The Cutting Edge* has gained popularity through its yearly broadcast around the holiday season.[2] Additionally it spawned three straight-to-video sequels.[3] Its continuing success reveals an ongoing appreciation of classic gender traditions. This film may be packaged as a love story, but it also caters to the male sports fan. Although the sport is figure skating, Doug's initial participation in hockey (a combat sport that establishes his manhood) allows for a male audience to connect. His continued critique of the feminine qualities of figure skating provides comedy. Kate's uptight and abrasive demeanor is handled as another comedic element, but in the end, it is the barrier the audience wants them to overcome to fall in love. It's important that as we work our way through this film, we recognize how much conflict Kate must overcome in her identity, but not Doug. By the conclusion of the film, Kate is no longer viewed as an athlete with a passion for skating; she is viewed as a girl who just wanted to be a girl. By redirecting her aspirations, we have sidelined respect for her as an athlete in favor for respect for her desirability as a lover.

The film opens on hockey skates, but they're not Doug's. He's busy oversleeping his Olympic practice after a night with what's-her-name in his bed. We are then introduced to Kate, who is in a militant figure skating practice arguing with her coach. Kate is introduced as "impossible," making demands and rebelling against her father Jack Moseley (Terry O'Quinn). We watch Doug and Kate fall and fail in their Olympic sport. Doug gets injured while scoring a glorious goal, leaving him with a vision problem that disqualifies him from any future opportunity in the NHL. Kate hits the ice as her partner drops her during their program, leaving her ineligible for the gold she's worked her whole life for. The film jumps two years later and we see that Doug works in a factory and Kate is training for the next Olympics. After Kate has rejected 35 male skaters, her coach Anton Pamchenko (Roy Dotrice) finds Doug and recruits him. We watch as these polar opposites connect and learn from each other to get back to the Olympics.

Overall the film becomes a discussion of acceptance. Kate can be tough because she is already established in a sport that promotes femininity. When Doug returns home and announces that he's becoming a figure skater, he is laughed at. When he masters figure skating, the film presents him as the "manliest" figure skater to the audience as we watch him refuse to wear the sequined attire and command that they do the hardest stunts (which require far more risk to Kate than him). He wants to skate to rock music; she wants to skate to Mozart. For Christmas he gives her a hockey jersey and she gives him the book *Great Expectations*. The only other male figure skater we meet is Kate's ex-partner Brian Newman (Kevin Peeks) who is outwardly, and stereotypically, gay. Doug brings a specific perspective into the sport of figure skating: a masculine point of view. He criticizes its antiquated uniform style and even challenges if figure skating is, in fact, a sport when he witnesses the subjective style of judging. It should be noted that in a private moment with his brother, Doug admits that figure skating is harder than hockey. However, granting one passing moment to respect the athletic demands of figure skating does little to diminish Doug's continuous masculine-based perspective.

The differences between Kate and Doug extend beyond gender difference; there is also a theme of class status. It is clear throughout the film that Kate is not skating for herself; she is skating for her father. Her mother was a professional figure skater and the pressure is now on Kate to win the family a gold medal. Whereas Kate shouts entitled demands, Doug is fueled solely by his personal passion to be on the ice. At one point in the film, Kate sees a picture of Doug smelling the ice and Kate admits she never thought of doing that. Kate has grown up in a wealthy family that chose her destiny; Doug has had to work for everything he has. As the underdog, Doug becomes our hero.

We see montages of Doug and Kate training as equals, muscles flexed, sweat flicking off their bodies. They each take a turn upstaging the other as they practice. Before we can get too caught up in this great imagery of equal toughness, we are reminded that this is a love story. They bicker and flirt and they both exhibit jealousy. We root for them to connect. After Kate sees Doug with another woman at Nationals, her jealousy is revealing to her fiancé and he breaks it off. She is now single and available to admit her feelings. It isn't long after that she does.

To celebrate getting into the Olympics again, Kate decides she wants to drink for the first time—but she drinks too much. When she makes a romantic advance, Doug refuses, not wanting to take advantage of her. When she recognizes he's going to reject her, she states, "Excuse my surprise, but really, what a disappointment … look at you, God's gift to reckless abandonment revealed as nothing but a prude in wolf's clothing." This is a direct slam to Doug's ego, but he cares and as our hero, he'll do the right thing, saying, "It didn't have to be like this…" before she kicks him out. Although his actions were admirable, later that night when Kate's female opponent comes knocking on Doug's door, he lets her in and spends the night with her. In the morning when Kate comes to apologize, she catches them both. This is rock bottom for our love story.

Throughout the story Kate is prim and proper and Doug shows her how to loosen up and live. If Kate and Doug's actions were switched, would she be thought of as a femme fatale or a floozy? Doug's sex drive, abrasive reactions and adventurous lifestyle are presented as a freedom. Kate's uptight demeanor reminds us of the confinement in femininity. When she finally lets go, she loses all control. There is no middle ground for Kate; she is either restricted or uncontrollable. Even though Doug does a respectable thing by not taking advantage of Kate, he lets another girl into his room immediately after, reinforcing the virgin-slut or good girl-bad girl dichotomy of our sexist culture. We can't condemn Doug for his action because we are to understand that he and his ego feel rejected, and he can ease his feelings by being with another woman. Meanwhile, Kate's rejection is handled by a night's sleep. In the morning when they confront each other, Doug admits, "From the first day I walk into your rink, you treat me like a hired hand and one night you get drunk, I'm supposed to roll over and thank my lucky stars? I'm sorry, I don't downshift that fast." As much as we can understand Doug's actions, it's unfortunate that Kate does not have the freedom to function in any gear other than highstrung and "good girlish."

As the film comes to a close, Jack calls a meeting with Doug to yell at him about not listening to Kate. In the heat of the moment, Doug defends himself by saying that he is not the problem, Kate is. Kate's failure in the last Olympics was her fault; her partner didn't drop her, she fell. Jack and Anton have supported her by blaming everyone else but it's simply no one else's fault. He yells, "You people are all excuses. You wanna point a finger? Gotta find that go-to guy. You should've started with a go-to girl, Jack!" Kate finally speaks, agreeing with everything he says. She then says, "Do you think I look at myself, at what I've become, and do you think I'm proud?" When Jack asks what she wants, she answers, "I guess I would like to go back to the beginning and have you say win or lose, I could just be your daughter." The film has placed all the blame on Kate. What's worse is that her story is not one of winning a gold medal; it's finding her place as a woman in a patriarchal society outside of her sport, be it lover or daughter. This is confirmed in the last shot of the film.

The finale supplies us with a truly prevalent lasting impression of priorities for cinematic female athletes. As Doug and Kate stand by the ice preparing themselves for their final skate, Doug declares his love for her. Kate is shocked, moved and then, in a returning gesture, agrees to do the challenging trick they've been working on. Now we are set up for the glory of a romantic climactic skating program. We sit on the edge of our seat as we watch them skate beautifully. They succeed in doing a stunt no one has ever done before in competition. After an entire film of training for their second chance to stand on an Olympic podium, the final frame is not Kate and Doug together holding their gold medals with a smile, it is their kiss. We've spent an entire film training yet it is not about what they were training for. The film opens with a hockey skate and ends with a kiss. This film isn't about their athletic dreams, it's about their love. If it weren't for Doug, Kate would not have found what she really wants, to be desired outside of her athletics. Why can't Kate be a girlfriend, daughter *and* a gold medalist?

The Cutting Edge is a love story with the world of sports as a backdrop. As Doug and Kate connect, we watch two athletes of equal ambition train and grow with each other. However, Kate's ambitious and demanding athletic demeanor is presented as her greatest weakness, which can only be cured by the attention of the male characters around her. She didn't want to skate; her father set her on this path. We are simply watching a female athlete execute skill rather than passion. Although Kate can be credited with molding Doug into a more responsible athlete, he is placed as the victim of her attitude for a majority of the film. He is the hero, the athlete who had to work twice as hard to get where he is and the lover who teaches her to loosen up, releasing her to lead her own life. It's unfortunate that *The Cutting Edge* does not provide us with a female athlete who truly wants to compete, but *Wimbledon, Love & Basketball* and *Blue Crush* do.

Break Point

Tennis, basketball and surfing have established leagues for women. Although spectator interest between the men and women's basketball leagues and surfing tours tips in the men's favor, tennis has afforded us female stars who receive equal, if not more, media and fan support. In 2013, three out of the top five highest earning female athletes in the world were tennis stars.[4] As I've said before, perhaps the greatest source of tension resulting in female athletes not being taken seriously is the differing rules and equipment between the male and female leagues in all of these sports. For example in women's basketball, the basketball is one inch smaller than men's and the three-point line is slightly closer to the basket. In tennis, women play a best-out-of three sets rather than— five. Women surfers only compete in seven events whereas men compete in ten. These allowances are presented as physical compromises due to biological differences between the sexes. However, they also aid in a continued effort to label women as weaker, actively placing women's leagues as secondary.

With this in mind, we take a look at three movies involving these sports that allow us to watch both a strong male and female athlete at play. Although a love story is present in *Wimbledon, Love & Basketball* and *Blue Crush,* it does not take away from these cinematic female athletes' success in their sport. However there is still a problematic difference of acceptance in competitive attitude for each gender and although all of these films confirm their female hero's success, only *Love & Basketball* and *Blue Crush* show it. The visual confirmation in seeing these female athletes competing is crucial. Let's briefly look at these three films in order from good to best, illustrating positively empowered conclusions for female athleticism.

Wimbledon, released in 2004 and directed by Richard Loncraine, is the love story between Peter Colt (Paul Bettany), the 119th ranked tennis player in the world entering the final Wimbledon tournament of his career, and Lizzie Bradbury (Kirsten Dunst), a top-ranked player trying to win her first. Peter has an endearing defeatist attitude, charm, and a true love and appreciation for what tennis has brought him. Lizzie has a cutthroat attitude with a hot temper and is at the top of her game. Once again, we are witnessing two different types of ambition between a female and a male athlete. Although Peter is older than Lizzie, and they are at different points in their career, there is no indication that Peter was ever as cutthroat as Lizzie. We are faced with another female athlete whose drive and ambition is overshadowed by her uncontrollable and unfeminine attitude. Whereas competing can accompany Peter's identity, competition *is* Lizzie's identity. Lizzie has lost her ability to understand anything else, let alone romantic love. She must be in control. Falling in love results in a loss of control. This is presented as her weakness.

Lizzie entices Peter to fool around, sharing that sexual encounters can release some tension and help his game. Although this works for her, it doesn't for him. However, Lizzie's romantic interest in him does. As she spends time with him and their connection grows, Peter's playing improves. Match after match, his confidence builds and he wins due to his skillful domination (or a turn of luck with his opponent suffering an injury). The film is clearly centered on Peter; however, Lizzie's journey is important to recognize.

When we first encounter Lizzie, she is a fearless powerhouse of an athlete. She has a temper problem, but her skills are unbeatable. Throughout the film as she falls in love with Peter, her focus is slowly withdrawn, leaving her distracted and weakened. Their love gives Peter power, but diminishes Lizzie's. In a pivotal sequence of events, after the press gets wind of their romance, they flee to Peter's apartment outside of the city. Their love grows exponentially in this getaway. Unfortunately their trip is cut short due to Peter's younger brother leaking their whereabouts to the press.

Lizzie's father Dennis Bradbury (Sam Neill) runs her life the way Kate's father runs *hers*. He shows up to retrieve Lizzie and remind her that her sport comes first; this adventure in love can come later. Differing from Kate, Lizzie wants to compete and agrees, telling Peter their love affair can continue after the tournament. The beneficial difference between this scenario and *The Cutting Edge* is Lizzie's passion to play. Although her father is directing her away from true love, she agrees that her priority is to play. He is not getting in the way of anyone but Peter (and the audience) rooting for their love. Lizzie wants to succeed in her sport first and then love later. But this story isn't about Lizzie.

We return to the tournament to watch Peter struggle, only winning his next match due to his opponent's injury. That night he sneaks into Lizzie's room against her wishes. She recognizes that her romantic interest in Peter is harmful to her game but he is persistent, knowing it's good for his. Lizzie surrenders because she truly does love him and from there, the story shifts completely for Peter's benefit. The following day, Peter dominates. We watch everything go his way. Lizzie is not afforded the same on her court. The film shifts between each of their matches, as he dominates and she struggles. In the end, he wins and she loses, sending him to the Wimbledon finals and her packing. Although Lizzie's loss is disappointing, what's worse is that we don't see it. The visual priority in play is handed to Peter. Even though Lizzie's game was off (we assume this is Peter's fault), it's a disrespect not to finish her athletic journey visually. We just watch Peter's victory and then cut to her reaction at her loss. In the end, their night of reconnecting is presented as an unknowing sacrifice Lizzie makes for his victory.

After her loss, Lizzie is sitting at the airport waiting for her flight home when she watches Peter's declaration of love for her on national TV. He also credits her for all of his wins (as he should). Before you argue that Peter deserves some credit because he was the one physically playing in his matches, not her, let me remind you that the film clearly states it was Lizzie's belief in him (not his family, his friends or his agent) that gave him the confidence to play so well. In further proof, no one could be credited more than Lizzie for his final championship win.

In the finale, we cut to the Wimbledon championship between Peter and Lizzie's ex-boyfriend, American superstar Jake Hammond (Austin Nichols). Peter is losing when it begins to rain, halting play and sending him back to the locker rooms. Lizzie is waiting for him. She not only gives him a pep talk admitting her love for him, but she literally tells him how to read, and therefore dominate, his opponent. Handing Peter a cheat sheet, she explains Jake's physical habits and cues to how he will serve and hit the ball. Once Peter returns to the court, he is armed with the secrets to get back into the match. However before the audience can credit Lizzie with his win, there is a specific moment where she is eliminated from the equation.

Throughout the film the audience has heard Peter's inner thoughts in a voiceover. Most of his thoughts have given us insight into how truly surprised he is at his survival through each round of the competition. Now this inner dialogue is specifically utilized to eradicate Lizzie's credit for the most important moment of his career. Once Peter and Jake are even for the set, there is a tiebreak that affords Jake a shot at a championship point. At this moment, Peter can either win the point or lose the match. We reenter his inner thoughts and find out his thoughts are jumbled; he can't remember what Lizzie has told him. From this point on, his match play is solely based on his own talent. Even though her cheat sheet got him back in the match, a fighting chance to win, it will not be credited for the survival of this point and with that, his championship point. This is his moment and his alone. This story is about Peter and it's important that he be credited with the win.

Lizzie's loss makes Peter's victory greater. He takes the sole spotlight for the conclusion of the film. There is an assumption that she is young and has a big future, so it's all right for her to lose, letting him have his moment right now. Why is this necessary? Wouldn't it have been just as exciting to have them both win? In the final moments of the film, we jump to the future to watch Peter and Lizzie on a tennis court with their young children. As the film fades to black, Peter's final voiceover tells us that Lizzie won Wimbledon twice. Why couldn't we have seen that? The visual success of a female athlete is important. I'm grateful that the final line of dialogue of the film is dedicated to Lizzie as an athlete, but it's placed as an afterthought not worth seeing. What *is* worth seeing is Peter and Lizzie with their child. She became a mother and that's more important than watching her win on a professional tennis court. There's nothing wrong with celebrating that she and Peter stayed together and had a family, but the film was set in the tennis world. Rather than watching Lizzie play with her daughter on a community court, why couldn't Peter have been sitting in the grandstands, with their children, watching Lizzie win her own Wimbledon championship match? These are the important images for women's sports that fall to the wayside. The visual confirmation that a female athlete's only priority is to be in a relationship and a mother is challenged in *Love & Basketball.*

Released in 2000 and directed by Gina Prince-Bythewood, *Love & Basketball* is a love story between two basketball players, Quincy McCall (Omar Epps) and Monica Wright (Sanaa Lathan). The film follows their relationship from when they are young dreamers through their experiences playing professionally, all while they weave in and out of each other's lives. What makes this film different is that Monica's determination and drive in her sport never wavers. Only after she has played professionally in Europe long enough to become homesick does she make the decision to stop playing. Then she returns home and, subsequently, declares her love for him. This film visually places these two athletes as equals. They each have struggles within their sport, gender and love for each other.

There is a very important visual we must appreciate in the final moments of *Love & Basketball.* Unlike *Wimbledon,* we don't just hear about Monica's success, we see it. The film shifts to the future as we watch Monica run out onto the court in the WNBA, turning around to smile at Quincy who is sitting in the crowd with their child. I want to make it clear that it's not so important that Quincy is in the stands as it's important that Monica is on the court. The empowerment isn't in watching a female athlete continue to play while a male player doesn't. It is simply watching a female athlete play. This is exactly the visual we should have had in *Wimbledon. Blue Crush* takes this lasting impression one step further.

Blue Crush, directed by John Stockwell in 2002, is the story of Anne Marie Chadwick (Kate Bosworth), a talented surfer training to compete in Pipe Masters surf competition in order to gain sponsors and turn professional. Anne Marie was an up-and-coming star when she was younger but a bad fall and a near-drowning experience has instilled a kernel of fear that she must overcome. She has the help of her two girlfriends, Eden (Michelle Rodriguez) and Lena (Sanoe Lake). This female support network is beautiful to watch. The female-centric cast doesn't end there; Anne Marie has her younger sister Penny (Mika Boorem) to watch over and provide for. It's clear that Penny's rebellion against Anne Marie as a mother figure is reflective of how Anne Marie must have been in her youth. However Anne Marie desires to grow into a good role model for Penny and by the end of the film, she does.

Before I continue to celebrate positive female representation in *Blue Crush,* it's important that we recognize an established sexual objectification in the film. Anne Marie, Eden and Lena are commercially beautiful women and we spend plenty of moments watching them in bikinis, swimming and surfing in various slow-motion montages. However, along with these moments, we also watch imagery of amazing athleticism as Anne Marie, Eden and Lena train. Additionally, we are introduced to multiple real-life female professional surfers. The local boys may give Anne Marie a hard time for trying to go pro, but the audience is granted visual confirmation that there are already established, celebrated female surfers.

Anne Marie, Eden and Lena build their incomes by working as maids at a fancy hotel. Here Anne Marie meets her love interest, NFL player Matthew Davis (Matt Tollman). This relationship eventually detracts Anne Marie from her training. She is wooed by his attention and his money, and the idea of an easier life starts to distract her from her surfing dream. Matt doesn't consciously veer her away from her training. In fact, Matt has little to do with the misdirection Anne Marie takes. Ann Marie's mother fled when things got too tough and now Anne Marie is doing the same. It's important to recognize that Anne Marie dictates her relationship with Matt. When Anne Marie hits rock bottom, feeling lost, she asks Matt what she should do and he replies, "Just be the girl I met on the beach... A girl who'd never ask a guy what to do." Even though Anne Marie's relationship with Matt is central to the plot, it does not define who Anne Marie is or validate her worth. When she says, "I really, really want to win Pipe Masters tomorrow," Matt simply responds, "Well, do it." Being an athlete himself, Matt can relate to her passion and he respects her athletic goals.

When we get to Pipe Masters, Anne Marie nearly drowns on her first run, but does score enough to move to the next round. But then her fear gets the best of her, putting her out of contention to win. After her female opponent advises and encourages her to take a wave, she crashes but this time she gets right back up and paddles out. Although she is out of contention to win, we watch Anne Marie successfully complete one incredible run, which is all she needs to get the attention of sponsors.

Blue Crush provides us with a final sequence that takes the progressive conclusion of *Love & Basketball* one step further: Anne Marie and Matthew kiss, but this is not the end. Earlier in the film Anne Marie had told Matthew, "I want a girl to be on the cover of *Surf* magazine, and that would be great if that girl were me, but any girl will do." In a truly empowering action, we switch to a replay of the end of Anne Marie's victorious run that freezes and turns into the cover of *Surf*. Our final frame is dedicated to her supportive female family. We watch Anne Marie, Eden, Lena and Penny all smile, arms around each other as we fade to black. The kiss from Matt is only one small part of her happy ending. Our lasting impression is of her becoming a celebrated surfer and we also revisit the amazing female support network that helped make it happen. This is truly empowering.

The landscape of a love story in these films allows the female athlete to exhibit more masculine-coded characteristics because she is already established as both desirable and heterosexual. It can't be denied that although *Blue Crush* exhibits empowering images of female support, that support is consistently dressed in a bikini. It can't be overlooked that both *Wimbledon* and *Love & Basketball* end with the proof that these competitive, tough women are still mothers. These nods are far more about a woman's duty than it is about a female athlete's happy ending. The requirement of having a family along with their sport is a recurring message cinematic female athletes give the audience. Before you ask, "Why can't they have it all?" let me ask you this: How many male-driven sports films do you see where after the big game, it is clearly pointed out that the players went on to have families? Winning the big game isn't enough for female athletes. Audiences must visually confirm that these female athletes can reconnect with their feminine-coded values after being entrenched in aggressive game play.

With this in mind, it's important we take a look at *Personal Best*. Another film founded on a romantic relationship, it explores a lesbian relationship. The rebellion against an established desirability by a man could create a different dynamic for our female athlete, but unfortunately the film transmits weakness, leaving us with a final impression of a female hero far removed from Lizzie, Monica and Ann Marie.

Backside Mechanics

Personal Best, directed by Robert Towne in 1982, is the story of Chris Cahill (Mariel Hemingway), a track and field athlete trying to get to the 1980 Olympic Games. Beyond the athletic struggles to train and compete, her journey is saturated with relationships. Chris' central relationship is with her female teammate Tory Skinner (real-life track star Patrice Donnelly[5]). This lesbian relationship has become the defining conversation about *Personal Best.* Although the film was not a box office success, it was a favorite among critics and the two points of celebration were its respectful portrayal of a lesbian relationship and its embrace of female athletes' active athletic bodies.[6] I find both these observations questionable. Firstly, Chris is never pronounced fully lesbian and therefore her happy ending is found with a man, Denny Stites (Kenny Moore). Secondly, the visual physicality of the female athletes in the film is downright sexual.[7] The film's biggest drawback is giving Chris no power. *Personal Best* follows a group of strong female athletes, yet centers on the weakest. In the finale, Chris's "strongest" moment comes in the form of a sacrifice for Tory, representing a weakness in competition and confirming the central theme of the film as feminine fallibility and need to be taken care of.

From the start of the film, we see Chris's weakness and vulnerability. In the opening scene, we watch a track meet where Chris struggles in the hurdles and then apologizes profusely to her father. Chris appears infantile in her demeanor. Her disappointment is not so much in her failure to compete well as much as letting her father down. This is the start of a continued problematic character trait in Chris. Her self-worth is not based on her own competition or growth; it is always based on her relation to, and acceptance from, other characters. Those other characters include Tory, her lover, Terry Tingloff (Scott Glenn), her coach, and Denny, the romantic interest she ends up with. These three characters become caretakers for Chris and any other dynamic to their relationship with her is secondary. In order to illustrate this action of Chris' caretaking-hand-off, we must look at the progression of relationships within the film and note that there is never a moment where Chris is alone.

After the initial track meet at the start of the film, we cut to a bar where Tory is celebrating her victory. When Chris nearly collapses in the bar from exhaustion, Tory brings her home. Chris shares her frustrations with Tory; Tory gives her advice and confirms her talent, giving Chris a much-needed boost of confidence. Tory is immediately seen as strong, confident and competitively dominant. She is also quickly introduced as fearless when she makes a romantic move on Chris so soon. They have sex. This sequence is the only time where Chris could be read as having a romantic interest in Tory. After this night, Chris' juvenile demeanor continually reassigns Tory's affection from lover to mother. There is never a moment where we truly believe that Chris loves Tory as Tory loves Chris. In a pivotal moment in their relationship, Tory tries to break up with Chris by suggesting they see other people:

> TORY: Look, either we're together or we're not together.
> CHRIS: Jesus Christ Tory, we're friends.
> TORY: Yes, every once in a while, we fuck each other. Either you move out or I move out and we really are just friends.

Needless to say, Chris's desperation for someone she trusts to look after her keeps them together. However, this is a far cry from a respectable portrayal of a lesbian relationship. This isn't about a fear of the world's intolerance of homosexuality because even in their private space, Chris does not connect with Tory. Tory is presented as a woman who knows herself, knows her sexuality and knows how she feels about Chris. Chris is presented as a woman who is confused and trying to hang on to anyone who will help her, even if that requires manipulating Tory to continue to be her guardian.

The other guardian who enters Chris's life is Terry, Tory's coach. After Tory and Chris share their first night together, Tory vows to get Terry to coach Chris. Tory and Terry have a strong relationship as friends and athletes. There is a shared respect and it is clear that Chris is jealous of that connection. Once Chris is on the team, it is quickly apparent that Terry's relationship with Chris will be different; he has romantic feelings for her. As Chris improves under Terry's coaching, Terry begins to steer her away from Tory by convincing her that Tory should be viewed as an opponent, not a partner. He even goes as far as encouraging Chris to compete in the same track event as Tory, the pentathlon.

Throughout the film thus far, Terry has appeared as a coach who truly believes in his female athletes. However, as he falls for Chris, we start to see that Terry's acceptance of his team of female athletes has limits. After Chris is accidently injured after taking advice from Tory, she loses trust in Tory and moves in with Terry. Once Terry has Chris's attention, he begins to admit his true feelings about female athletics. Terry blatantly states the assumed biological struggle (eventually played out in the conclusion of this film) for female athletes to compete when he says:

> TERRY: All right, one thing you gotta understand. I could have been a man's coach. Backfield coach, Oregon State. I had the job. I had the job. I actually had the job. Do you know what I'm saying? I had the job. Oh, well. Coach of the Year. I was Coach of the Year, last year. You know what that means when you're a woman's coach? Jack shit. I mean, I could've coached football. Do you actually think that Chuck Noll has to worry that Franco Harris is going to cry because Terry Bradshaw won't talk to him, hmm? Jack Lambert can't play cause Mel Blount hurt his feelings? That Lynn Swann is pregnant? That Rocky Bleier forgot his Tampax?

This is a speech about women's alleged weakness: the reason men relegate women to different sports or different rules, the reason women will never be taken seriously in sport. This is the exact accusation that confirms elements of womanhood (menstruation, pregnancy, emotions) as "lack." The implication is that since men don't have these natural hindrances, sports (and therefore competition) are just naturally a better fit. The conversation continues:

> CHRIS: I'm sorry. I … I didn't mean to upset you. Listen, she didn't mean it.
> TERRY: She didn't mean it. You know what you're like? There's a joke about a faggot who makes a pass at a Marine in the men's room on the 40th floor of the Empire State Building. The Marine throws the faggot out the window. The Marine gets down the street, passes the faggot in the gutter. The faggot gets up on one elbow and says, "Yoo-hoo, I'm not mad." So why don't you just go home? So why don't you just go home, kiss, make up, eat each other. Whatever the fuck you do … I actually did it. Well, why don't you hit me? Be nice to see if you got the balls to—[*She hits him then immediately regrets it and apologizes*] Why do you always have to do what I tell you?

A speech that offends both women and homosexuals, this scene becomes the primer to understand the underlying message, and problem, with *Personal Best*. The film is hinged on Chris as the epitome of all this alleged lack. She lacks independence, she lacks a belief in herself and most of all, she lacks the "killer instinct"—which the film places as a sports requirement. What's worse is that Tory, who is introduced as so strong, grows weak with her feelings for Chris. She loses her competitive edge to her emotions and eventually loses her competition because of it. *Personal Best* may be complimented for its avoidance of placing Tory's central problem as homosexuality, but the film does punish her for being a woman. Tory can't help herself but care and the more she cares, the more she struggles to compete.

Perhaps there is no stronger confirmation of these ideas than the conclusion of the film. After Chris rejects Terry's advances, she has about one minute of independence before she meets Denny, an Olympic water polo player whose complete separation from the world of Terry and Tory creates a safe space for Chris. In their introduction, we witness that Chris is physically stronger than Denny as they train. In a comedic play on him trying to assert his manhood, Chris unknowingly upstages his every move in the weight room. Unfortunately, this established physical strength difference does not translate to their emotional connection. Chris continues to surrender to a vulnerable state of need for approval, support and guidance. I understand that the support of a lover cannot always translate to a weakness being present, but the film continually places Chris in an endless cycle of desperate need for approval and therefore any hint of this with this new love interest simply continues this character trait. When asked by a fellow athlete about her newly inspired confidence, Chris just smiles and looks at Denny. It is Denny who gives her the encouragement to resurrect her competitive edge when she's struggling. It is Denny who is her happy ending.

The finale is set at the 1980 Olympic Track and Field Trials. At the start of the pentathlon, Chris struggles in the hurdles, her strongest event. She then struggles in the shot put. Denny calls her over and gives her a pep talk, which gives her the confidence to win the high jump. It rains in the middle of the competition, leaving the runway to the long jump slick. When Tory goes to jump, she slips and hyperextends her knee. She has to get into the top three to qualify for the

Olympics. Currently in fourth place, she only needs to beat one competitor in the final race to make it. However Tory has surrendered; she knows she can't win with her knee the way it is. Chris comes to visit her in the medical tent to convince her to compete. More than convincing, Chris offers to sacrifice her chances to win the entire event to help Tory. If she runs at her fastest pace (putting her at risk to tire herself out before the finish), she can tire out Tory's opponent, allowing Tory to pull out a victory in the end and slipping her into third place. Chris's action should be viewed as a completed character arc. She is now taking care of Tory and she is now a confident athlete who knows her strengths. However, the action of sacrifice is reflective of the very weakness the film has assigned Chris. Much like in *A League of Their Own*, the victory of this film for our female athlete isn't in winning the competition; it's placed in her action of sacrifice for the one she loves. Sure, Chris' actions could be seen as a competitive play for a teammate, but that's not the message sent to the audience. Tory has resigned to losing and understands that perhaps her time as a competitor has come to an end. For Chris, it's not about the competition; it's about how she feels about Tory. This is not a "killer instinct" for competition; it's a killer instinct for nurture.

Tory agrees to run, but doesn't agree to Chris's offer. She wants to finish the race for herself. However, it is quite clear that Chris does as she promised and as a result, Tory wins the third place spot. With the boycott of the 1980 Olympics in Moscow, our story ends here. As they step up on the victory stand, they share this final exchange:

CHRIS: Well, what do you think?
TORY: Well, he's awful cute ... for a guy.
CHRIS: Are you shittin' me? Hey!

They laugh and the film fades to black. Keeping in mind the battle for female athletes to avoid assumptions of homosexuality, the female romantic relationship is not the central problem of this film; the problem is connecting femininity with weakness. Chris and Tory's athletic conflicts hold little weight in comparison to their emotional struggles. There is emotion involved in competition, but the emotions they struggle from are presented as weakness due to their gender. Furthermore, although one could compliment *Personal Best*'s display of freedom within the spectrum of sexuality, it cannot be overlooked that the film's happy ending is Chris's heterosexual conclusion. Even worse, the film makes a point of showing Tory's approval of this. She wants what's best for Chris and both Tory and we know it is Denny.

Personal Best is a story of relationships. Sports certainly play a far greater role than a background setting; however the presence of competition only aids to a conversation of weakness. Chris is the weakest character and her strongest moment (helping Tory) could be viewed as her weakest in competition (sacrificing her win for Tory's). It's problematic that Chris never fully admits romantic feelings with Tory and that she ends the film in a relationship with a man. This muddled exploration of sexuality sends a disempowering message about homosexuality. It doesn't take it seriously. Her relationship with Denny confirms a re-correction of heteronormative ideas. *Personal Best* introduced an intimate portrayal of female athleticism, but rather than embrace the strengths of these female athletes, the film promotes their emotional weaknesses. These weaknesses continue socially constructed ideas of femininity. Our hero, Chris, is defined by her subordination and secondary nature to everyone around her.

As I've stated earlier, love stories create a specific freedom for the female athlete to succeed. If she has established a connection with a male character, she is afforded a level of access to play. So what happens if there is no love interest? Could the "feminine" qualities of her sport serve as enough to solely focus on her struggles as an athlete? We conclude the chapter with this question and an exploration of the film *Stick It*.

A Gainer

Directed by Jessica Bendinger, *Stick It* (2006) is the story of Haley Graham (Missy Peregrym), who was once a world-class gymnast and now spends her time rebelling as a juvenile delinquent. After getting arrested too many times, she is sentenced to train at Vickerman Gymnastics Academy, owned and run by Burt Vickerman (Jeff Bridges). Before I begin to critique the story elements of *Stick It,* it's important to praise the film for its portrayal of the athleticism in gymnastics. As Haley shares in a voiceover, there are 2000 Navy SEALs and only 200 elite gymnasts: "Don't be fooled by the leotards, people. The things gymnasts do make Navy SEALs look like wusses, and we do them without a gun." With an established respect for the difficulty of gymnastics as a sport, *Stick It* never shies away from promoting positive values of a female athlete's toughness. The prominent problem in *Stick It* is who coaches and inspires this toughness. As we work our way through the film, it's important that we recognize a lost opportunity to expand our positive female representation beyond Haley.

We are introduced to Haley as she is reaching the bottom of a downward spiral. One of the best gymnasts in the country, she walked out on her team at the Junior Olympics, costing them a gold medal. The reason she walked out was because in mid-competition she found out her mother was cheating on her father with her coach. She now has a troubled relationship with her parents and, with that, any figure of authority. Once she is sentenced to the Vickerman Gymnastics Academy, she and Burt are quite the match. Burt is a coach known as an outcast in the gymnastics world due to his gymnasts getting injured all the time. He is also money-hungry, manipulating the mothers of his gymnasts to pay top dollar, promising elite status even though only a few can actually make it. The age discrepancy between Burt and Haley preclude the possibility of a love story, yet allows us to witness another recurring relationship we've seen for cinematic female athletes: father and daughter. With Haley's troubled relationship with her father, Burt's position as her coach and mentor translates to a father figure in many literal ways as well.

The relationship between Haley and Burt is ultimately a positive one. They challenge each other and connect to truly better one another. It is not unusual that Haley would have a male coach in gymnastics. Although a popular sport for women, gymnastics is a sport in which both men and women compete. However, men and women compete in different ways within the sport. It's regressive that the film has a male coach coaching women's gymnastics. Yes, male coaches do exist in the real world, but the choice to hand the coaching, and parenting, to Burt in this story follows another recurring problematic pattern for cinematic female athletes: the absence of a female mentor. Had Haley been under the guidance of a female coach and mother figure, we would have the opportunity to recognize two female athletes and an acknowledgment of female athletes who came before Haley. We don't live in a world where female athletes succeed under male coaches and then just disappear. Even if there is a heavy presence of male coaches in female-driven sports, in a cinematic landscape, could we at least imagine a woman in the position to mentor and lead a female athlete to success? By handing the reins to Burt, *Stick It* is continuing a gender tradition of granting access and permission for athletic opportunity via a male figure. Haley may become a female role model for viewers, but it is clear that the origin of her power lies with Burt.

Gymnastics serves as one of the most rigidly judged sports in its pursuit for perfection. Haley makes it a point to tell the audience that the effort to succeed in gymnastics is pointless because you can't win. There will always be a deduction due to an unreachable human level of precision and the subjective style of judging. Burt even admits, "There's nothing fair about a girl landing a double pike and losing a tenth 'cause her toes weren't pointed." Further, Haley argues that the judging system "makes conventionality good and innovation bad." This stab at conventionality is the heart of the film. Throughout the film, it's made abundantly clear that Haley's biggest conflict is her disgust at being judged: She is judged for breaking the law, she is judged for being a tomboy and she's judged for being a quitter. Unfortunately, Haley's only option to stay out of jail is to return to a sport of judgment.

In order to get Haley to start taking his academy seriously, Burt bribes her with the incentive that should she fully train and compete in the IG Classic in the following month, she could win some restitution money to pay the court, thereby earning her freedom. Haley and Burt begin their journey for redemption together. At this point, one would assume Haley is headed back to Nationals and that redemption will serve as her completing the competition with her team. However, the film shifts focus from direct athletic redemption to challenging gymnastics as a sports altogether. We'll return to this when we discuss the conclusion of the film.

As Burt once says to Haley, for someone who hates judgment, she certainly hands a fair share of it out herself. Throughout the film she has an attitude about her teammates and continually judges their commitment to the sport. She is presented as far more talented and brave than her teammates and although she makes jokes at their expense, she still inspires them to challenge themselves as women both on and off the mat. Unfortunately, her teammates don't teach her much. Though they support each other, she is always placed as an outsider. This allows all of her support to come solely from Burt. It would have been beneficial for her to connect with her female teammates seeing as there are no positive female role models for Haley in this film. Her support system comes solely from her two male best friends and now her male coach. Her mother is the source of her troubles and the only other females we hear from are the judgmental, fame-hungry mothers of the other gymnasts and the gymnastic judges who unfairly score her competition. We watch female coaches in the background but we never meet one. Perhaps this is why Haley only desires to connect with male characters. By presenting Haley as the only strong woman, we are given the impression that strength only comes from interactions with men.

During the IG Classic, Haley finds out her father has been paying Burt four times his usual rate to train her. Burt wasn't giving her a chance out of the goodness of his heart, his kindness and support were in exchange for large sums of money. This causes Haley to repeat her Junior Olympic actions and walk out on the competition. Even though this time her forfeit does not affect the entire team's outcome, it does reflect an absence of change in her character. As an athlete, she has walked out on herself. This confirms that success in gymnastics holds little relevance in this story. This is a movie about Haley finding someone to believe in her. That someone is Burt. If there weren't such a lack of camaraderie with her teammates, they could have helped her through this and stood as the support system she so desperately desires. Adding insult to injury, when Haley encourages her teammates to push the limits of their athletic ability and try the hardest tricks, they fail in landing them and they blame her for their lack of success. Because of this, we continue a private space where only Haley and Burt can affect each other.

Once she reveals to Burt that she walked out on the Junior Olympics because of her mother's betrayal, Burt now knows she is not just some petulant teen, she's a child in need of someone she can trust. Burt may care about money, but he cares about Haley more. He proves this to Haley by using the payments from her father to clear her debt with the courts. Additionally he writes a positive reference letter asking for

Haley to be given a clean slate. When Haley is called into the office of Judge Westreich (Polly Holliday), she reads his letter and finds out that she is now free. Before she leaves, Judge Westreich advises, "Be good, sounds like you're built for it... There are a lot of great people who had jerks for parents. We gotta stick together." This could be the female role model we've been waiting for, but it's too little too late. Although Judge Westreich is demonstrating a supportive belief in Haley, Burt beat her to the punch with his letter. Coming second, Judge Westreich is simply agreeing with Burt and freeing Haley. Now we can confirm Haley's growth and commitment to Burt when she returns to the gym on her own terms.

Even though Haley lacks female role models, it cannot be denied that she grows into being a role model for her teammates. After she's made amends with the girls, she shows them the importance of having autonomy and standing up for what you believe in. She encourages the girls to embrace confidence outside of gymnastics. Most importantly, she leads them to come together for a common cause. In the conclusion of the film, one of her teammates is unfairly judged due to her bra strap showing. It is quickly clear that her teammate is being penalized for having Burt as her coach. His complicated past with the gymnastics world, much like Haley's, is obstructing fair judging. When it's time for Haley to compete, she pulls her bra strap out, effectively forfeiting her turn. Soon the other girls join in to stand united in protest against the judge's unfair motion.

Competition after competition, the gymnasts declare who will win by forfeiting their turn. After a glorious montage of the girls proudly revealing their shoulder straps, it's Haley's turn to compete in the category the girls have chosen her to win. She stands on the corner of the floor mat reflecting on what she wishes for. She thinks:

> There are things you wish for before big moments. I wish my friends were here. God, I wish my parents were different. I wish there was someone who got what was happening, and could just look at me and tell me we weren't crazy, that we weren't being stupid. Someone to say, "I'm proud of you. And I got your back. No matter what."

Immediately, Burt interrupts her thoughts and calls her over. As if he heard her every word, he says, "Listen, I, uh ... I just want you to know ... that I'm so proud to be your coach." This is a beautiful moment and it's clear that Haley and Burt could not have grown into the people they are right now without each other. The problem is, Haley's speech to herself gave Burt the absolute power of validation. We recognize what she has done for him as well, but this story is about Haley. And for Haley, Burt's support is paramount. This supportive growth and connection could have been incredibly beneficial to the cinematic representation of female athletes had Burt been a woman.

While *Stick It* provides us with some necessary support of female athletics, the foundation of the story is based on deconstructing a sport rather than competing in it. In a story so rich with critiquing conventionality, it's a shame that it continued such a conventional relationship. It's important that I compliment *Stick It* for embracing Haley's toughness as an individual, rather than taming it. Haley's characteristics of aggression and passion don't change much throughout the film, but rather adapt and redirect toward a more beneficial platform. I can't deny the relief I felt that Haley didn't suffer a makeover to gain a boyfriend by the end of the film, but I did feel disappointment with the focus shifted off of her fully completing a competition. It is honorable to stand up against a system you believe is unfair, especially a system based on conventionality. Centering the film on this premise makes its lack of female representation all the more disappointing. The system of male dominance in sport is also unfair. Here we had an entire film showcasing women's gymnastics, yet the most influential supporter of Haley is a man. Why couldn't the fight against conventionality include a female coach?

Since all of the films in this chapter center on sports that have established leagues for women, we should see a backdrop filled with a range of positive female representations for our heroes to interact with. However, with the exception of *Blue Crush*, our heroes' support systems come in the form of their male love interests or father figures. Although *Personal Best* has a female love interest, our female athlete hero still enacts a subordinate nature and two men also anchor her story. We are continuing to watch a pattern of centering these cinematic female athletes' purpose in relation to male characters. Our heroines' conclusions then rely on these relationships. Just because these stories are set in a familiar territory for women doesn't mean that we can dismiss having the central focus rest on their athletic goals. Just as our onscreen female athletes could have benefitted from female mentors, we as the audience can benefit from these cinematic female athletes as our role models. They need to lead us into an understanding that the exciting conclusion to her sports story does not have to include winning the guy or winning his approval, it can just be winning.

5

Illegal Substitution
Replacing One (Wo)Man with Another

If it looks like a duck, swims like a duck and quacks like a duck, then it probably is a duck. If she looks like a man, plays like a man and sounds like a man, then she probably is a man. This inductive reasoning can help reveal a separation of biological sex and the action of constructing gender performance in our society. RuPaul once wrote, "We're born naked and the rest is drag."[1] Drag is the act of dressing and enacting the opposite gender. When we think of drag, we think of men dressed in hyperfeminine outfits who stand as entertainers. But the root of drag is the simple act of presenting yourself as the opposite sex. Also known as cross-dressing, this performance is evidence that gender is socially constructed.[2] Through dressing in clothing marked for the opposite sex and enacting mannerisms and actions associated with masculinity or femininity, one is revealing society's accepted (and promoted) characteristics for men and women while simultaneously demonstrating that the supposedly opposite sex can also favor and expertly display these characteristics. So, could a female finally prove her worth among male teammates on the field if she played just as well as the men but no one knew she was a girl? Without the socially constructed pretense that comes with her female gender, could we finally see a competition simply full of athletic bodies and skills?

There haven't been many cross-dressing films centered on female athletes. In fact, I could count them on one hand. The same goes for male athletes. These films are quite revealing of gender stereotypes and perhaps the small number of them reveals a decreasing willingness to challenge gender ideology. People want to believe women's inferior athletic abilities are inherent traits, but the truth is, although women and men may differ biologically in strengths, they differ more within their sex than they do with each other.[3] There are some women capable, with the right amount of training, to compete with men, just as there are some men, with the right amount of training, who still couldn't. However, this is not just about men versus women, this is the simple acknowledgment of women playing sports. As discussed before, the allowances and differences between women's and men's sports continue a gender divide that restricts female athletes and male athletes from being thought of as equals. So in a scenario where she can pose as an equal physically, without any pre-conceived notion based on an understood gender construction, could she be seen as simply an athlete rather than a "female" athlete?

Drag sports films haven't been particularly popular at the box office, but it's important that we examine a few for their direct spotlight on the conversation of gender and sports. In order to examine the male-to-female drag scenario, we're going to take a look at *Ladybugs* (1992) with reference to *Juwanna Mann* (2002). In order to examine the female-to-male drag scenario, we will be analyzing *She's the Man* (2006) with reference to *Motocrossed* (2001). Even though these films exhibit empowering visuals of women and men playing together and differing strengths that allow women and men to better each other, we still see the same patterns of active correction to their assigned gender. These athletes—in drag—weave in and out of the world of the opposite sex, yet certain plot points assure the audience that they are still firmly rooted in a recognizable feminine female or masculine male gender. Drag really gets down to the basics of what we define as gender, a costume of superficial identity that we must embody in order to "fit in." Our real identifications and proclivities are veiled behind our ability to "act" the part. This is the foundational problem for cinematic female athletes. Their ability to compete does not play a predominate role in their success, their ability to simultaneously present as "genuinely" female does.

Disadvantage Rule

Ladybugs (1992), directed by Sidney Furie, is the story of Chester Lee (Rodney Dangerfield), a corporate worker who, desperate for a promotion, falsely sells himself as a soccer coach to his boss. When he finds out his company's championship team has lost all of its championship players, he convinces his soon-to-be stepson, Matthew (Jonathan Brandis), to become Martha, dressing in drag to help them win. Comedy ensues and we watch the team improve and eventually win, thereby earning Chester a promotion, a wife, a newfound relationship with his stepson and a new profession of coaching youth athletics, all while avoiding any recognition of talent or value in female athletics. *Ladybugs* is a form of protest against women in sports, plain and simple. The female athletes *are* the butt of the joke. Through its comedy, the entire film promotes a message of women's inability to play sports and a failure for them to support and learn from each other, leaving a lasting impression that even if they win, that success is not accountable in the long run for continued playing opportunities.

The film opens with Chester sitting in a conference listening to a motivational speaker. The mantra he has paid to learn is "I am great, I am wonderful, everybody likes me." However, these declarations play little part in Chester's journey. A short introduction portrays Chester as weak, vulnerable and easily manipulated. However, he's also clever as we watch him comment to and about other men and flirt with every grown woman in the film. His flirting proves heterosexuality and his clever humor asserts his masculinity. Although a jester, his place as male entertainer gives him value. This is our hero. Matthew, the son of Chester's girlfriend, is introduced watching music videos of scantily clad female butt-shaking. Right away, we know he's straight, he's masculine and no matter how many dresses he wears, he likes to sit in a beanbag chair and objectify women.

Chester's boss Dave Mullens is a power-hungry, full-of-himself, stereotypic corporation man who only believes in winning. Dave has a commercially attractive wife, Glynnis Mullen (Jeannetta Arnette), whose every movement is accompanied with sleazy saxophone music denoting her as a sex object. Throughout the film, Chester is aided by his sidekick, his secretary Julie Benson (Jackée Harry). Quite funny herself, she is assigned as Chester's assistant soccer coach. Although tough, her hyperfeminine and diva-like asides have little impact in the story and it is clear that her place is simply to set up jokes for Chester to execute, rather than inspire and help coach the girls. These characters serve as comedic exaggerations to their gender. They both celebrate and poke fun at themselves, yet they play an important role in the film's active effort to send a message that boys will be boys and girls will be girls in the most constructed sense.

In Chester's first meeting with the team, it's revealed that the team members who had helped win the championship have all graduated and moved on. What's left is a bunch of players who lack ability, confidence and experience. Chester asks each of the girls to stand up and introduce themselves by sharing how many goals they scored last year. Needless to say, they haven't scored any. Each young female athlete stands to introduce herself and effectively also introduce her representation via the construction of femininity. Sally Anne Welfelt (Johna Stewart-Bowden) introduces herself as she shifts between model poses and flaunts her desire for good-looking guys. Carmelita Chu (Jennifer Frances Lee) simply shares that she collects butterflies. Penny Pester (Jandi Swanson) is quickly marked as socially awkward by her shy demeanor and by her large beauty-hiding glasses. There are only two girls remaining from the Ladybug dynasty: Nancy Larimer (Crystal Cooke), who appears smart and generally athletic, and Kimberly Mullen (Vinessa Shaw), Chester's boss's daughter. Chester placates her and favors her no matter how athletically challenged she is.

The first game is an absolute embarrassment, which initiates our drag storyline. Chester reaches out to Matthew, who has been struggling with his grades and has recently been kicked off both the junior varsity football and soccer team because of it. Chester is minimally interested in building a relationship with Matthew; he is more interested in what Matthew can provide for his soccer team. His intention is clear. On the flipside, Matthew is not ready to slip on the dress simply in an effort to connect with Chester; he has a crush on Kimberly, whom he knows from school.

If the male gaze within this film wasn't apparent thus far in this story, then it's made crystal clear when Matthew first spots Kimberly on the field. The film shifts to a montage scored with "All I Have to Do Is Dream" by the Everly Brothers as we watch Kimberly, in the blink of an eye, switch from her soccer uniform to a bikini, running in slow motion. The montage continues as we watch Matthew and Kimberly run into each other's arms, Matthew leading her down a red carpet into a private jet, both of them eating fancy hamburgers and getting married. The whole time Kimberly sports short dresses, jewelry and loving eyes for Matthew. But it's just a dream, a comical insight into his teen imagination, right? No. This isn't just for Matthew; it's for us as well. We watch and desire Kimberly. Kimberly isn't desirable in her soccer uniform; she's desirable in a bikini. Matthew may come off as a silly teenager, dreaming of himself in a leather jacket and of hamburgers on a silver platter but he is our portal to dream of Kimberly outside of this athletic playing field. Kimberly is now something more than a soccer player. We needed this moment to assign her desirability. This not only separates her from her teammates, but now she also stands as a heterosexually driven (and therefore acceptable) reason for Matthew to sign on to the idea of putting on a wig and becoming Martha to be closer to her.

Soccer is a team sport. One player cannot win the game and that is confirmed as we watch the Ladybugs lose their first game with Martha, even though Matthew easily dominates the playing field. After the game, Chester gives Matthew a talk about how teamwork and sportsmanship is necessary. At the start of the scene, his speech is positive, stating, "I don't want *you* to play, I want the team to win." He talks about a need for harmony on the team and that Matthew carries the most faults in their loss. Chester's positive speech takes a turn for the worse when he redirects Matthew's problems to his inability to enact what a *girl* does and does not do. An obvious turn for comedy, this eliminates any positive sports*person*ship message of what a player should or shouldn't do to be a better team member, and instead assigns the blame on being female:

> CHESTER: A girl doesn't give the opposing team the finger and tell their coach "up yours." A girl doesn't refer to the referee as a blind bastard. A girl doesn't slap another girl on the ass and say, "You're hot stuff." And a girl doesn't say, "I gotta take a leak so bad, I can taste it." Matt, you have to start acting like a young lady.

This scene effectively marks this soccer team as female and females as traditionally feminine. This places the issue outside of athletics and better coaching, instead centering the problem on acting like a lady. It's also equating sportswomanship with weakness. Although Chester is discussing an abrasive competitive spirit, the nature of aggressive competition is marked as masculine. Not long after this scene, we begin

Matthew's transition to a lady. Chester begins the lessons of gender construction as follows:

> CHESTER: Matthew, I told you before, you got to act like a lady. You have to be considerate, loving, giving ... Matthew, just remember, a lady is sensitive, she's tender. Women are like a beautiful bed of flowers. [A girl with bright purple hair walks by.] Of course, there's a weed here and there.

All of these gender lessons for Matthew are gender lessons for us. Although Chester can be seen as a joke himself, these essentializing statements are actively assisting in our thought process. We laugh but the film continues to illustrate the truth in his statements.

Chester brings Matthew into a department store to have him try on dresses. This sequence turns into a comedic gag of dialogue that is misinterpreted as pedophilia. Matthew can't zip up his dress and asks Chester to come in and help. There they stand behind the curtain as we hear line after line to be misheard. Matthew says the dress doesn't fit right and Chester responds, "If it's too tight, you'll get used to it." Meanwhile we watch as a mother sits within earshot, horrified, misinterpreting the situation. Certainly posed as a joke with levity, it's distracting in its offensive nature against men, women, coaches, fathers and every other human being. Directly after this sequence we watch Matthew stand in a sports store boxing in his dress. Obviously he can't prevent himself from acting macho and this extreme visual aids us in understanding that the dress in no way shapes Matthew as anything different than a boy. Although I wish this stood as a statement that clothes are just fabric covering our bodies, the film's continued presentation of archaic gender stereotypes takes away any conversation of a gender spectrum.

One of the most troubling layers in *Ladybugs* is the idea that girls can't and don't support each other. Teamwork and team improvement only appears to stem from Matthew. Even worse, his methods for their improvement are infantilizing and sexist. In their first game since Matthew's transition into a "lady," he gets Carmelita Chu to focus on the ball by covering it with shiny butterfly stickers. It's not about teaching her to focus on the ball, it's appeasing her irresistible necessity to watch butterflies in the air. As a self-appointed leader he shouts, "All right, look at the pretty butterflies, Chu!" as she dribbles the ball. Chu then shoots and scores a goal not from her desire or newfound skill to play soccer, but from her love of butterflies and her inability to look and interact with anything else.

Matthew and Chester are credited with giving Penny Pester her confidence as a woman. During the game, Chester is about to take Penny out because of her lack of defensive skills but Matthew turns to her and tells her that they need her. This outward admission of confidence in Penny injects her with the desire to play and prove herself. Wouldn't it have been nice to have this sentiment come from one of her female teammates? Why does it have to come from Matthew? The girls are improving and part of that improvement should be a belief in each other. Instead, it is portrayed as acceptance from Matthew, and therefore male acceptance. Before you challenge me based on the fact that he is in drag and therefore viewed as a female from Penny's perspective, let me remind you that this analysis is for us, the audience as well. Penny may believe Martha is supporting her, but we know that Martha is fictitious and only Matthew, the boy within the costume, could possibly enable Penny and the rest of these female athletes to succeed on the sports field. Sports are masculine and Matthew, as a male, has an innate ability to play and lead. Needless to say, Penny Pester helps score a goal soon after.

Chester's influence in Penny's growth comes after a game they win. She is sitting in the bleachers watching her teammates flirt with boys on the field. She admits to Chester that she doesn't think boys like her because she's not pretty. Chester shows her a mirror and encourages her to put down her hair and take off her glasses to reveal her "beauty." He admits that if he were younger, he would ask her out on a date. To boost her confidence, he even shares that she probably would have rejected him, to which she disagrees and gives him a kiss on the cheek before she runs off to join the girls. Her worth is wrapped up in physical desirability, which he can give her.[4] In this moment, we are to praise Chester for his positive encouragement, even though his encouragement was positively sexist with its gender-assigning instruction. It also is a form of sexual harassment for Chester to express sexual interest in Penny, even if that interest is projected as not viable. This film is full of moments to remind us that these players aren't just soccer players; they are to be recognized as girls. After one of their first wins, we're treated to a moment where all the girls on the team are celebrating by giving Martha kisses on her cheek. In my many years of playing and watching both women's and men's sports, I have yet to see the traditional celebratory high five, hug or even a pat on the behind turn into kisses on cheeks. So this is yet another moment where the film mocks femininity as it reveres the man whom viewers know is really responsible for the win.

Of all the female representations we meet in the film, perhaps no one is more damaging then Coach Annie (Nancy Parsons). The position of coach in sports carries with it an understanding that this person has a mastery of sorts in that sport. Since the film relates competitive nature to masculinity, a competitive female coach would equate to a masculine, and therefore butch, persona. Coach Annie with the Beavers (insert laugh) attacks Chester like a bull with her words of intimidation at their introduction, declaring that her team is undefeated and that his team will get crushed. However, everything about this interaction is to demean her. I don't want to support trash talking; however I do want to point out that the film fails to create any understanding of a spectrum for women's behavior. These female characters are relegated to either act "ladylike" or be unruly. There is no in between.[5] Matthew can yell at refs, but if this female coach wants to act competitively, she becomes the butt of jokes for Chester such as, "Hey Annie, I want to take you to the zoo. Yeah, they'll thank me for returning you!" and "What a lady. At Christmas they hang her and kiss the mistletoe." He even refers to her as a dog. What's worse is, during the game, she gets so angry that her team is losing, she throws a chair and accidentally hits one of her players. Her competitive nature is hurting her team. After the Ladybugs win the game, Coach Annie comes over to make peace and celebrate with Chester. Chester is busy molesting Glynnis and when he is done and has nowhere to turn except Coach Annie, he simply turns his back on her, creating one last laugh at her expense.

After a montage of the Ladybugs improving and winning game after game, we watch Kimberly overshoot and miss yet another goal. Dave asks Chester to remove her from the game. Although Chester defends her, he recognizes that this request is attached to a possible pro-motion and pulls her. After this, we finally witness a short display of communication improvement in the team as the girls call out each other's names as they pass the ball. Unfortunately, it is still Matthew who scores the game-winning goal. This moment of admiring our team of female athletes finally communicating and working together is short-lived. Right when the team begins playing like a team, the film redirects back to Matthew and Chester, so we can watch their drag conflict reach a climax.

The big reveal takes place when Kimberly shows up at Matthew's house in hopes for some girl friend support. There's a mix up when his mother Bess (Ilene Graff) comes home too early and Matthew displays a juggling act (referred to as a "drag race" by Chester) where he spends time with Kimberly as Martha in the living room and then dashes to the kitchen as Matthew for Bess. Needless to say, he eventually loses his ability to keep up with the sham and Bess catches him as Martha. The film takes a quick turn, as everyone must pay the piper for their actions. Cut to the championship game where Chester reveals that a week has passed without reconciliation with anyone. His opponents are the Flames, a team run by a drill sergeant, Coach Bull (Blake Clark). Although this coach resembles Coach Annie of the Beavers, this time the jokes at his expense do not center on him being an animal or being ugly; Chester simply states, "They ought to tell that guy the war's over." Coach Bull's aggressive competitive nature is presented as more acceptable because this is a man exerting a form of explosive hegemonic masculinity. He has the right to reside at the furthest reaches of the male gender spectrum, Coach Annie cannot. This place does not exist in the female spectrum. It is important to point out that on this opposing team, we watch female athletes show immense skill and athletic ability. However, this team is not our focus and certainly not placed as heroes. They are simply presented as militant aggressors, following his direct orders. Coach Bull literally orders them when to score and encourages them to fight dirty.

Matthew shows up to the game to support Chester and offers to play as Martha. He recognizes that Chester's actions were centered on an effort to provide for his mother. However, Chester stops Matthew from transitioning. Chester wants to win but he's not willing to sacrifice any last hope to be with Bess in order to do so. They have now connected. This conflict has been resolved. Now Matthew can run off to save Kimberly. In fact, his reveal to her is incredibly quick; he just walks into her house and removes his wig. We don't even stick around to see her reaction; we just hear a scream as we return to the game. Kimberly's quick acceptance of Matthew's hidden identity illustrates how she was just a tool to enhance his masculinity. Her place was to solidify his heterosexuality while in drag. She has served her purpose.

Back at the game, Chester announces that Martha will not be playing. The team immediately loses all confidence. Even with Chester's efforts to pump them up by giving a great speech about how playing their best makes them winners no matter what (a speech he should have given long before this moment), the team mopes onto the field already defeated. We are then subjected to watching the opposing team's unbelievable skill as they pass, use trick plays and score using a bicycle kick, all executed by their drill sergeant's orders shouted from the sideline. One Ladybug player resorts to violence and pushes her opponent down to the ground. They all start to fight and chaos ensues. At halftime, Matthew returns with Kimberly and it's time to tell the rest of the team the truth.

When they find out that Martha is Matthew, the team is shocked. As a comedic aside, Sally Anne Welfelt can't help but immediately play with her hair to spruce up her appearance. Chester continues his pep talk:

> That's right. Martha is Matthew. And I'm showin' you this for one reason. You don't need Martha any more. You don't need a boy to help you win. You're women! You don't need anyone! You're liberated! You got the vote! You can burn your bras … when you get them. Now get out there and put out those Flames!

However inspiring, this speech isn't enough to cause them to magically play better. Because this speech is a caricature of women's liberation, it does little to liberate the team. Chester is liberated. He stands up to his boss, he's honest with Matthew and he recognizes his self-worth and the importance of supporting these kids, stating, "What good is being the best if it brings the worst out of you?" This supportive sentiment is not transferable to the girls.

When they return to the game, their self-worth and confidence improvement is revealed through tricks and not athletic skills. For example, Nancy Larimer talks trash to one of the opponents to throw off their game and physically pushes another girl to score her goal. This celebrated misunderstanding of violence as empowerment exhibits an act of solo aggression rather than teamwork or sportsmanship. The next goal results from Sally Ann Welfelt's anger when she breaks a nail by bumping into an opposing player and falling down. Her mother announces to the bleachers that her daughter has broken a nail and the sideline fans all start to chant, "Get those nail breakers!" Now Sally, fueled by a ruined feminine aesthetic, dominates the field and scores. The tying goal takes place when Penny turns to the sideline and dedicates her efforts to Chester, taking off her glasses and letting down her hair. In this "pretty" state she can now outplay her opponents, single-handedly scoring, with hair blowing in the wind. Chester shouts, "Beautiful, I told you you're beautiful!" All of these goals are attributed to specific feminine ideals. The other team scored their goals by athletic skill and, from what we know of the coach, a simple drive to win and dominate. Our Ladybugs must find their skill and power from a feminine accepted place of a diva-like attitude, manicured nails and a makeover. Fortunately we do get to witness a short montage of Chu saving goals *sans* shiny butterflies on the ball.

The Ladybugs win the game on a goal scored by Kimberly. She is tripped and awarded a penalty kick. Chester assigns the kick to her. After a shared look with Matthew, she proceeds to kick it perfectly in the corner of the goal. They win and celebrate. It just so happens that Matthew's mom was there to see it all, of course. Kimberly and Matthew kiss. The boss approaches Julie and shares that he heard a little rumor that Chester had once dressed a boy as a girl and put him on a soccer team. He calls it an imaginative strategy.

This introduces our last scene, which is perhaps the most influential and damaging laugh at women in sports. We jump to the future and see that Chester has gotten his promotion, he's married, Matthew is dating Kimberly and everyone's happy. Chester now sits on a bus with Dave and a group of boys dressed in baseball uniforms. Logic would inform us that Chester has decided to continue coaching youth athletics, but has now moved on to boys' baseball. However this last joke is on us. The bus pulls up to the fields and Chester stands up and shouts, "All right, boys, this is the big one, the championship game and you're gonna go out there and play the game of your life. Because you're men. Are you with me?!" The boys shout in excitement and exit the bus. As we watch Chester get off, another coach approaches him to ask if it's true that he dressed a boy to be a girl on his soccer team. Chester laughingly denies it and then turns to call his team to the field and we see that the boys are all wearing wigs. As they run by we see that the bus reads "Girls Softball Team." After a film of reaffirming harmful social constructions of femininity and simply ignoring feminine athletic ability, the message is clear: Women can't win.

The ending is a humorous gag, but it's very harmful. The film's representation of Chester winning by playing with boys in drag fails to condemn him for cheating; instead it celebrates his supposedly clever and ballsy strategy in making a mockery of girls' sports. It makes him *manlier*. Everybody laughs. He's a hero. And girls, once again, are a weak subplot simply to aid the male hero on his own journey, which in this case doesn't appear to have advanced much. With this action, any growth in Chester's character has been eliminated. This effectively erases some of his more profound moments and returns us to the same sexist trickster we met at the start of the film.

If we remember his paid-for mantra at the start of the film, "I am great, I am wonderful, everybody likes me," we've learned that Chester is not great, he's not wonderful and everyone likes him because they see him as a "winner" or because they're in on the prank and appreciate his cunning scam—a scam that confirms boys as the elite and deserved players of sports. One could argue that *Ladybugs* also presents a critique of masculinity, but even if Chester, Matthew, Dave and Coach Bull serve a few jokes at their own expense, they still hold the dominant power in the story. I'm tired of hearing arguments that comedy is forgivable in its discrimination. Comedy can stand as the most vulnerable avenue to impress ideas upon us. Yes, we should be able to laugh at ourselves, but when those of a socially powerful group laugh at those whom they lord over, this perpetuates damaging ideas. We have to remember comedy can also be a space of healing. It can lighten ideas that are in need of conversation. It can also appear in situations, such as men and women playing sports together, in a context where female athletes are uplifting and not the butt of the joke. *Ladybugs* does not do this. It posits the girls *as* the joke.

The fact that his female soccer team wins in the end carries no weight in the long run for Chester. It's crystal clear that in choosing to put an entire team of boys in drag, he hasn't developed a belief in women's capabilities as athletes. Taking into account that it's a comedy, wouldn't it have been funnier (and better) if the ending was a bunch of girls on the bus and when he steps off the bus and someone approaches him accusing him of putting his players in drag, he turned around to reveal that all the girls are dressed as boys? That would empower female athletes, and be a clever gag after a story chronicling his growth coaching and improving a team of girls.

Ladybugs is a sad reminder that in 1992 we still had a long way to go in the support of female athletics. Female athletes were still struggling for mainstream interest. It would be seven years before our women's national soccer team would win the World Cup, and those seven years were a continuing fight to remove sparkly butterfly stickers from their soccer balls. It's important that we recognize the essentializing nature of *Ladybugs*. Although the film's jokes may try to critique gender performance, the male characters still come out on top. It's imperative that we not dismiss the power of these gender portrayals simply because they are placed in a comedic setting. Comedy creates a space where we can openly discuss and critique some of our most taboo subjects. Female athletics are certainly not taboo, but Chester's treatment of his female team continues to set these female athletes as outsiders of the sports world and continues promoting false assumptions of the female identity.

With this in mind, I would like to take a brief moment to discuss a male-to-female drag film released ten years after *Ladybugs*, 2002's *Juwanna Mann*, directed by Jesse Vaughan. Although not a box office smash,[6] it does pose some interesting and differing approaches to a gender athletic discussion than *Ladybugs*.

Juwanna Mann is the story of Jamal Jefferies (Miguel A. Núñez Jr.), a self-obsessed professional basketball player whose unsportsmanlike conduct gets him ejected from the UBA (a fictional version of the NBA). In order to continue playing, he decides to dress in drag and play in the WUBA (a fictional version of the WNBA). Jamal gets the idea to dress in drag while watching a group of kids play basketball in a driveway. There is a young girl dominating her male opponents and he is reminded that there is another league for professional basketball. Unlike a male dictating the lessons of how to be a lady in *Ladybugs*, *Juwanna Mann* provides Jamal with his Aunt Ruby (Jenifer Lewis) to assist in his transformation into Juwanna Mann. Having his source of female lessons come from an actual woman is already a step in the right direction.

Let me be the first to admit that not everything in this film should be celebrated. For example, Jamal's big drag reveal comes when he slam dunks the ball, a form of play his agent previously specified was not allowed in the WUBA.[7] When he shatters the glass of the backboard and lands on the ground, his wig comes off. By establishing the slam dunk as a play designated for male basketball, Jamal's big reveal plays a dual role: It reveals that he was wearing a female disguise and it reconfirms the action of a slam dunk as male-owned. Female basketball players have, in fact, slam dunked in the WNBA and they have yet to be revealed as having false hair or being a man.

Another problematic element is Jamal's continual objectification of his teammates. À la *Ladybugs*, Jamal falls for a woman on his team, Michelle Langford (Vivica A. Fox). But what sets this story apart is that she and her attractive teammates are not what inspire Jamal to dress in drag, it's his desire to play. Although we are constantly reminded that he is heterosexual (no matter how well he seamlessly transitions into his drag persona), *Juwanna Mann* does exhibit some important validation of teamwork. And unlike Matthew, Jamal does learn a few things from being in a woman's shoes.

Jamal joins a women's basketball team, the Charlotte Banshees, and his ego causes plenty of friction with his new teammates. In his first game, he dominates. Just as in *Ladybugs,* Jamal's actions as a ball hog are not rewarded with a win. However in this film, the goal is not simply to win, it's to play. Jamal is introduced as a dominant player in both the men's and women's league, but just as he is not the only good player in the UBA, he does not stand as the best in the WUBA. We see other athletically dominant women throughout the film. Additionally, Jamal improves his game, learning skills from his female teammates. Jamal's journey is founded in the lesson of how to be a good teammate, not to expose athletic differences between the sexes. These women are talented athletes and he must learn to play with them to win. In addition, he must overcome his self-centered attitude to compete in either league, regardless of gender.

There is also an interesting education of the sexes between Jamal and the Banshees. When Jamal finds out that Michelle's boyfriend Romeo (Ginuwine) is cheating on her, he begins to give his female teammates love advice and insight into male behavior. In exchange, they unknowingly give him an insight into female behavior. Jamal even has the experience of being objectified as a woman from the romantic (and persistent) pursuit of a rapper, Puff Smokey Smoke (Tommy Davidson). *Juwanna Mann* opens a conversation about both genders and the film doesn't shy from respecting female athletic ability in the process.

Right before his drag reveal, Jamal has to choose between attending a meeting with the UBA commissioner to try and get back into the UBA or play in a playoff game with the Banshees. He chooses to play with the Banshees, effectively ruining any chance he has to return to the UBA. He chooses his team over himself. It's in this playoff game where his team, and the world, finds out he is a man. Unfortunately, the moment he truly proves he's changed becomes the moment where he loses everything.

During halftime of the Banshees' playoff game, Jamal returns to the locker room to apologize. They are struggling and he tells them:

> When I first got here, I got to tell you, I thought women's basketball was a big joke. Hell, I thought anything that wasn't about Jamal Jefferies was a big joke. Turns out the joke was on me. That's because I thought that the most important thing about basketball was being a star. That's until you guys taught me the only way to truly shine is to be a part of a team. So if you guys wanna hate me, Lord knows I understand you if you do. But you're gonna have to hate me after the game because you guys never needed me to win this and you don't need me now. I needed you. So come on, go win it.

This impassioned speech may earn Jamal credit for inspiring their confidence to dominate this game and get to the championship, but at least they legitimately play and don't win through jokes at the expense of being female. The Banshees continue on to the championship and win it without Jamal. After the championship, Jamal sits in front of the basketball commissioner defeated as it becomes clear his actions have only hurt his chances of returning to the UBA. Just then, his female teammates come bursting through the door to speak on his behalf:

> MICHELLE: With all due respect, sir, and on behalf of the Charlotte Banshees, we in no way feel that Jamal Jeffries has disgraced our league. Without a doubt, he may have disgraced himself and he is certainly paying the price for that. But we forgive him ... and we feel that you should too.

They then present him with a team championship ring. The commissioner changes his mind and the board welcomes Jamal back into the UBA.

Although there are still gender-essentializing jokes at play in *Juwanna Mann,* it's important to recognize an improvement in the visual representation of respect for female athletes. Even Jamal Jeffries, egotistical and one of the most celebrated players in the UBA (and now the WUBA), recognizes the talent in the WUBA. Additionally, he is one of many WUBA players who are celebrated for their skills. As much as I want to criticize the specific use of a female team to teach Jamal how to show emotions such as respect, the action of Jamal choosing to play the Banshees' playoff game over possible entrance back into the UBA shows the film's priority to portray teamwork (male or female) as the true victory. This is a vast improvement over *Ladybugs.*

Now it's time to shift gears and see what happens when we turn drag the other direction.

Blind Side

She's the Man directed by Andy Fickman in 2006, and is the story of Viola (Amanda Bynes) whose love of soccer and passion to prove herself inspire her to dress in drag and join her school's rival boys' soccer team. Because Shakespeare's *Twelfth Night* inspires the story, the focus is far more on the complicated relationships of everyone involved rather than Viola's involvement in sport. However, by choosing to center her drag complications in a sports arena, we see some important visual conversations.

She's the Man kicks off with positive female athletic imagery right away. The opening credits play over images of Viola playing soccer on the beach. It is quickly apparent that Viola isn't just good at soccer, she's better than most of the boys. This is confirmed by her boyfriend Justin (Robert Hoffman). As the story begins, Viola finds out that the girls' soccer team has been cut because not enough girls signed up. She marches right over to the coach of the boys' team, Pistonek (Robert Torti), and asks to try out. She isn't asking to join, she is asking for a chance for her and her teammates to show their skills and earn a place on his team. Without a soccer season, these girls won't have the chance to play for college scouts and earn scholarships. Pistonek is beside himself at this proposition and calls over his team so that he can announce this notion as entertainment. The boys laugh in agreement as the coach announces, "You're all excellent players, but girls aren't as fast as boys, or strong, or as athletic. This is not me talking, it's a scientific fact. Girls can't beat boys, it's as simple as that." At first, this statement excited me. This is setting up the ceiling to be broken by our female athlete hero. However, the biggest problem with *She's the Man* is that this plays a very small role in the conclusion.

Keeping in mind that the focus of *Twelfth Night* is a crisscross of relationships, Viola's athletics goals take a back seat to the attraction that take place in the film. However, there is enough content within her specific sports storyline to analyze. There's no need to thoroughly summarize the relationships that get intertwined, so I'll just give you the highlights: Viola dumps her boyfriend Justin at the beginning of the film. When in drag, she is posing as her twin brother Sebastian (James Kirk), who has left the country to tour with a band. Her parents are divorced, giving her and her brother an easy alibi by making each of their parents think they're with the other. Sebastian currently has a girlfriend, Monique (Alexandra Breckenridge). While in Sebastian's identity playing with her new team, Illyria, Viola falls for their star player Duke (Channing Tatum), who has a crush on Olivia Lennox (Laura Ramsey), who ends up liking Viola as Sebastian. I only share this chaos so that I can get to what's important, the sports storyline. Of all the reasons that could be chosen for a female to disguise herself as the other gender, sports would seem logical. As one of the most well-known fields of sex segregation in the present day, it's a believable scenario.

Throughout the film, Viola is battling a timeline of when her brother will return to the country and when she is to be inducted into the Debutante society. Much like in *Whip It,* Viola's conflicting storyline is pressure from her mother Daphne (Julie Hagerty) to become a Debutante. With such Debutante lessons in the film as "Chew like you have a secret" and "When debutantes disagree, we say it with our eyes," the Debutante world represents an extreme subordinate femininity. Daphne, an avid member of this community, does not support nor has any interest in Viola playing soccer. Viola constantly reminds her mother that she has no interest in being a Debutante, insisting it's archaic. Viola appears to display feminist forward thinking, saying things such as "Heels are a male invention designed to make a woman's butt look smaller and to make it harder for them to run away." But as the film unwinds and becomes complicated in relationships, we soon lose sight of these ideas.

The lack of female representation in this film is troubling. Other than Daphne, a bubbly vulnerable 1950s mother, we share a few moments with Monique (desperate and aggressive) and Viola's friends who only serve to make Sebastian desirable when they pretend to be his ex-girlfriends. Fortunately, Olivia Lennox (Laura Ramsey) appears smart, strong and uninterested in machismo. But she had little influence in the story other than complicating Viola and Duke's interactions. The only other characters are boys and men. Her physical makeover is created and directed by Paul (Jonathan Sadowski), a boy presented as stereotypically gay. Paul appears to have knowledge of both gender worlds. In the scene where Viola's friends pretend to be "Sebastian's" ex-girlfriends, he literally instructs their every move to play seductresses. Duke, who becomes Viola's soccer mentor, also becomes her love interest. It just so happens that Duke once made Justin cry on the soccer field, which impresses her. To round out the cast, we have Principal Gold (David Cross), whose sole purpose is to serve comedy by being daft, and Andrew (Clifton MaCabe Murray), whose obsession with Olivia is exaggerated to a level of campy humor.

The main issue with the portrayal of Viola's journey as a female athlete is continuity. The film opens with Viola's boyfriend admitting she is probably a better soccer player than half of his team members, yet when she has her first tryout with Illyria, she doesn't make the cut. It's not necessary for her to be the best on the field, but we've been sold on the idea that she is equal to, if not better than, some boys, so why is she not good enough initially to join the team? We soon find out that the cinematic purpose of this rejection was so that she can bargain with Duke; he'll help her improve her soccer skills if she'll teach him how to win over Olivia. However, this is the first deception of her power. Why couldn't she join the team and simply become friends with him through her skill? With Duke's coaching and training, Viola does improve enough to join Illyria but by simultaneously placing Duke as her love interest, he initiates many of the compromises that Viola, as a cinematic female athlete, must make to play.

One night while Viola is sleeping, we get to watch a very interesting dream sequence where she is playing soccer with Illyria. It opens with two players leaping up and knocking heads. Another player gets kicked in the face. It's quickly apparent that this is an overly violent melodramatic display of the game. The entire dream is darkly saturated as we watch their coach Dinklage (Vinnie Jones) scream at Viola to get in the game. As she stands up, we see she is in a debutante dress. She panics as she looks down at this restricting uniform. The coach's screams are becoming increasingly aggressive so she runs onto the field, tripping on her dress. There she is, dribbling the ball in a princess dress looking frightened as the boys charge her while making animal-like growling noises. Her dress rips a bit as she approaches the goal which Justin is defending. She goes to shoot but completely misses the ball, flipping up in the air and landing on her back. Everyone laughs at her and a giant sheet of water comes splashing down on her as she wakes up in the real world to the Illyria team throwing water on her to start a hazing initiation ritual. This dream could appear as simple performance anxiety for her but it's a perfect representation of the female athlete's trials navigating the sports field. The inability to play in her dress speaks of the struggle to be competitive while still conforming to feminine ideals. The men enacting violent animal behavior adds to the assumption that men's competition is naturally tougher and not safe for women. Her missing the ball and falling on her back neglects to send an empowering belief in herself or women on the field at that. Women are still restricted by ideas of beauty, ideas of weakness and in the end Viola can't even dream of conquering those.

According to her male teammates, Viola isn't cool. Many jokes center on the idea that she feels and shares too much to be "masculine," which is exactly the reason Olivia likes her rather than Duke. Olivia is tired of boys trying to be macho. As I mentioned before, in order to make Viola "cool," Paul sets up a scene where Viola (as Sebastian) is seduced by her girl friends, posing as ex-girlfriends. By posing as desirable to women, she gains the respect from her teammates, so her "odd" reveals of emotion that put her masculinity in question will be laid to rest. However, it is not solely on Viola's teammates to accept her "feminine" traits, it is also the world around her that must accept her new "masculine" traits. As we watch Viola attend her first debutante luncheon, she rips meat off of a bone and slurps her soup. Exaggerated for comedy, this sequence demonstrates that Viola's time as a boy has infiltrated her ability to have basic manners.

Throughout the film, Duke helps Viola improve in soccer, helping her earn a starting position for the big game against her old school. This game will serve as the setting for her drag reveal. Without Viola knowing, Sebastian returns to the U.S. the night before the game. Viola isn't sleeping in Sebastian's bed because Duke thinks he saw Viola kissing Olivia, who was actually the real, and unknowing, Sebastian. When Sebastian returns to school, everyone assumes he is the soccer-playing Viola in drag they have been living with. He is rushed to the game in Viola's place. Viola, meanwhile, sleeps in and when she shows up late to the game, she sees her brother out on the field, failing miserably to play with the team.

This switch plays an important role. In the middle of the game, Principal Gold comes storming onto the field and accuses Sebastian of being Viola, a female in drag. Because Sebastian is now the true Sebastian, he is able to prove that he is in fact a biological boy by pulling down his pants. This is a great moment, allowing a direct visual display of the difference between gender and sex. The school had believed Viola was a boy from her acting and athletic ability without this biological proof. Now when it's necessary, it's provided through a comical mixup. Once halftime starts, Viola pulls her brother under the bleachers, explains everything and then switches places with him. Now that the team and the crowd believe Viola (as Sebastian) is a biological male, we can simply watch Viola play with her male team.

It's a wonderful visual watching her run and skillfully play among her male teammates. Unfortunately, after a few moments of this tremendous display, our attention is diverted to Duke's personal frustration with the fact that he thinks Viola (as Sebastian) kissed Olivia. He won't pass the ball to her, which costs them a goal. She tries telling him she'll explain everything after the game but the referee stops the game because of their confrontation. Justin steps in to taunt them both and a fight breaks out. Olivia rushes the field to see if Sebastian is all right, which cues Viola to reveal her true identity. She slowly pulls off her sideburns and takes off her wig as she tells everyone what she's done and why. Then Duke challenges her biological proof and she lifts up her shirt. However unnecessary this sexual objectification moment is, Duke follows it by accepting her as a female teammate and announces the team's best chance of winning will include her playing. As Potensky protests by throwing the manual, Dinklage rips the booklet in half saying, "Here in Illyria, we don't discriminate based on gender." Prior to this moment, Dinklage had consistently demeaned girls, using them as an example of weakness, so I'm a bit skeptical about his change of heart.

Now we are treated to an even greater visual than the one after half-time. We get to see an acknowledged and accepted female player playing among men. We watch Viola excel with dominant soccer skills and great teamwork. Then an opponent slide tackles Viola, giving her a penalty kick. Usually I scoff at the idea of a penalty kick's power versus scoring during active game play because penalty kicks are a controlled space where you can set your shot, take your time and execute it by yourself. However in *She's the Man*, the penalty kick simply serves to set up to a much higher caliber goal. As Viola kicks the ball, Justin blocks and redirects it with his hands toward Duke, who then head butts it back toward Viola, who leaps up and bicycle kicks it into the goal winning the game. This time *she* makes Justin cry. We've gotten to see Viola play with the boys as an accepted teammate and score using one of the most difficult soccer techniques. Had the movie ended right now with this positive portrayal, so would my book. Unfortunately, it doesn't.

The story continues as we watch Viola win Duke's forgiveness and partake in the debutante ball with Duke on her arm. We finish the story back on the soccer field with her playing; however the final freeze frame is dedicated to an image of Viola being held up in Duke's arms. A believer of the power in final impressions, Viola in Duke's arms (edited to repeat three times no less) diminishes the independence Viola has exhibited throughout the film. Further, by showcasing her successful inclusion into the institution of being a debutante, we lose all of Viola's constructive criticism of its dated construction of femininity.

The truth is, there's enough drama in this film that we don't need Viola to struggle at soccer at the beginning of her time at Illyria. In *Ladybugs* and *Juwanna Mann,* these male players immediately dominated in the women's leagues. Why couldn't Viola immediately dominate in this men's league? It's troubling that her strength and playing ability is always in flux. Although this film carries positive imagery, it's ultimately a straightforward display of the requirements of a cinematic female athlete: She can play with the boys as long as she has a boy to lift her up in the end.

Most of *She's the Man* is silly and outlandish; however, the sports side is taken seriously. Although the conclusion is troubling to Viola's empowerment, it cannot be denied that the different levels of watching her play (as Sebastian and as herself) do create positive images that challenge a gender divide in sports.

I'd like to briefly share one last film, a film that I find truly boundary-breaking. I've tried to focus most of my analysis on popular films with theatrical release but I think it's worthwhile to shine light on a smaller made-for-TV film called *Motocrossed* (2001). It provides us with multiple positive female representations and allows our cinematic female athlete to control her success in her sport and her romantic relationship on her own terms.

Motocrossed, directed by Steve Boyum, is a Disney Channel Original Movie that follows the story of Andrea Carson (Alana Austin), who steps in to race motocross for her injured brother Andrew (Trever O'Brien). She doesn't just step in to fill Andrew's racing spot, she literally dresses in drag to replace him. Motocross is the family business and when Andrew gets injured, their whole season and family income is in jeopardy. Because Andrew's injury occurred in a race Andrea challenged him to, she feels responsible and driven to make amends with the family stress she's caused. When she offers to compete in his place, their father Edward (Timothy Carhart) rejects this idea, claiming he would never have his daughter compete in such a dangerous sport. When Edward heads overseas to get a new rider for their team, the family finds out the first race of the series will be run sooner than expected. Andrea knows the family needs a racer to stay in competition for a shot at the championship so when they can't get hold of Edward to tell him of the schedule change, Andrea hatches the plan to cut her hair and pose as her brother.

What makes *Motocrossed* different is the power awarded to Andrea's mother Geneva (Mary-Margaret Humes). It is the mother who signs off and steps in to support our female athlete. After some initial shock, Geneva truly believes in Andrea. It quickly becomes a family affair with Andrew helping train Andrea and their little brother, Jason (Scott Terra) helping as a mechanic. But it is Geneva who gets her hands on a rulebook and puts forth the effort to learn the sport in order to coach and support Andrea. Geneva recognizes that Andrea really does love to race and sees

123

this as both an important opportunity for Andrea and an important lesson to her sons.

Much like in *She's the Man*, Andrea's love interest Dean Talon (Riley Smith) makes a deal where in exchange for advice in how to win a girl, Dean will help Andrea (who he thinks is Andrew) improve. However, this does not distract from Andrea continuing to race in an empowering fashion with her mother by her side. They learn and improve together. This is incredibly powerful. When Edward returns with European racer Rene Cartier (Michael Cunio), who has a bad attitude, Geneva and her sons fight for Andrea to continue racing. When Edward disputes the issue with fear for her safety, her mother argues, "If you're willing to let Andrew take the risk of riding, don't you owe Andrea the same?" They're both his children and they're both talented racers. Why does gender affect whom he protects?

After Edward finally sees how toxic Rene truly is, he agrees to Andrea's drag solution. In a very powerful plot choice, Edward hands the coaching reins to Geneva, announcing, "Why mess with a winning team?" Andrea then proceeds to race with her mom coaching and wins!

When her gender is revealed at the end of the race, there's an uproar. However, the race organizer shares that there is nothing in the rulebook that says a girl can't race. Andrea is the first girl to win a pro race. Her family is offered a factory contract. Everything falls into place thanks to this mom-and-daughter team. At the end, Dean shows up to their house to apply for a rider spot on their team. Andrea proposes they race for it. The film ends with them both freeze framed, side by side, in the air on their dirt bikes. This romantic relationship takes a backseat to her racing storyline.

When I watch this film, I'm bursting with excitement. Even though there are feminine identifiers such as Andrea's high-pitched scream elation over NSYNC tickets and Geneva helping a group of girls do their nails, there is such a strong support of female representation that those moments become part of Andrea and Geneva's personality, not defining values of their character. Andrea is a competitor and her strongest ally is her mother. This is a wonderful example of empowered choices and we need to see more of them for cinematic female athletes.

Using drag to access gender-specified sports teams should allow all of these films to expose false assumptions of athletic differences based on biological sex. Even though the films illustrate gender acting that is so outlandish (borderline silly), the supporting characters still believe our heroes are the opposite sex, which allows the audience to watch a discussion about the differences, or lack thereof, in sports between girls and boys. With romance still present in each of these stories, we get to have a comedic but interesting insight into the opposite gender's strengths and weaknesses in wooing each other. Since we've repeatedly observed that neither gender really knows what the other wants, perhaps the simple answer is if we, of all genders, talk to each other more about what we truly feel and want. This could alleviate manifested pressure to fit into one female or male mold.

Throughout this chapter, we have explored films that offer us the opportunity to watch girls and boys, women and men, play side by side. Although *Ladybugs* denied support of female athletics, it now serves as a reminder of how far we've come. *Juwanna Mann, She's the Man* and *Motocrossed* represent growth in the acceptance and support of women as athletes. In each of these films, we watch men and women learn qualities and skills from each other to improve their game. It's a shame these films weren't a smash at the box office because they open an important conversation about a genderless view of athletic ability—conversation I hope can take place soon, without a disguise necessary.

6

Measured and Recorded
Cinematic Female Coaches

The role of coach carries with it prestigious respect and enormous power as the epicenter of decision-making and leadership. Real world sports politics and money would place the decision-making ultimately in the hands of the team owners (which we'll discuss in the final chapter of this book). For the sake of the films discussed in this chapter, the coach is the closest conductor to the players. A coach is a teacher, a guardian and a boss (on and off the field) to their players. They explore both layers of technical instruction and emotional connection with their team in order to succeed. Furthermore, a coach's success is contingent on their players' success, creating a relationship of necessity that goes two ways. With such complexity in utilizing many facets of skill and emotion that are mental rather than physical, it's hard to imagine that this job would carry an advantage being placed in one gender or another.

A majority of coaches are men because most sports programs are run by men.[1] The factors that we've discussed throughout this book that align sports with masculinity make this statistical truth appear logical. Young boys are initiated into manhood while playing and watching sports and therefore follow through into sports careers. The lack of female presence is not representative for a lack of trying. The support network and the experience necessary for women to reach higher positions in sport simply do not exist. With an old boys' network within sports, women lack the strategic business connections to be hired. Additionally, if a sports program were to look objectively at résumés, women's lack of opportunity would continue to illustrate a less qualified candidate.

Unlike the steady increase of women working in previously male-sanctioned jobs such as law and medicine, the number of female coaches has decreased over the past decades. As discussed in this book's introduction, prior to Title IX the rising number of female athletes was matched by the rising number of female coaches. After the passing of Title IX, this increase not only stopped for female coaches, it decreased.[2] As women's sports programs were folded into male programs, the very women who assisted in the passing of this great amendment were denied its benefit. Even if the presence of female athletes continued to grow, stunting the female mentor continued to promote any affiliation with sports as the male domain and an agent of masculinity.[3]

As with all representations and positions in the sports world, the lack of role models stunts the progress of possibility. Most casual sports fans can name Pat Summitt, coach of the Tennessee Lady Vols basketball team, because she has the record for the most wins in the history of both men's and women's NCAA basketball. She had to break into the record books to become somewhat of a household name. This lack of publicity for female coaches makes Pat appear to be an exception rather than a representative of the talent in women to coach. It comes to no surprise that this lack of presence (and access) translates to film representations. There has only been one film released each of the past four decades that features a female coach.

Three of the four films discussed in this chapter focus on the sport of basketball: *Coach, Eddie* and *The Mighty Macs.* As we mentioned with *Love & Basketball,* basketball is the only sport out of our four American dynasties (football, baseball, hockey and basketball) that has a women's league. The spectator interest between the men's (NBA) and women's (WNBA) league favors the men, but the fact that the WNBA continues to exist is a continuing benefit for all women's sports. Even with this established access for female involvement in the sport of basketball, these cinematic female coaches face the same patterns that we've seen with our cinematic female athletes. Whether it is a romantic relationship or the act of sacrifice, with the exception of *The Mighty Macs,* we witness active cinematic choices to divert attention from these heroines' strength and skill. What might be the most interesting and surprisingly empowered cinematic portrayal in this chapter comes from the man-land sport of football, *Wildcats.* The heroine of *Wildcats* is the daughter of a professional football player and has inherited a knowledge and love for the sport. She may not have played it, but she knows football like the back of her hand and she's far more qualified than some of her male peers. These cinematic female coaches have the requirements and the drive to coach their sport. Now all they need is the access, support and belief that they can do so.

Foul Shot

The first cinematic representation of a female coach I've found was in the 1978 film *Coach,* directed by Bud Townsend. Honestly, I was hesitant to include this film because it appeared to resemble soft-core porn far more than a work of sports entertainment. However the film attempts to balance the heroine's overt connection to sexuality and objectification with some awkwardly placed feminist declarations. These declarations can most certainly be credited to the post–Title IX era that was still in its infancy. Although there is ultimately more resistance than support in the representation of this cinematic sports heroine, there are some moments that appear to embrace the confidence that females can and will stake their claim in the sports world. That said, let me state for the record that I find this film incredibly damaging.

Coach opens with a sequence of our heroine, Randy Rawlings (Cathy Lee Crosby), running in the Olympics. We watch her push her body to the limit in slow motion. The only thing we hear is the sound of her heavy breathing. Much like the subsequent film, *Personal Best,* this is a very intimate space. She crosses the finish line victorious and we watch her atop the podium receiving her gold medal and wiping a tear. Proud and taking it in, she stands in bliss. We then immediately cut to her as an aerobic instructor in a gym with older women. Although she looks to be enjoying herself, this is quite the visual statement for a female athlete's future. She isn't a track coach. She isn't involved with the Olympics in any way. Additionally, the film's portrayal of aerobics consisting of women twisting their waists and then looking up and doing facial exercises simply encourages a difference between sport and "feminine" fitness.

When we are first introduced to the basketball team that Randy will eventually coach, they are struggling. It is quickly established that the elderly man sitting on the sidelines, Fenton Granger (Keenan

Wynn), funds and dictates the team. He is also the grandfather of one of the team members, Bradley William David Granger (Channing Clarkson). With the team losing yet another game, Fenton successfully encourages the current coach to resign, creating the available coaching position.

Before I launch into Randy's journey to acquire that position and coach the team, it's important to discuss the underlying values within this film. Although there are varying degrees of masculinity on display, the film utilizes this variety far more in a "misfit" formula than exploring their difference. The boys who could be seen as categorically "nerdy" or a joke are simply tools for the film to focus on girls, such as when one clumsy boy spills his drink on a girl's lap and the camera just sits there while he tries to mop it up. For all intents and purposes this film quickly reveals itself to be a movie for men. In the first ten minutes there is a party scene where we watch women physically and emotionally cater to male players and then perform a striptease, exposing their breasts. This humor is *for* men rather than providing a dialogue *about* men. The boys are lazy and full of themselves, yet on most accounts we're laughing with them as they are placed as our gateway to sexualize the females around them. Almost every subplot is about a boy trying to get a girl or having a girl chase him.

One boy on the team does not partake in these actions: Jack Ripley (Michael Biehn), who doesn't seem interested in playing along with objectifying these girls and who also seems invested in the betterment of the team. He takes on a leadership role, advises his players on and off the court and seems to walk the line of respecting females. That's not to say that he doesn't still enable moments for his teammates to continue in their sexist manner. Jack will quickly become the most damaging element within this film. His slightly more mature stature will simply enable him to stand as a romantic candidate for Randy. That's right, this film presents a romantic and sexual relationship between a coach and her high school player. We will discuss this incredibly problematic story element shortly.

Since "Randy" is both a female and male identified name, her impressive résumé (including an Olympic gold medal) is attached to the assumption that she is male and thus, the school offers her the job as their new basketball coach before even meeting her. She doesn't know this, of course, and when she shows up to meet the principal and the board (made up of teachers and Fenton) to confirm getting the job, the following exchange takes place:

RANDY: I'm your new basketball coach.

FENTON: But you're a girl.

RANDY: Well, thank you very much.

FENTON: Miss Rollins, I'm afraid there's been some bitter mistake here. We really do need a P.E. instructor for our basketball team, but it's a boys' basketball team.

RANDY: Well, if there *is* a misunderstanding, it's not on my part. I happen to have a telegram here with a firm job offer. As a matter of fact, the telegram almost begged me to take this job.

FENTON: I'm sure everything you say is true. But we will not have a lady basketball coach in Granger.

RANDY: Mr. Granger, I'm not sure you are aware of the fact that women are protected against discrimination. It's called the Equal Employment Opportunity Act.

FENTON: Miss Rawlins, I wonder if you would do me a personal favor. I wonder if you would go look for a husband and let me find a coach.

RANDY: Mr. Granger, I want this job and if you try to stop me from having it, I will take this telegram to my lawyer and I will file suit against you personally for breach of contract and violation of federal law. And I will call every single member of this board as my witness.

With that, the board votes in her favor. This is one of the few scenes that prevent this film from being solely defined by a frat house party genre. Although after we *bare* witness to plenty of flagrant sexualized females, this moment of progressive empowerment feels out of place. It almost feels as though this scene is from a completely different film. This will become much more apparent as we continue.

The first time Randy is introduced to the team, they immediately begin sexually harassing her. Even though she proves her worth by making back-to-back three-point shots (the farthest shot you can make for the most points), they still laugh and scoff at the idea of a woman coach. They pretend to touch her butt and make verbal sexual advances. Fenton even instructs Bradley to give her a tough time and try to drive her out. Once we've established she's not welcome, Randy goes to work. She announces what she's going to teach them and then puts them in a cold shower, promising she'll continue to put them under the icy water if they can't control their "irresistible urges." After Randy asserts herself, the boys begin to listen. They begin to practice under her guidance and we start to witness the building of respect for her knowledge.

Throughout the film, one board member, Tom (Otto Felix), continues to make advances on her. It's clear to the audience that she's not interested, but he's persistent. As annoying as this character may become, this adult option is only offered to become a later conflict between her and Jack. Jack and Randy's relationship is the biggest problem with this film. Sure, the nudity is demeaning. Sure, the boys are disrespectful and one-note in their misfit charades. But nothing is more offensive than the portrayal of Randy engaging with her player with no consequences by the film's end. This film is a boy's fantasy. Even this strong female who fought for her job and is more than capable of being an excellent coach can't resist the charm of a teenage boy?

There are many levels to why this is problematic. In the context of this book, what comes to the forefront is the fact that she must be desired and conquered by a male character after displaying such strength and winning a dominant job. However, in the context of the sports world, and the teaching world, being involved with a student, player or anyone predominantly younger and involved in the pupil-teacher dynamic is controversial for a reason: It's an abuse of power. There are many instances in the real world where romantic relationships have grown from coach-player dynamics considering the intimate layers of that relationship. A player relies on a coach not just for the instruction of skill and command of strategy but the personal involvement in knowing their mental strengths and weaknesses that may be triggered in competition. When you are experiencing the stress of learning your mental and physical limits, a coach can help you push those limits and learn how to best utilize your strengths so those limits don't withhold possible athletic goals. This is an intimate space with one's self and a trust that binds you together. This trust can easily shift from a safe space to an abused space.[4]

This real world controversy that can involve both female coach to male player and male coach to female player is not approached at all in this film. It is simply a device used to illustrate a love story. At no point do we see Randy coach Jack in a way that would connect them; she is simply presented as the ultimate catch because of her beauty and ability. Jack, placed as a bit more mature than the rest of his teammates, is presented as having a chance with her. There is never a moment where the age dynamics of Jack and Randy's romance are challenged. After their first flirtatious evening together, Randy says, "It's getting kind of late, I don't want your parents to worry." In another scene she even calls Jack's parents to find out where he is, which is a blatant reminder that he does in fact still live at home and is at the age where his parents should know his whereabouts. Randy doesn't bat an eyelash at the reality of what she is a part of.

I found myself continuously reminded of their age difference and disturbed by her allowance for him to feel that she was his. Although Jack may be placed as the film's controlling factor of Randy's objectification, my frustration must be pointed at the older party because he, as the younger party, should not carry the power in this relationship scenario. However, we must analyze the older party as not Randy, but the producers of this film for condoning such an action and continuing to put Randy on display, and for the pleasure of, Jack and the audience. That is the true abuse of power.

From the beginning, Jack is placed as our male gaze surrogate. After the film's introductory striptease party, Jack goes to the beach and sees Randy running along the ocean's edge. Much in the cinematic tradition of introducing love interests (as we saw in *Ladybugs*), we peer through Jack's point of view that shows Randy running in slow motion. Additionally, the first time Jack walks into her office, he (and we) see the side of her breast as she's getting dressed. Jack is consistently placed as our tool to objectify Randy.

It should be noted that Randy and Jack do in fact keep their relationship a secret from the school and the other players, which is the only indication that they recognize their actions are not all right. In one scene when Jack walks into the gym, he caresses her backside and she flinches, looking around. She recognizes it's wrong, yet the film handles it like any other love story equipped with montages of their dates filled with laughter and a happy soundtrack. Throughout the film, their relationship is handled in such an innocent way that when Jack becomes jealous of Tom, the harmless board member, we are supposed to root for our two lovers to overcome the misunderstanding.

When the team heads to their first game, the opposing coach gives Randy a hard time and Jack reacts violently, causing the game to be forfeited. Instead of condemning Jack and her team for wasting an opportunity to play by fighting, she thanks them and admits she's proud of them. Randy is misconstruing their "protective" attack as them playing for her. Furthermore, it is after Jack's attack in her honor, that their romance is officially initiated.

As their relationship flourishes, we finally see the team begin to respond to Randy. After the first forfeit, Fenton tries to fire Randy and she offers the deal that the first game she loses, she'll hand in her resignation. He agrees. What follows are some wonderful images of Randy and her team finally working together. Unfortunately, the crosscutting of the Randy-Jack love story clouds this empowerment. The team wins, she and Jack make out, the team wins, they are intimate in the shower, and so on. In one scene after they've had sex, Jack says, "I love you." Randy starts to laugh and says, "I just can't any more." Although this could be interpreted as Randy not taking this relationship seriously, she never gives the impression that this was just for her pleasure or that she didn't fall for Jack as he did for her.

Sometimes, it's hard to remember that this film began centered on Randy's goal to coach basketball. There is one scene late in the film that returns us to a feminist conversation. Bradley is sitting at the dinner table with his mother (Patricia Garrison), Bradley's girlfriend Darlene (Kristine Greco), Fenton, and the rest of his family when he proceeds to stand up for Randy as follows:

MRS. GRANGER: I can't understand why she isn't at home with her husband raising children.
BRADLEY: She doesn't have a husband, Mother.
FENTON: Perfectly natural for Bradley to be smitten. She's a very attractive lady.
BRADLEY: I am not smitten.
MRS. GRANGER: I really can't understand this. How can she stand the odor of a gymnasium? It's so unfeminine. No wonder she can't get a man.
BRADLEY: She could get any man she wants. She happens to like being a coach.
MRS. GRANGER: Well, I liked sports when I was young but you just didn't let people know that. How do you feel about her, Darlene?
DARLENE: Well, I certainly think she has the whole team behind her.
BRADLEY: She's worked like crazy, Mother. She's given it her best shot.
FENTON: Bradley, how do you like being told by a woman what to do?
BRADLEY: She knows what's she's doing, Grandfather. I've learned more from

133

her in the last month than I have in the last two years playing with Bresnehan.

FENTON: Well, she has been lucky so far.

BRADLEY: In spite of what you've done, she's made *us* into a good team.

FENTON: A team? A team of panty waists! A team...! [*laughs*]

MRS. GRANGER: She's more to be pitied than censured.

BRADLEY: Look, I'm not gonna take this any more! We're gonna win the game. And we're gonna win the conference championships! And it's gonna be because of Randy Rawlins. And you can come and see for yourself!

This is an empowering scene. This player is standing up for Randy as his coach. He is acknowledging her gender and he's letting her skill speak instead. Unfortunately, this film continuously cancels itself out. Conversations like these present moments of respect for Randy's talent and ability regardless of her gender, but the film also projects a parallel sexual perversion of her character. There just isn't enough of these proactive empowering scenes to hold weight against her and Jack stripping in the shower.

The final sequence takes place in a game. Randy is credited for the vast improvement in the team and she's got the whole school, including Fenton, behind her. The team is playing hard but struggling. After a pep talk at halftime, Randy has the team riled up and ready to win. Unfortunately, the film hands Randy one last negative blow to her character, this time to her coaching ability.

There is a running gag where Jack has hypnotized another player, Ned (Jack David Walker), to learn things. Ned has trouble finding confidence in himself in both learning and playing basketball and hypnosis seems to alleviate that. At one point Jack hypnotizes Ned to believe he is professional basketball player Sidney Wicks. This enables Ned to play in a highly skilled and dominant fashion. When Randy learns of this, she commands Jack and the others to stop utilizing this technique and to start encouraging Ned to consciously recognize that this skill exists within him. The trigger to put him under hypnosis is the term "jabberwocky" and when the team is struggling at the end of the game, Randy decides to trigger Ned.

The problem has nothing to do with cheating the other team by using this "secret weapon," it has more to do with cheating Ned. Wouldn't it have been great to have Randy help Ned find this natural ability within himself like she originally asked of her team? That is what a coach should do. Instead, she buys into a tool Jack has created to win. And with that tool, and Jack's winning shot, they win the game. In the midst of celebration we cut between consecutive shots of each player scooping a girl into their arms and kissing her. Jack picks up Randy. The team members then pick her up on their shoulders and chant, "We're number one." This becomes a freeze frame and we fade to credits.

Coach is a confusing collection of different perspectives that attempts to cater to so many audiences that it lacks a fluid theme. It literally places implied feminist scenes side by side with scenes of absolute objectification. Perhaps this movie represents the problems of using a pill-in-the-peanut-butter approach to feminist conversations. In the end there's too much nudity and objectification to truly respect Randy's role as a coach. Furthermore, there is no way to envision Randy's character as anything but a sexual fantasy by presenting a romance between her and a teenage boy. It's almost as if her empowering scenes were simply foreplay for Jack's initiation into manhood.

This film was not ultimately successful, but the fact remains that this was our first portrayal of a lead cinematic female coach and this film was released post–Title IX. The late '70s were a high time of feminist progress and although this film uses those conversations to get its heroine into the job she deserves, it continues the tradition of segregating her to concepts of objectification. *Coach* is the most troubling representation discussed in this chapter. The most positive representation came eight years later in the form of *Wildcats.*

Forward Progress

With the exception of *Wildcats* (1986), all of the films in this chapter are centered on the sport of basketball. As we've established, basketball is a recognized professional women's sport. *Wildcats* focuses on the sport of football. Women's sports history is rich with female athletes who have played hockey, baseball and basketball, yet the football field continues to stand as an isolated realm of hegemonic masculinity. In a sport where players are referred to as "weapons" by commentators, the battlefield of football remains a mainstay producing patriarchal ideas opposing gender equity. Because there aren't women playing football, it's not difficult to see why there aren't women coaching it. Football remains, in the public eye, an uncharted territory for women that only continues to enforce gender difference. Even though the female coach in *Wildcats* has to handle some recognizable cinematic hurdles we've faced before while entering a male-identified space, this heroine finds a balance and ultimate success and can truly stand as a positive role model.

Wildcats, directed by Michael Ritchie, is the journey of Molly McGrath (Goldie Hawn) achieving her lifetime dream to coach football. She is the daughter of a famous football player and has lived and breathed the sport from birth. This is made clear in the opening credits while we watch old family footage of her as a child playing with a football, on the sidelines with her father's teammates and receiving a football helmet on Christmas while her sister gets a doll. We then cut to see a grown-up Molly dressed in football gear, growling. Unfortunately she isn't playing the sport; she's just dressed in the gear as a gag for her yearbook picture. Her sister Verna (Swoosie Kurtz) is taking the picture and even though Verna wasn't illustrated for her love of the game in the opening family footage, she is very supportive of Molly and will play a key supportive role throughout the film.

Molly is the coach of the girls' track team. She's a good coach which appears to be confirmed when Principal Walker (George Wyner) repeats a direction she gave her team earlier, confirming that she knows what she's doing. Although a small gesture, I can't help but point out that this male peer's comment to her team feels as though it's a necessary validation of this female coach's ability.

Molly loves her track team, but she desperately wants the now-available Junior Varsity football coaching position. When she approaches Principal Walker about the job, he tells her that as long as it's okay with the other football coach, Dan Darwell (Bruce McGill), the job is hers. Dan is introduced while hitting on Molly and her sister, which would suggest a less than hopeful verdict. Verna suggests Molly meet with him off-campus, like a social date to butter him up. So she brings him to play racquetball, which backfires because she's better than he is. When she brings up the coaching position mid-game, he simply dismisses it. Much like Randy, Molly utilizes the term "discrimination" in her retort, which changes Dan's tune and he offers to discuss it with the principal, simply saying, "You know me, babes, I'm a modern guy."

When Molly meets with the principal and Dan, it's revealed that he has already given the job to the unqualified Home Economics teacher. In a twist, Dan offers Molly the job of coaching Varsity football at Central High School, the school across town. This is an obvious effort to set her up to fail: Central is a "tough" school so Dan is pleased with what he believes is a diabolical plan to put Molly in her place. Molly leaps to her feet and confidently states, "I'm going to take that job. You think a woman can't be tough enough? Well, I'll show you tough," and she storms out. In a comedic nod, she forgets her purse and has to return for it. In a feminist nod, it serves as a reminder that such strength and confidence disconnects a woman from the construction of femininity. This is certainly a pattern we've witnessed before. However, in this film, even though Molly will always have her purse, she will also continue to embrace her strength.

Before we head to Central High School, we are introduced to Molly's home life. Molly is a divorced mom of two. Her ex-husband Frank Needham (James Keach) is not supportive of her love of football. When he spots her taking out her dad's old playbooks for her new job, he simply says, "Finally getting around to throw that stuff out, huh?" Her kids Alice (Robyn Lively) and Marian (Brandy Gold) spend time with both Molly and Frank even though it's made clear that Molly does a majority of the caretaking. I won't bury the lead by sharing that Frank's new wife Stephanie (Jan Hooks) is an antiquated version of femininity. She dresses like a child's doll and is very soft-spoken. Stephanie enacts weakness and caters to Frank, all things we can assume Molly didn't do and therefore lost compatibility.

There are some obvious analytical assumptions that can be made by introducing this scenario as Molly's backstory. Number one, Molly's connection to football has made her too "masculine" (categorized as "difficult" for women) to control and therefore she can't have a successful relationship with a man. Frank's introduction also confirms Molly's heterosexuality. Another is that we must establish that she has children so she is worth rooting for because she is responsible enough (even in her football-driven sensibility) to care for these two young girls thus far. Although these critiques are what first come to mind, *Wildcats* effectively uses these elements of Molly's character to exhibit different empowered choices revealed throughout the story. She is divorced because she and

Frank are different people. She won't cater to his need for control. In fact, Frank and his wife are presented as humorous jokes that we root against. There is no love story in this film other than the love Molly has for her daughters. Even though Frank uses them against her, by the film's end she fights for what's best for her and her daughters rather than sacrificing one for the other. Although this film features some truly empowering actions when it comes to Molly and her family, the reason we're discussing it in this book is because of Molly's other kids, the football team at Central High School.

Central is presented as a formulaic "wrong side of the tracks" school. In the neighborhood, there are half-demolished buildings and fighting in the streets. Molly even spots people drinking alcohol on school property as she parks her car. When she walks into the school, a group of guard dogs chase her. Principal Ben Edwards (Nipsey Russell) says that the dogs are there when the armed guards are off-duty. The school has no money and therefore the football program has no funding. There is no assistant coach, no team practices and they've only won one game because their opponents' bus broke down. But this is Molly's only chance and she's taking it.

When Molly enters the locker room to meet the team, they are waiting for her in uniform from the waist up, holding their helmets over their privates. In unison, they put on their helmets. Molly is certainly caught off guard, simply stating, "Be on the five in field minutes." But her shock doesn't last long: When the team is on the field harassing her with catcalls, sexual innuendos and vulgar humor, she lays down the law. As she begins to teach them conditioning, the team's star players don't want to work out so they storm off the field. The second string players hang around and Molly trains them to beat the stars in a scrimmage to prove she can coach. Unfortunately, even though the second string players prevail, the stars continue to resist Molly as a coach.

There are many moments where Molly wants to quit. The most symbolic and recurring thing that keeps her going is a stopwatch her sister gave her, engraved with her sister's and her daughters' names. This inspires her to keep fighting for her team's respect. When her office is vandalized, the pocket watch is damaged and this puts her over the edge. Molly's had enough and stands up to the team, offering a very interesting proposition: a physical challenge. She is going to run with them and keep running until either she or all of them drop. If she drops before any of them, she'll leave. But if they all quit before her, they have to listen to her.

This is a very interesting turn of events. To have a female prove her worth amongst males via a physical challenge takes her out of the coaching role, placing her side by side with her players, while also dismantling the assumption that they are physically stronger than her in every way. It is true that women are biologically stronger in endurance sports, such as running, but the visual confirmation that Molly can outlast these men (in dramatic fashion in the rain no less) is very empowering. Little do these football players know, but Molly has run the Boston Marathon twice. Men dominate the world of physical strength because we only think of size and brute strength as indicators. But there are different categories of strength that can be appreciated as athleticism and even if Molly can't stay on her feet when a player tumbles into her, she can certainly outrun them all. At the end of the run, when she's outlasted the team, she shouts, "You owe me a stopwatch, you pussies." When a player responds "Fuck you!" she simply says "Fuck you *what*?" causing him to confirm her newly awarded respect: "Fuck you, Coach McGrath."

Now the team is listening and learning. In their first game, they lose but they play a great game and they play together. As she leaves the field with the team, her daughters unsuccessfully try to get her attention. This is the first time the film hints that her daughters feel neglected. When she gets home, Alice has dyed her hair. When Molly doesn't respond in anger, Alice confronts her about the neglect. Rather than this scene playing out in a fashion that criticizes Molly's ability to be a mother and coach, it instead presents an incredible payoff to what she's trying to accomplish:

> ALICE: You don't even care if I do bad at school. It's all your fault you came home late and we didn't have any supper. All you care about are those stupid boys. You don't even care about my hair. You didn't even notice it. I hate you. [*Alice storms upstairs.*]
> MOLLY [following her]: Okay, I hate your hair. I really, really hate your hair. I didn't want to be one of those mothers who doesn't understand. But I didn't. So I guess I am.
> ALICE: What?
> MOLLY: I wanted to be able to talk calmly about your hair. Marian, come here, honey. [*Marian joins them on the bed.*] You are the most important people in my life. Much more important than any football team.

ALICE: If we're so important, then how come you play with them instead of making us dinner?

MOLLY: I was late because I had to do the shopping. I am now a football coach and I want to be the best one I can possibly be just like I want you to be the best at whatever you decide to do.

MARIAN: I want to be a helicopter pilot.

ALICE: Don't be stupid, Marian, you can't be a helicopter pilot.

MOLLY: Of course she can. She can be anything she wants to be, as long as she works hard enough at it. So can you. So can I.

ALICE: Daddy says you're going to quit.

MOLLY: He did, huh? Well, he's wrong. I'm not going to quit. I'm going to see this through but I need you to help me. Can you do that?

The girls agree to help. What began as a scene to cause worry about Molly's ability to both coach and mother has instead turned her into a positive role model for her children. She wants to inspire them by following her dream. This scene also brings forward another complexity of women's responsibilities: Whereas many male coaches may be accompanied by their wife who will watch over the kids while they can focus on their sports programs, women are expected to pull double duty, caring for their kids *and* running their sports team.[5] Frank is nowhere to be found. We know he doesn't support Molly's goals in football, but he doesn't seem to be supporting his kids with his time either. Frank's only purpose is to create obstacles for Molly's success.

In this chapter, Molly is our only coach with kids. Although her kids ultimately support her, they are used against her. When Molly's team wins their first game, she invites the team to her house for a party. Frank shows up to pick up Alice and Marian and through a series of misunderstandings, such as Molly holding beers she confiscated from players, Frank believes the kids are unsafe. He threatens to take custody away from her. Her lawyer Walt Coes (M. Emmet Walsh), an old teammate of her dad's and very supportive of her aspirations, alerts her that Frank's lawyer has submitted the statement that her job is "endangering the safety and welfare of the children." He assures her that the odds are in her favor but as the film continues, it is clear that Frank doesn't agree. Molly would quit to keep her daughters and Frank knows that.

I have to commend the film for always returning to the football field after these threats. This isn't *A League of Their Own* where we don't see Dottie play after she faces conflict; Molly always returns to the field.

Between Frank's attacks on her custody of the kids, she continues to succeed in coaching. When Dan admits that this was all a prank to watch her fail and tells her, "So you won a few games? You're a laughing stock, you're the joke of Chicago, you don't even know it!" she doesn't quit and run home to cry about it: The film cuts to the next game when she pumps up her team by saying, "They say we're a laughing stock? Don't get mad, get even!" and they go on to win the game and many more in a montage leading to the playoffs. Molly's conflicts are simply fueling her fire to follow her dream.

Frank proposes that he'll drop fighting for custody if Molly will quit and instead teach Jazzercise at a conservative girls' school where he wants to send Alice and Marian. Molly refuses. After her team makes it into the championship, Walt tells Molly that Frank is taking her to court. Once again, Molly is faced with quitting. It's at this point that the stopwatch comes back into play. Like a magical talisman, the watch returns right when Molly needs it. This time it's a gift from the team and it's engraved, "Coach, we owe you. Love, from your pussies." It works and she's inspired. In many ways, the watch is symbolic of the message that it's time for Molly (and all women) to take control of their lives and aspirations. The watch continuously saves Molly from continuing an archaic cycle of submission. It's time to move forward. First it came from her sister, a bonded partner of support, then it came from her team, the group that represents her accomplishing her dream.

Unfortunately, that dream is about to hit its harshest resistance. At a party celebrating the football team getting into the championship, Alice drinks some punch that's been spiked. When one of the players and his girlfriend give her a ride home, Alice decides to call Frank to tell him off. When he comes to pick her up, between the player and his girlfriend making out on the couch and their daughter drunk, Molly knows that this is all the evidence Frank needs in court to win.

In court, the judge rules that if Molly doesn't take the Jazzercise job, she won't be allowed visitation rights with her children during football season. It's hard to imagine a more literal translation in the assumption that during her time coaching football, Molly is unfit to be a mother. This ruling also offers the concept that in the offseason she can turn her coaching (and football) identity off just as it was turned on. Simply put, the acts of mothering *and* coaching cannot exist simultaneously. Furthermore, her daughters would not be allowed to attend any more games or interact with any players. This does more harm than good, considering some of the most empowering images were those of watching Molly coach with her daughters by her side cheering. However, from Molly's perspective, she knows she can't fight the law and she can't lose her daughters so she surrenders and agrees to Frank's terms.

The film cuts to the championship game and Central is struggling. At halftime, Molly's players sit defeated in the locker room. She knows she's lost her team in more ways than one when she surrendered in court. For the first time, her team saw Molly not fighting for something she believed in. Now they're simply following suit. However, a few players, Marvel (Willie J. Walton) and Krushinski (Woody Harrelson), spark a wild turn of events when the following conversation takes place:

> KRUSHINSKI: Hey, look, it's nobody's fault. They're champions, and we're a bunch of dildos.
> MOLLY: Oh that's nice. So what do you want to do? You wanna quit?
> MARVEL: Why not? It worked for you.
> MOLLY: What's that supposed to mean? I sent plays in. You just didn't execute... Oh, I see, this is about yesterday. Great. I suppose you think I was chicken shit for what I did in court, huh? I suppose you think I got beat because I was afraid to fight. Yeah, you do. And you figure if your coach is such a loser, then that gives you all the right to be a bunch of losers too, doesn't it? *Doesn't it?!*

With that, she storms out of the locker room and straight to Frank's seat in the crowd and says:

> MOLLY: Frank! The deal's off. You're not sending our girls to some school they don't wanna go to and you're not taking them away from me! And I'm not quitting my job here either. If that's not okay with you, then you can sue me and I'll fight you all the way to the Supreme Court! [*She kneels beside him to speak quietly.*] Frank, I don't want to be a quitter any more. I don't want our girls to see a quitter. For them ... not for me.
> FRANK: Okay. We'll work it out.

Molly fixes everything by her own power. This is a female role model. The help she receives from her team and her sister doesn't take away from this victory. They were the support system anyone would need to overcome adversity.

The team starts to dominate and they win, all while Molly's daughters stand by her side. This film has awarded its heroine everything she wants: She gets her dream job, she wins the respect of her players and her school, she keeps her daughters and stands as a positive role model for them and the audience. Molly didn't need to reconcile with her husband or find a new one; she just fought for her independence and kept the focus on coaching football.

Wildcats is a wildly inspiring film. At the start of Molly's job at Central, she tells her team to forget the past, she will help them be better now. Perhaps we should do the same. We are better now and we need to forget the false assumptions that have held women back from opportunities such as coaching football.

Eddie, directed by Steve Rash, came out in 1996, a decade after *Wildcats.* Unfortunately, the fact that *Eddie* was released after *Wildcats* does not translate to even further advancement in empowered choices. In many ways, *Eddie* returns us to persisting patterns of controlling our heroine.

Sixth Woman

Eddie (Whoopi Goldberg) is a diehard fan of the New York Knicks. That is made clear in her introduction while we watch her as a limo dispatcher who would rather give play-by-play of the game on her company microphone than dispatch travel requests. Furthermore, she leaves a different Knicks trivia question on her answering machine every day, has a closet complete with every player's jersey, and when she's at live games the volume of her voice cuts through the crowd noise like a train whistle in a library. She's avid, to say the least. One day while driving a customer, she calls in to a sports talk radio show to share her thoughts on the new Knicks owner. As fate would have it, her customer in the back is that very owner, Wild Bill Burgess (Frank Langella). When she becomes aware of this, she showers him with advice. He seems entertained by her passion. Later, while we watch Eddie at the game, they announce a fan competition to become honorary coach for a night. Bill spots Eddie in the crowd and rigs the game to get Eddie down on the court and she wins.

What is missing from this introduction is the fact that Eddie coaches youth basketball. This is revealed later in the film. Instead, what is prioritized is the notion that she's passionate but summarily a comedic loud-mouthed, unruly fan. Had we caught a glimpse of her legitimate application of her love of the sport (working with youth on the court) we might have seen that she had some qualifications for her "won" role as coach of the Knicks. In the sequence where she coaches youth, a mother approaches her and complains about her son being benched. Eddie tells her that he's benched because of his grades and then explains the importance of an education over playing. Right away we see that she is grounded, caring and a responsible coach. However, for the sake of comedy, the film's opening relies on the idea that she's a crazed fan who wouldn't have any shot at turning this opportunity into a real job. It's omissions like this that make *Eddie* an important film to look at.

Wild Bill Burgess is a businessman. All he cares about is money and his flagrant spending certainly confirms that from the start. The first time this new Knicks owner introduces himself to the crowd, he enters the court on horseback with the horse outfitted in basketball sneakers. When a rogue firework starts burning a commemorative jersey of a famous player in the rafters, it is quickly revealed that this is reflective of Bill's feelings toward the legacy of the team. It's not about the game; it's about the investment. Eddie becomes his greatest investment.

Since the Knicks are struggling, both in the league and attendance-wise, Bill knows he needs to make a dramatic change. After recognizing that the current coach John Bailey (Dennis Farina) won't play along with his circus, Bill chooses to aggravate John to quit (if he fires him, he'll have to pay out the remaining millions of dollars in his contract) and in turn hires Eddie to coach for the night. In the first game she coaches, he tells the team to listen to the assistant coach Carl Zimmer (Richard Jenkins), and just let her make a show. This appears to be a smart choice considering Eddie's first interaction with the team is her "fan'ing" out on them, simply telling them how excited she is. She offers no direction. As the game progresses, she is hesitant and afraid to speak up. In fact, the only time she gets out of her seat is to get the crowd to chant "Defense!" After the game, Bill realizes that there aren't many coaches available and they cost far more than he'll make back so he offers the job for the rest of the season to Eddie. It's an obvious move to make money and forfeit the season; even Eddie is hesitant and assures Bill that the Knicks need a real coach. Bill simply responds, "That's what you are, Eddie. In your heart, you are a coach." In *your* heart. Throughout the film Bill continues to encourage Eddie to stick it out but we know it's a show. When Bill says, "I believe in you, Eddie. I believe you need the Knicks and the Knicks need you," this may be true but it isn't always clear that this is due to her coaching ability.

Although the city rooted for Eddie when she was a fan who had the golden ticket for a night, they don't seem to be on board with her turning that into a career. There are two montages that express the city's feelings about having a woman coach. The first is when they are struggling and a construction worker (John DiMaggio) says, "I'll give my tickets to my wife." Even real-life Mayor Rudolph Giuliani can't help but laugh before switching into political mode and stating, "It's a real break through for equal rights. She'll bring something very special to it." In the second montage, when the Knicks are starting to benefit from Eddie's coaching, that same construction worker recants: "I wish I could get my tickets back from my wife." In sports, if you win, you're in. However, all Bill cares about is that this publicity charade is selling tickets. By the end of the film, that will play an important role in Eddie's future. We'll address that shortly.

As with both Randy and Molly, Eddie's initial introduction to a male team is cause for resistance. Eddie has two descriptors going against her: She's a woman and she's a fan. These players aren't introduced to her in any fashion that would signify that she has the talent to help them. She is just another heckler in the crowd, and even worse, she's a woman. The first time Eddie is on the sidelines, she is quiet and afraid. Who can blame her? She just went from giving her advice from the nosebleed seats, where she felt she bore no responsibility, to giving her advice mere inches from the players' faces where they have to listen. However, as Eddie begins to realize how lazy the players are off the court and how their "million dollar egos" are more to blame for their struggles than anything, the fan inside of her finally detaches and we begin to watch her coach.

Carl, Eddie's assistant coach, has all but given up on the team. He has surrendered to their egos and has no authoritative power over anything. But, he does appear open to working with Eddie. The first time we watch Eddie prove her worth is when she walks down the aisle of the

Knicks jet and basically runs down each player's items to work on. Some players respond, some wave her off, but the audience can see that she has good advice to give. Additionally, it's the first time we see that she's not affected or afraid of confronting these players. Comparing the sequence where Molly is speechless at her players' nudity in the locker room, it's worth sharing that Eddie laughs at her naked team in the shower.

After another loss, Eddie turns to veteran player Nate Wilson (John Salley) for advice. He tells her that she should care about the personal issues of the players, not just their skills on the court. For example, one player is going through a difficult divorce so he's been distracted. Another player doesn't speak English but nobody has bothered to find a way to communicate with him. Although my initial thought was disappointment that she didn't think of this herself, at least Eddie wasn't essentialized to innately focus on their emotions and feelings. I have to commend the film for asserting her focus on coaching skills before exploring her nurturing capabilities. By ordering her thought process in this way, we are not aligning the emotional connection with the players as a specifically female skill; it is simply another layer of good coaching.

As she starts to reach out to the players and help them on a more personal level, they begin to respond. She replaces the largest ego, star player Stacy Patton (Malik Sealy), with Nate, which helps change the ball-hogging-star dynamic to a collaborative team. The Knicks start to improve and it's thanks to Eddie's efforts. There are a few humorous asides to her being a female coach such as auditioning male dancers to join the female dancers who perform between game breaks. Beyond her coaching duties, she makes a conscious effort to involve the fans, leading supportive chants to support the team. Eddie's growing into a great coach and the film is embracing it.

However, as we've seen before, right when everything is strong with our heroine, the film diverts the story. Bill calls a meeting with Eddie and reveals he's moving the Knicks to St. Louis but he's negotiated a deal to keep Eddie coaching. The fact that Eddie can remain the coach is great but Eddie is a die-hard fan whose focus becomes solely to keep the Knicks in New York. Bill asks point blank, "What do you care where you coach as long as you coach?" but she has roots in New York and this may be the reason why Eddie isn't introduced as a coach at the start of the film, she's a fan. The driving force of this story is now confirmed: It's about the pride as a fan and not the opportunity to coach. Obviously this is a little unsettling when discussing empowered representations of female coaches, I do have to credit Eddie for standing up for herself once Bill reveals his motives in the following conversation:

EDDIE: Why did you buy this team?
BILL: I bought the players for skill. I bought the cheerleaders for tits and ass. I bought Bailey for experience and I bought you—well, what does it matter?
EDDIE: Oh, no, don't stop now. Why me?
BILL: Fun. I bought you for fun, Eddie. I got me a circus and you're my clown. You got no real skill, no profound talent. You're loud, you got a big mouth. You're funny, but you're an amateur, hon. You're all hat, no cattle. As long as you put on a good show, I'm gonna ride you just like I ride my horse. And if he can't carry me, he's gone. And if you can't carry me, the same things gonna happen to you. You know, hon, like we say back home—
EDDIE: No, it's like *we* say here at home: Fuck you and the horse you rode in on.

In this interaction, it's important to recognize that Bill's "using" of everyone and everything is somewhat genderless. Although I could go on about how this feels like a deep revelation of the object, subordination and ownership of women, the truth is that this man would sell his male players just the same. Not to credit this as empowering because it's blatantly oppressive, but we cannot overlook the fact that he sold the team with *her* as the coach. Although this is the climactic scene for Bill's villainous intentions, the film's intentions are far worse once it's established that Eddie would rather see the Knicks in New York than coach at all.

Before we reach the conclusion of the film, it's important to remark on the scene that immediately follows this confrontation. The film cuts to Eddie at home watching some old video footage of a policeman working with youth on a basketball court. The camera pans by framed photos of Eddie and this policeman, including a photo of them getting married at a Knicks game. The information is clear: This was her husband and he is an integral part of her love of the Knicks and the game of basketball. A rosary hanging on the frame tells us he's passed away. This is the first time we've learned that she ever had a husband. When Eddie first walked on the court to win the honorary coaching opportunity, she said to herself, "It doesn't get any better than this." Now we watch her husband in the video say that same thing. This scene feels like an afterthought, a simple action of confirming she is, in fact, heterosexual. Although it also stages a dramatic element to what defines her "roots" in New York, why can't we watch her peruse her Knicks jerseys, listen to her answering machine or admire the New York skyline? Why must we introduce her husband to remind her of her love for the city? At least this scene is placed so deeply in the film that Eddie is allowed credit for everything she's accomplished without the pretense that her husband was informing her skill or enabling her actions. However, even if the film is simply placing her husband as another important aspect of her connection to the city, this scene is a perfect example of the patriarchal checklist we are all too familiar with in the treatment of our cinematic sports heroines.

At the end of the film, the Knicks have a shot at getting into the playoffs. Nate, our veteran captain, gets injured and Eddie is forced to put Stacy back into the game. Thanks to Eddie's coaching and communication, Stacy has ditched his ego and is now an integral and important part of the team. Near the end of the game, during a timeout, Eddie walks out to the middle of the court and announces Bill's plans to sell the team. She declares a protest and puts the team in a position where they'll forfeit if Bill doesn't drop his plans. Carl is the first to join her and the players and fans soon follow suit. Even the opposing team joins Eddie on the court. Bill surrenders. The Knicks go on to win the game and the film concludes on a freeze frame of Eddie being held up by a teammate.

Ultimately *Eddie* does support its female heroine. However, there is confusion as to whether her goals were to be a coach or to be a loyal fan to the Knicks. Having the source of the team's problems be their personal lives presents a dialogue more about fandom then Eddie's coaching ability. We as fans just want to see players score; we don't take into account that they are human beings. With this in mind, the underlying theme of the film didn't seem to be about Eddie so much as it was about the players. They change far more than she does. However, the fact remains that Eddie did manage to be a fan *and* help the team as a coach, which is empowering to watch.

All of the coaches in this chapter have the skill and knowledge to improve their team but face immediate discrimination because their teams are made up of men. In concluding this chapter, it would be beneficial to briefly discuss one more film, 2009's *The Mighty Macs*, directed by Tim Chambers, which portrays a female coaching a team of female athletes.

And One

Based on the true story of Immaculata College winning the first-ever women's college basketball national championship in 1972, *The Mighty Macs* offers confident feminist intentions by staying honest with this highly impactful moment in women's sports history. Unlike *A League of Their Own*, *The Mighty Macs* sacrifices little to embrace the strength of its female athletes and especially the female coach behind it all, Cathy Rush (played by Carla Gugino). Cathy brought the highest success to a team that struggled to recruit, had no home court and little equipment to play with. Above all, the team was from an all-girls Catholic college which saw basketball far more as an activity to "suppress their hormones" than a sport of competition and future profession. All of this is cinematically fluid in the story on the screen. Furthermore, Cathy ultimately receives more support than stress from her husband, Ed T. Rush (David Boreanaz), an NBA referee.

Cathy doesn't face any conflict that sacrifices her empowerment. Each conflict simply triggers another inspiring argument she shares. In one of the few scenes where Ed challenges Cathy, he infers she's wasting her time: "You're trying too hard to change these girls, Cathy, and they don't want it!" Cathy responds, "It's not that they don't want it, it's that they have been told for so long that they can't have it, that they can't even imagine wanting it." This film doesn't utilize the mentalities of its time period like *A League of Their Own*, it challenges those notions by celebrating those individuals who wanted to change and make progress. Any moment with the girls where they are tethered to traditional ideas of a female's role in society, Cathy is there to teach them about their options. The largest conflict in the film surrounds funding for the team and the school. By the film's end, the team's success is seen as one reason the school is saved, which certainly speaks to the power of sports programs.

One of the most impactful messages Cathy teaches her team is that they will win the championship because of the things that others cannot see; their inner beings and the traits that make them who they are. A beautiful message, this reminds us that having the skills to compete and/or coach is only one part of succeeding in sports. *The Mighty Macs* is an amazing and loyal slice of women's sports history. Its heroine is empowered and empowers others. The visual representation of this is incredibly important. The only problem is that *The Mighty Macs* lacked the budget to reach mainstream audiences on a mass level. The film was created and distributed independently which weakened the impact of these important female representations. As Cathy's voiceover reveals, "When I look back, I'm not sure any of us could explain the mystery of how we won, or why we won, but maybe all we did was look around us to see other women committed to something they believed in. Somewhere along the way, you forget how important that is." As I've written over and over again, role models are the gateway to continued progress. If we can create more stories embracing characters such as Molly and Cathy, while having those stories reach mainstream audiences, we will be creating visual representations of role models that are absolutely necessary.

The truth is that there are many successful female coaches around the world, but because they aren't featured on Sportscenter, or have the lead job in a male sports league, they don't get the proper publicity to lead the next generation. As the assistant coach in *The Mighty Macs,* Sister Sunday (Marley Shelton), says to Cathy, "You taught me that not only is change possible, it's as vital as breathing." This is a truth we must all embrace to continue progress. Progress hinges on less representations like Randy, balanced with sexuality and a distraction of men, and more like Molly, a woman who takes control of her own life in order to accomplish her dream and earn the respect of her players.

Coaching is a role that does not require physical dominance; it's about mental strategy, which should represent an equal playing field. If you know the game, you can play the game from the sidelines regardless of your gender. All of the female coaches in this chapter succeed in projecting this message in one form or another. Until films such as these and *The Mighty Macs* can reach a mass audience with mass interest, we will continue to only access these strong female representations once a decade.

7

Principal Interest
Cinematic Female Owners

Throughout this book, we've discussed players of all sports and in the previous chapter we took a look at their leaders, the coaches. The truth of the matter is, none of this would be possible without money. From the co-ed sports of our youth to the highest echelon of professional play, these programs require investment and that investment must reap rewards, sometimes that are not synonymous with on-the-field success. For example, the Lombardi trophy (the award given to the victor of the Super Bowl) is only one part of the team owner's ultimate success in the NFL. Fans, endorsements and star players are just a few of the other necessities of a professional sports organization. The fate of a team, its players and its legacy rely on one position: the owner.

Financial numbers aren't as exciting as a hail mary to the endzone to win the big game or the look in the eyes of a fierce competitor. It's easy to see why owners may be easy to vilify in cinema. Fans can believe that these owners don't know, or forget to care about, what it's like to physically and mentally leave everything on the playing field. With this in mind, it comes to no surprise that some of our most popular and classic films have placed a woman in the role of the owner. The societal disconnect of women and sports makes this position available because it does not require the experience of playing the game. It is a job of business and although business is also historically the male domain, women's presence in business has progressed far more than their professions on the playing field. Furthermore, placing a female in the position of owner in these films offers a distraction from the sometimes harsh truth of this profession: Owners don't see players as human beings, they see them as investments. Having a woman embody this notion is incredibly damaging. Instead of seeing her as a savvy businesswoman, these films choose to use her to embody the questionable practices of sports owners.

As we saw in *Eddie,* Wild Bill made the most offensive decision when he wanted to sell and move the Knicks. According to cinema, this is an owner's ultimate villainous action. With the exception of *Secretariat,* which I will briefly discuss at the conclusion of this chapter, *Any Given Sunday* and *Major League* follow in this cinematic path. Even worse, *Slap Shot* has a female owner who would benefit financially from folding the team (simply shutting them down) rather than moving them. Placing these actions in a female representation provides a two-fold message. First, it continues the tradition of separating women from sports. Although an owner could be said to know a sport the best because they must carry expertise on every level of the organization, they are not the celebrated heroes on the field fighting for the honor of victory. Instead, owners are simply seen sitting in their comfortable luxury box looking down at dollar signs and firing those who do not produce. Second, much in the sense of the highly skilled female athlete on a misfit team, a highly skilled and knowledgeable cinematic female owner becomes the sign of a problematic team. Having these male players and coaches answering to a woman creates a conflicted gender power dynamic these male teams make clear they are not happy with.

All of the female owners in this chapter have inherited their position from a father or husband. The assumption is that even the owner's wife or daughter has to have some sports knowledge after so many years in the box by his side. And she does, just enough to ruin the organization in each of these films. As long as a woman did not work her way into this position without the unfortunate passing of a man in her life, there is an underlying hope that patriarchal roots in sport can be redeemed if she is defeated.

With the exception of *Secretariat,* the films discussed in this chapter do not center on their cinematic female owners. Because their screen time is minimal, we will weave them together to illustrate common patterns they share.

Personnel Management

Major League, directed by David S. Ward in 1989, is about a struggling Cleveland Indians team owned by ex-showgirl Rachel Phelps (Margaret Whitton), who inherited it from her late husband. Her only desire is for the team to finish dead last so she can move them to a more glamourous location in Florida "for a mansion in Boca Raton." As a comedy, we watch the trials and tribulations of our team of heroes as they battle both her and the harsh conditions she damns them to. Throughout the journey, we laugh as she prances around in debutante garb and cheers at their dismay. The more she throws at them, the more they overcome to succeed. She has no regard for the players or their livelihood and, most importantly, the game itself. She uses what little she's learned of the game from her late husband to build a facade of legitimate business intelligence. At one point, she hands out the spring training roster and one of her board members points out that one of her scouted players is dead. She replies, "Cross him off then." Throughout the film, she sits in her owner's box (which is more like a Floridian patio dressed with plants, a pink palm tree ashtray and tropical umbrella drinks) dressed in outlandish gaudy outfits and roots for the opponents. In the final big game, she wears all black as if she were attending a funeral as she roots for the Indians' defeat.

Director Oliver Stone's *Any Given Sunday* (1999) takes a raw look into all of the aspects of a professional football franchise. Franchise owner Christina Pagniacci (Cameron Diaz) inherited the team from her late father. We get visual confirmation of her success and capability by seeing her on the cover of *Forbes* magazine and her degree from Cornell University. Christina as an owner differs from Rachel because she is presented as an extremely informed, sports-knowledgeable, hard-edged businesswoman. Her owner's box is simple and classy like the current luxury boxes of the rich. She wears nondescript business clothing. However, she is like Rachel in that she's entertaining the idea of selling the team and she has little regard for anyone but herself. Christina's even tough on her own mother. At one point she admits, "I would cut my father's ass if we were losing." She knows the game and it's business. She is, by all philosophical accounts, a man. Her success in the film is harnessed with her lack of classical femininity. Even the manliest of men cannot overtake her.

Any Given Sunday posits Christina as representative of a new generation in sports. Coach Tony D'Amato (Al Pacino), referred to as "Coach Stone Age," represents the old classic way of doing things. After a heated argument with Christina, Tony says, "You know how your dad and I negotiated my contract? We had a beer, we shook hands." She replies, "Well, I don't drink beer, Tony." It's not so much that she doesn't drink beer as her recognition that a handshake doesn't stand up in court as a viable business method. It's a new age and a new business. This is why Tony wasn't made franchise manager by Christina's father: Her father recognized that Tony was too "old school" in the way he approaches everything. Although the film critiques this character trait in Tony, it ultimately celebrates him for it. Tony may not be as savvy a businessman, but he believes in the sanctity of football and the film honors this notion by allowing him to be solely responsible for helping their star player, Willie Beamen (Jamie Foxx), overcome his ego and fall in love with the heart of the game. This heroic motion overshadows any connection Christina has to the sport and her team; thus, her business knowledge and toughness are misconstrued as villainous actions holding Tony back, rather than Tony's antiquated methods holding the team back.

Any Given Sunday more than any of the other films in this chapter celebrates the "old boy's" club of sport. Beyond embodying the tent poles of masculinity in Tony's character, this film visually translates the correlation of football with gladiatorial competition and smashes us in the face with anti-femininity rhetoric through the players' and coaches' interactions on the field. Placing Christina at the head of this inflamed masculine world equates to an inflamed backlash to her as a female. At one point the male commissioner of the league says, "I honestly believe that woman would eat her young." This statement would not be relevant if a man had been the one to challenge the commissioner because Christina's actions are simply not how a "lady" should act.[1] It should be noted that Christina does in fact have a boyfriend. However, we only see her interact with him once in a conversation where she forgets about a work trip he has and doesn't seem to care much about him leaving. We never see or hear of him again. Instead of our usual cinematic strategy to place a boyfriend to prove she is still desirable or at least tameable, he is simply introduced to become another piece of debris left in her wake.

Christina is our most modern representation of a female owner and she exhibits some truly fearless and powerful moments. However, the film provides plenty of hints that she's abused her power as well.

When Willie Beamen begins to shine on the field, she asks her assistant, "Where did we get this guy?" and he simply insinuates that she carelessly fired the talented scout who is now credited for saving the team. When the team's doctor puts the players' health at risk by letting them continue to play hurt, it is revealed that Christina has endorsed his actions.

Any Given Sunday is a film of extremes. Perhaps Christina's biggest hurdle is the spectrum of extremes in the other female representations that accompany her. In this cinematic world, there are only soft cheerleaders, seductive or wild prostitutes, abusive and controlling wives and her drunken, regretful mother. The only redeemable female character is Willie's girlfriend Vanessa Struthers (Lela Rochon), who is educated and calls him out on his actions when he begins to get caught up with the fame and money. Although she leaves him, she comes back once he's changed, which is used as another device to celebrate his growth as a character. Without the character development given to the men in the film, these women are simply tools to be used to establish this as a masculine territory. Christina is no different.

In director George Roy Hill's *Slap Shot* (1977), a struggling professional hockey team turns to a more violent game plan to bring in crowds and save their fledgling organization. In this film, the team members want the team to be sold. When the mystery owner, Anita McCambridge (Kathryn Walker), is revealed to our hero Reggie Dunlop (Paul Newman), Reggie pleads with her to sell the team by saying, "We've been doing real good, you know." She replies, "Well, my accountant is certainly pleased." She then tells him that she could sell the team but she won't, it wouldn't be profitable. Although this interaction should demonize her because of her lack of respect for the men's livelihood, Anita is handed an inch of redemption. She confesses, "I've never let the children watch a hockey game. I have a theory that children imitate what they see on a TV screen. They see violence, they'll become violent." Although this statement causes Reggie to storm out of her house, she does effect change in our hero. His eyes are opened to the violence he has taught his team and the city of Charlestown where the team plays. Although Reggie reverts to his violent ways once they are losing the championship game and he learns there are NHL scouts in the crowd, the actions that take place in the championship game do verify that Anita has voiced the exact message the movie was trying to convey.

During the championship game we watch both the team and the fans fighting in a riot-like atmosphere. Ned Braden (Michael Ontkean), the only team member who won't fight (and is ultimately deemed a wimp and not a man), plays on the ridiculousness of the violence by providing a striptease on the ice. The blood-soaked players, fists still against each other's faces, complain that he is disgusting. The crowd agrees. This plays as a comical critical conversation about the layers of violence, which is a theme that runs throughout the film. It's clear that Anita's argument isn't so far-fetched.

Although Anita chooses to be far removed from the team she owns, Rachel and Christina are very much involved in every aspect of their organization. They have unbridled access into every private space their players and coaches occupy, which in the case of the locker room, can be played out as unapologetic sexual harassment.

The locker room has come to represent a private and sacred space for men to, by all classical readings, be men. This is where the coaches "shame" them to pump them up to conquer the field of "battle" and this is where they can say anything and everything without political conflict. This being a "safe space" for explosive hegemonic masculinity, it's not hard to imagine this as one of the most vulnerable spaces for a woman.[2] In both *Major League* and *Any Given Sunday*, Rachel Phelps and Christina Pagniacci enter this private space and defile it. When Rachel enters, she struts around the room, touching and patting the players, and even knocks on a player's jock strap cup and says, "Cups still work though." She calls them a bunch of "pansies" in response to the coach's complaint about a lack of working equipment, invoking them all to motion a fist in unison behind her. When Christina enters her players' locker room, she confidently strolls by all the naked man, even turning to one and saying "Pete, don't stiffen up on me" with a smirk on her face. This is the ultimate penetration and domination of the male world. Men are at their most vulnerable naked state, figuratively and literally, and now a woman is deconstructing them. The aforementioned shaming that the male coaches inflict on their players has nothing to do with sensual insinuation or touching. That is a form of shaming that is centered on accusing these players of being weak so they'll fight to prove themselves, not making them feel powerless where they can't do anything. Although some of Christina's players seemed aroused by her actions, this only makes it more problematic. Can you imagine if a male owner did this?

So how does a woman in such a powerful position get defeated? All three of our female owners suffer different forms of punishment for asserting such power in these masculine territories.

In *Any Given Sunday,* Christina suffers in two forms. First, and most obvious, Tony is awarded the last laugh at the end of the film. Once the team completes their season, Tony announces that he has a job managing a new team and he's taking her star, Willie Beamen, with him. On the surface, audiences celebrate that Tony's "old ways" still carry value. To sweeten the pot, Christina turns to Tony in the press conference before his announcement and admits, "Thanks again for helping me understand what I'd forgotten." She's referring to the love of the game, the pride of a team and her father's legacy that she almost sold. The second, and far more damaging, way that Christina's image is controlled is inspired by a conversation between Tony and Christina's mother, Margaret Pagniacci (Ann-Margret). Christina may credit Tony for helping her remember the importance of her franchise, but it is her mother who helps her remember she's a woman. In a scene where Christina is eavesdropping on her mother talking with Tony, she hears the following:

TONY: Christina is gonna destroy this team.
MARGARET: What is it you fear? You've got so much fear inside you, Tony.
TONY: I'm losing the team, Maggie. I'm losing control. Everything in my life's about control. I lead men. I control. Did Art think I was past it?
MARGARET: I don't know.
TONY: Do you care?
MARGARET: Oh, Tony, you never understood Artie, did you? He wanted a son more than anything else in the world. And when you really think about it, what Christina is it's just such a tragedy. You know, she will sell the team. And everything that her father stood for is gonna die. And what will you do Tony, after football, with nobody to control?
TONY: Stop it. What are you doing?
MARGARET: Hey, I blame you for a lot of things. You were like Artie. A monster. You've gotten older. Better, yeah. But for a long time, I hated you. That game took my husband, my daughter, my youth. Left me with what? All those Sunday afternoons at the stadium. And time just kept slipping away, didn't it?

Margaret, who has been belligerently drunk throughout the film, is revealed to not be so lost after all. She becomes a voice of reason in the chaos of all the money, violence and smothered masculinity. But when she mentions Artie's desire for a son, she is simply pointing out how her daughter has become that son rather than a strong woman who has perhaps gotten caught up in the business of the game just like her father. "It's such a tragedy" that she has drifted so far from her gender. In the final game, Christina turns to her mother and admits, "I feel like things are changing, you know? Things are out of control. Maybe I'm just out of control. I'm sorry for the way I've been behaving." Although there is truth to the fact that Christina has overstepped her boundaries as an owner, this admission to change is not a victory in her favor. It's important to recognize that this is happening with her mother, and not with any member of her organization. This is contained as a female-centered moment, and a generational one at that. If Christina had said this to one of her staff members, perhaps she could elicit some respect for recognizing her abuses of power. Instead it is a private moment to be recognized in a feminine space. As the team wins the game, she and her mother cheer together. It's not so much that we shouldn't appreciate Christina's growth in character, but her growth ends up appearing to be a weakness by the film's end. She changes but Tony does not. And the final victory is awarded to Tony when he announces that he has another team and he's taking her best asset to win with him.

Although Anita in *Slap Shot* seems to prevail in her message, she is ultimately defeated in her image. She may win in business, but according to Reggie Dunlop's final words to her when he storms out of her house, her son will end up a "fag" if she doesn't get married again. The implication is that she won't be able to instill masculinity, and therefore heterosexuality, in her son as a single mother. In Anita's only scene, the film has still awarded a slam to her as a woman.

There may be no more violent cinematic answer to a dominating woman than the punishment of Rachel Phelps in *Major League*. In the locker room, after the manager alerts his team to her plot to ambush their season, he reveals a life-size cardboard cutout of her that is covered by pieces of cardboard "fabric" and concludes, "I figure it's gonna take 32 more victories to win this thing. Every time we win, we peel a section." There are many issues with this action in addition to the overt sexual assault. First, this action is one of dominance bonding.[3] These men are bonding through the domination of her body. Although this is not her physical body, this representation of her body can achieve the same sense of control. By determining that this is the way to inspire the team to win, we are celebrating a truly heinous component of the construction of masculinity. Second, there is an assumption that all these men will enjoy the stripping of Rachel and view it as a reward, which could stem from immense homophobia in sports.

What follows after the introduction of this "inspiration" is a montage underscored with uplifting music as we watch them battle for victory and reveal more and more of Rachel's flesh. We watch players slide into base, hit home runs and make extraordinary catches while Rachel's arm, stomach, waist, crotch and the edge of her breast are revealed. The montage quiets as we pan up her now naked body (only dressed in high bikini bottoms) with one final piece covering her breasts. The players sit at a long table, a supposed celebration meal in the locker room, and cheer as the coach rips off the remaining section to reveal her breasts with only her nipples concealed by golden stars. The fact that this film is a comedy does not excuse this action. These players are not being laughed at for cheering for this nude artificial reproduction, they are being celebrated.

DVDs allow us a commentary track where we can listen to writers and directors elaborate on the creation of each scene. Although this could be a space of reflection and perhaps further conversation about what they've created, writer-director David Ward and producer Chris Chesser simply validate the very problems Rachel's punishment provides. They spend the entire sequence of Rachel's undressing discussing how the extras lacked consistent attendance, which made continuity difficult. They also note how great the actors were at playing baseball. There is no mention of the action being portrayed on the screen until the very last piece is removed (revealing her breasts) when they share, "Now it's interesting ... she was concerned about what the body would look like ... that she was given ... that they were peeling the dress off of ... she was fine with this body... But what's interesting about this is, this is before the days of silicone. Basically, that's a real woman's body. The way a woman's body actually looks if she's built like that." There is no consideration for the act of undressing Rachel, only that once undressed, she is worthy of our eyes. The necessity to embrace the fact that she is "all natural" seems to negate the fact that we shouldn't bear witness to her naked body at all. Even though this was a cardboard replica of her, the retaliation of her uncontrolled subordination is quite clear.

What we see of Rachel in live action is quite linear through the entire film. She is, in fact, a cardboard replica in her lack of range in character. There is no arc to her storyline. On the contrary, Christina Pagniacci is a multifaceted character who evolves. Whether it is her troubles with Tony or reconnecting with her mother, she is afforded multiple scenes where we watch her grow and change. Even in the small amount of screen time that we share with Anita McCambridge's character, we see more than one layer of her character through her family, her business sense and her views of violence. Pure and simple, Rachel Phelps is a villain. Her goal is to have her team finish dead last and to demean them at any cost.

In the original screenplay for *Major League*, there was a twist at the end. This ending was filmed and later cut for the theatrical release. As with *The Longshots*, the DVD of *Major League* hands us another round of empowerment that just didn't make the cut. It appears that Rachel Phelps outsmarted them all and was in on the whole thing from the beginning. The manager, Lou Brown (James Gammon), storms up to her office before the big finale game to hand in his resignation and the scene goes as follows:

RACHEL: Oh, hi, Lou, what can I do for you?
LOU: I wanted to hand in my resignation before you had a chance to fire me.
RACHEL: Well, what do you mean?
LOU: I know what you've been trying to do to this team. After the season, I want no part of it.
RACHEL: I knew I could count on Charlie to tell you. I was just afraid he'd wait too long.
LOU: Why'd you want him to tell me?
RACHEL: So you'd tell the team, hopefully, getting them mad enough so they'd knock themselves out trying to prove they belonged in this league. I think it worked.
LOU: You're trying to make me believe that you wanted us to win all along? Bull! What about the plane, the bus, the bad hotels?
RACHEL: We were broke. We couldn't afford anything better. Donald left the team nearly bankrupt. If we'd had another losing season, I would've had to sell this team. I knew we couldn't win with the players we had. So I decided to get new players and see how they'd do with the proper motivation. There never was any offer from Miami. I made it all up.
LOU: Why should I believe any of this? Now that we're winning, it's easy for you to jump on our bandwagon.

RACHEL: If I really wanted you to lose, all I had to do was to send your best players back to the minors. But I didn't do that, did I? You think this was all an accident? I personally scouted every member of this team ... they all had flaws that concealed their real talents, or I wouldn't have been able to afford them. But I knew if anyone could straighten them out, you could. You see, I scouted you, too... Oh, Lou, I love this team.

It is in this moment that the world turns upside down. The female owner has succeeded. She has dominated the sport on every level. This ending is a game changer. In the film that carried the harshest punishment for its female owner, *Major League* would have afforded the greatest reward. It revolutionizes women in the sports world. That is only one of the reasons it couldn't make the theatrical cut.

Rachel Phelps is introduced as a one-dimensional character. It would be inconsistent to open the floodgates and let this depth occur. David Ward set her character so strongly in an evil one-dimensional role that he set up this twist ending to fail. Producer Chris Chesser explains, "The reason we changed it was, that while we tested the picture with that twist and it worked, we've discovered that audiences, by that time, really loved to hate her. Margaret Whitton did such a good job of making that character evil that the audiences loved to hate her so we felt like, let's just give them what they want." Ward revealed that after removing the twist, the film actually scored 15 points higher amongst audiences. They even had to reshoot and replace the original ending of her celebrating in her owner's box as the team is winning the championship with footage of her unmoving dismay. He adds that the only reason they got the script developed was because of the twist. That unique quality attracted the studios, yet in the end the audience wanted more of the same old one-dimensional villain, which sadly rested on the shoulders of a capable female character.

No audience would see this twist coming, yet the twist almost seemed so far out of left field, that no one might believe it. Her whole demeanor in the unreleased scene is coherent and confident. It is nothing like the barrage of infantilizing absorbent femininity we've watched as she throws tantrums at their victory. She was playing them the whole time. Maybe if this ending had been released, she would have been viewed as even smarter and the men as even dumber at buying into this "act" she pulled off as the prerequisite image of an "ex-showgirl" wife.

She controlled every male character. This revolutionary ending never stood a chance. *Major League*'s action of mocking men is only successful if, in the end, they are no longer the butt of the joke. Rather than positioning her as the hero she deserved to be, we continue in the tradition of defeating her for having that power.

I'd like to conclude this chapter by taking a look at *Secretariat*. Although the female owner owns a horse and not a team of players, horse racing is very much a male-dominated arena and she must fight on many levels to earn respect and take her place in the sport.

Across the Board

Secretariat (2010), directed by Randall Wallace, is based on the real-life story of Penny Chenery (played by Diane Lane) who bred and raced Secretariat, the winner of the 1973 triple crown. This is a Disney film; recalling our discussion of Disney's traditionally conservative female representations, Penny hands us one of the most feminist Disney heroines we've ever seen. Furthermore, this story is based on real-life events. The facts of her winning cannot be tarnished or questioned. However, in the cinematic world, we've learned that it's not about the fact of winning, it's how you win that defines your character. Rest assured, how Penny wins can more than make up for the flaws promoted in Rachel, Christina and Anita.

Secretariat opens in 1969 with Penny serving breakfast to her family. Her husband is dictating a shopping list for her to complete in order to host a client of his. Although this introduction embraces Penny as a dutiful wife, this is a far cry from the Penny we will conclude with. Penny's real story begins when her mother passes. She rushes home and is faced with the struggling state of her father's farm. He is a respected breeder of racehorses and his farm is losing money because he's too ill to run it properly. Penny puts her father on a pedestal and he does the same for her. She has immense pride in everything he accomplished while her brother Hollis (Dylan Baker) wants to sell it all. Hollis isn't greedy, he just never had the relationship with their father that Penny had and therefore doesn't have the same emotion invested into his father's legacy. Penny decides to stay to help her father, sending her husband and children back home without her. At this moment in the story, under these circumstances, this action seems understandable and she is supported by her husband Jack Tweedy (Dylan Walsh). As the movie progresses and the time she dedicates to her father's farm overtakes the time she gives her family, her husband begins to cause a lot of the tension for Penny.

It's important to stay sensitive to how much Penny credits her father for her every move. It is true that she has learned everything she knows about horses from him and that the farm is his, but there are many influential decisions Penny makes on her own accord yet the film always finds a way for her to credit her father. This celebration of the father is most certainly a pattern we've witnessed throughout this book. However, I can't help but celebrate certain moments where *Penny* is celebrated for her decisions, and her decisions alone. One of her strongest supporters is her father's secretary Miss Ham (Margo Martindale). Miss Ham spends most of the movie translating to Penny how proud her father is of her, but she also helps with some much-needed confirmation that Penny is doing something that is okay even if it takes her away from her family.

The first time we see Penny take a stand is when she fires the trainer who took advantage of her father's state by trying to sell his horses for less than their worth to a stable he was working with. Penny is stern and strong and we see a glimmer of the capabilities of this heroine. With moments like this and moments where she marches unapologetically into a Gentlemen Only club, we are quickly faced with a heroine we can get excited about. Soon we watch her make the decision that will change her life forever. It appears that her father had set up a coin toss with the richest man in America to see which owner will get which foal of the union of his best stallion and her father's best two mares. There is one horse that everyone thinks will be the best choice, but Penny knows this is the wrong one. When she loses the coin toss, she wins the horse she already wanted. That foal grows up to become Secretariat.

Because of this acquisition, the trainer she scouted, Lucien Laurin (John Malkovich), joins her on her journey. Lucien never challenges Penny because of her gender. He respects and supports her and treats her as any other horse owner. This is a common thread with the other male characters on her team, the stable hand Eddie Sweat (Nelsan Ellis) and her rider, Ronnie Turcotte (Otto Thorwarth). The only men in her life who give her a tough time, other than opponents in competition and the media, are her brother and husband. Throughout the film Penny has to repeatedly reject coming home to her family in order give the proper attention to her new racing career. This is only punished in one moment where she misses her daughter's play and we witness her heartbreak while listening to it through the phone. Fortunately, most of the film is dedicated to Penny's journey to conquer the horseracing world. I want to be clear that I don't believe any semblance of her care for her family should be omitted; it just shouldn't overtake her success.

A scene that was deleted from *Secretariat*, but can be found as an extra on the DVD, is worth noting in the conversation of family. The scene shows Penny breaking down after her husband and children drive off. It's already been established that she misses her family and wants to repair her marriage. If the film continuously reminds us of this fact, her family problems will upstage her horseracing accomplishments. Cutting this scene allows us to see her sacrificing time with her family as another part of her journey, not a sacrifice that tarnishes it.

As we watch Secretariat grow, we also watch Penny try to balance her racing career with her household chores and tending to her husband. One night while Penny works late, Jack enters and the following conversation takes place:

PENNY: I'm almost done.
JACK: I know this is hard for you. How long do you think you can keep living two lives at once?
PENNY: The yearlings are looking good, especially the red one. We've cut expenses. We're breaking even.
JACK: I thought the point was to sell the farm, not break even.
PENNY: When I went off to college, I felt like that colt. Full of promise. Full of adventure, like I could make something work. I gave up a career to have our family, and this colt is part of our family now. I just want to see him run.
JACK: So after two years of juggling all of this, it isn't ending, it's just beginning.

Penny isn't swayed by Jack's disappointment. She's driven to follow through with something she feels she sacrificed long ago. It's her turn now and she's not taking no for an answer.

As Secretariat wins each race we are gifted the visual of Penny gaining more and more confidence and earning the respect of those around her. We also continuously check back in with Penny's ailing father who is quickly being surrounded by Secretariat's awards and trophies. Secretariat wins "Horse of the Year" and inspires Lucien to raise his glass and declare, "To its owner, who took on the old boys and won." She certainly did. Unfortunately, directly after this moment, Penny learns that her dad has suffered a stroke, redirecting the attention and credit back to her father. Although Penny's source of strength is her father, watching Penny stand her ground on important decisions is an empowering sight. She refuses to sell Secretariat even though her husband and her brother reveal that the family can't afford to cover the inheritance tax on her father's property. Because her father has left the welfare of the horses to Penny in his will, as the old saying goes, Penny is willing to "bet the farm" on Secretariat and no one can stop her.

It pays off. Secretariat wins the Kentucky Derby and then the Preakness, leaving only the Belmont Stakes to win to become the first horse to win the Triple Crown in 25 years. There is an interesting cinematic touch during the Preakness where instead of sitting in the stands with Penny, we are at home with Jack and her children as they watch it on TV. This isn't meant to illustrate her absence but instead celebrate how they are involved and proud of her success.

Before the Belmont Stakes, Penny receives some much-needed, and hard-earned, validation from her husband. Penny didn't need Jack's approval to succeed, but after he gave her such a tough time throughout her journey, she deserves to hear his support *before* she proves him wrong and wins. As they stand at the Belmont Ball, he admits:

> JACK: There's something I need you to know. I want you to win. And win or lose, you've taught our children what a real woman is and what it is to believe in yourself, and I never could have taught them either of those things. And you've taught me something, too.

After this beautiful admission, we watch Penny as she admires all of the important people in her life dancing together and smiling. She made sacrifices and they paid off. In the end, the reward was not just hers, it's also awarded to everyone she's touched. Penny is a role model. As she says to Secretariat before his final race, "I've realized something, I've already won. I made it here. I didn't quit. I've run my race. Now you run yours." She has won, no matter how this story ends. But as we find out, Penny gets it all. She gets her family *and* she gets to build a legacy in horseracing. Secretariat wins the Belmont Stakes and although the film finishes with Penny in the winner's circle with every influential person in her life, the final frame is reserved for her and Secretariat. This was her story and the best part is that we know this female's achievements happened off the silver screen as well.

It's true that there are constructed feminine qualities this film celebrates in Penny's character such as how the press continuously reminds us that Penny doesn't like to be in the limelight. They say she's selfless. But we know that she had to make some selfish decisions to achieve her goals. Selfish decisions are not within the construction of traditional femininity and amazingly enough Disney rewards Penny for hers. She certainly shed tears while missing her family, but she didn't quit for them. She may have strung her choices together on threads of advice her father gave her but it was Penny we saw make these decisions, not him. Remembering the actions of our previous cinematic female owners, we have to pay tribute to Penny for not selling her horse no matter the price. She kept Secretariat even if he might cost her more than she has. She just wanted to see him compete.

This is the truth of many owners. Many business-savvy people invest in teams because they love the game and want to be part of a sport. However, with the exception of Penny, these cinematic female owners represent the raw and unflinching darker side of the business of sports and in doing so easily become the villain. Do their actions mirror real decisions that exist in sports today? Yes. But in order to divert the harsh reality that sports are not always run by people who simply love the game, we embody that truth in a female representation and therefore *she* is the problem, not the way *owners* may handle their teams. By placing a female face on the problem, we are simply making women the target again.

There are women who are fully capable of taking on powerful roles in sports organizations, yet lack the opportunity simply because sports are still marked as a masculine territory. Sexism is the true star of the sports world. Everyday women are fighting for a place in the business of sports. Until we can watch Christina Pagniacci and Anita McCambridge be tough without hurting their organizations, we will continue to project a false argument that women are still too disconnected from sports to support it. Until Rachel Phelps can come forward and tell the truth about her success, the world of sports will continue to be the breeding ground and last frontier for patriarchal ideology. The good news is that we have been gifted Penny Chenery and with her story being the most recently told, let's hope it's a sign that we're headed in the right direction.

Conclusion

The cinematic portrayal of female athletes, coaches and owners can be an important source for women's empowerment. Fiction affords a freedom to challenge, create and celebrate women's accomplishments and imagine new possibilities. Rather than continuing archaic, predictable character dynamics, non-sexist innovations re-imagine the world outside of hegemonic, socially constructed definitions. Gone are the days where you only find women in sports films to create added conflicts for male sports heroes or pose as added trophies, mere symbols of a male athlete's on-the-field success. Now in some feature films, we can find leading heroines whose prominent roles in the sports world embody empowerment and influence a vision of equality. However, this has yet to become common.

Throughout these chapters I have presented the recurring patterns utilized in film to promote female subordination. It cannot be denied that these females are breaking barriers simply by existing in these sports. On the other hand, we cannot overlook what plot choices dictate her ultimate resolution. Let's reflect on the different conflicts and resolutions we've found throughout these films and offer guidelines for more positive portrayals.

First, I would like to discuss the lack of female athlete role models who are completely autonomous. These films are dominated, driven and controlled by male characters and these male characters often control every aspect of these female athletes' lives. It is not impractical to believe that these female athletes would only have male coaches, managers and trainers considering they are entering some sports that specifically lack female presence. However, it is problematic that men also direct their private lives. They stand as the prominent parent, husband or boyfriend whom she turns to for support and direction. In some cases, such as

Bad News Bears, Little Giants, The Cutting Edge, Wimbledon and *Girlfight* there is an absence of the mother completely. If these female athletes are breaking barriers with their passion and ability to play in a male-defined sport, then we need companion female characters who break their own barriers in supporting her, such as *Motocrossed.*

For several of the films that do have mothers, such as *Whip It, Love & Basketball, She's the Man, National Velvet* and *Million Dollar Baby,* they are only introduced to challenge and cause conflict for our female athlete. These films have continually placed our female athletes in comparison to the "traditional" women around them. In the case of *National Velvet,* Mrs. Brown helps Velvet achieve her dream but then serves as a reminder that Velvet must put her sport aside to become a "traditional" woman. There are other forms of empowerment for women than simply playing sports. We need more supporting female characters who present alternatives to what being a woman can mean. A few of these ideas are offered by Becky's aunt in *Little Giants* when she says, "Girls can run countries, they can sit on the Supreme Court, they can discover radium, but they can't play peewee football?" Perhaps we can watch a female athlete whose mother is currently sitting on the Supreme Court or discovering radium. If the person in charge of these female athletes is male, then that designates the world they're in. If these stories are based on our heroine's choices, or the choices of those around her, then let those choices be made by women.

Romantic interests are the easiest way to add conflict and resolution to a story. Does she get the guy or doesn't she? This is also the easiest method to celebrate gender definitions. What does she need to do to get the guy? Romantic relationships are a common plot device in every genre. They stand as an easy method to establish one aspect of the story that can be relatable to all audiences. An audience may not have experience playing football, but they've all had a crush or a relationship of some kind. However, in the specific world of the female athlete, a romantic relationship is often used strategically to ease the audience into the idea of her entrance into masculine territory. This is of course particular to heterosexuality.

As I have established, there is a distinct fear that female athleticism is associated with homosexuality. This creates a difficult predicament for how to challenge this plot dynamic. If she is heterosexual, then it seems like she is being saved from audience speculation or judgment. If she is homosexual, it furthers the homophobic presumption that all female athletes, because they are strong and/or "masculine," must be lesbians. So perhaps the answer is to present alternative power dynamics within the couple regardless of their gender. In *Pat and Mike,* we watched a role reversal in gender power. Although this simply swapped recognizable gender definitions, it presented a new view of a woman in charge. However, it would be best to move beyond emulating established male and female roles altogether. We need to create a dynamic that encompasses shared respect and shared power. We witnessed this in *Girlfight.* This is an important step towards re-imagining our positions in romantic relationships.

Another conflict we repeatedly see is the female athlete's struggle to be recognized as a skilled athlete rather than an anomaly. In the misfit storylines I've addressed, it is clear that the only thing missing for these female athletes is their invitation to play with skilled male athletes. They all have an elevated skill level in their sport. We need to stop making her gender the central issue for her placement with these unskilled boys. This continues the attention to solely reside on her being female and not her ability to play. We need to watch female athletes who play with skilled teams and among skilled players, such as the possibilities afforded in *She's the Man* and *Motocrossed.* There is no need to lose the misfit formula entirely. Should a film choose to use this storyline, make the female athlete unskilled as well. However, you must then place skilled females throughout the teams they face off against. The focus here is the acknowledgment that some athletes are simply more skilled than others, regardless of their gender. This includes female team sports. When watching cinematic portrayals of female athletes on female teams, we find an array of female-specific conflicts. In *A League of Their Own* and *Ladybugs,* these females simply stand as recognizable female stereotypes attached to their role as athletes. We need to embrace the diversity among women as athletes and as individuals. We cannot continue to compare them in order to celebrate the one who best fits the patriarchal female social construction.

These constructions continue into cinematic portrayals of non-team sports. Should she be an athlete competing in a solo sport, her conflict has less to do with her ability to participate, and more to do with her ability to be balanced with a female role such as girlfriend, daughter, wife or mother. By making these female athletes focus on whether or not they fit into a definable box, they are not allowed to fully find their potential as athletes. Effectively, their attention is diverted from their sport or even worse, they use their sport to enact these roles (e.g., sacrificing a win). In these stories the heroine has to recognize that her sport is outside the acceptable definition for her gender role in patriarchy. It is here that her choice matters most. Rather than trying to juggle both or surrendering to her "rightful place," she needs to take a stand. She needs to expose the deceitful power of definitions in the first place. She's already taken the first step by simply following her desire to play. Now we need to let her be skilled, let her prove her worth in her sport and then let her play.

The conflicts that our cinematic coaches and owners dealt with weren't so different from our female athletes. These women also faced the pressure to conform to recognizable female representations and suffered if they didn't. Whereas the female athlete can prove her worth on the playing field, women in managerial positions must prove their worth by instructing and directing the team to win. This takes a different set of skills that, logic would inform, is genderless. Although we get to witness a few occasions where cinematic female coaches prove this (e.g., *Wildcats* and *Eddie*), the position of owner created the harshest conditions for our female representations. With the exception of Penny, these women made poor decisions to help promote them as villains. Their knowledge of the sport and skills to run an organization should be celebrated and not used against them. What would help most is the visual confirmation of many female coaches and owners throughout sports films. Some may be good, some may be bad, but as long as there is a spectrum, then these female representations won't carry the burden of solely aligning powerful women with negative connotations. Much like the suggestion to have both skilled and unskilled girls in misfit storylines, we can place female coaches and owners in many minor roles throughout all sports films, such as the coach of an opposing team or another owner simply networking with our lead character. Not only will this enable the visual representation of gender equity in the sports world, but also it would allow cinema to introduce captivating new characters instead of reproducing men and women defined by antiquated ideas of gender.

Before you conclude that these changes preclude all possible elements of entertainment, let me remind you that competition in its own right is dramatic. The simple desire and strategy to win is a driving force for a climactic play in a game. Stories can include unskilled players, villainous rivals and even love stories, but be centered on the competition of the sport and not whether the players are men or women.

In truth, sports should be gender-blind. In reality, sports come down to a set of rules for strategic plays to win. Yes, the idea of winning, losing and domination are rooted in masculine ideology; however, if we strip a sport down to the bare rules we will see that elevated elements of violence are not necessary. Sports come down to scoring and how you score can come down to creative and strategically skilled play. The problems of violence are created once a sport is defined as a "combat" sport. These sports have an added strategy involving how hard you can hit players to render them ineffective. In a country where the sport of football is most popular and profitable, we have become accustomed to a certain amount of hitting to make things entertaining. As long as fighting is why people go to hockey games and montages of big hits in football are the highlights, sports will continue to be a breeding ground of hegemonic masculinity. We need to reclaim sport for what it is, an athletic realm based on physical skill and strategy, not brute strength and domination.

Film is a venue where we also see this celebration of "combat" sports. Everything is magnified in film for dramatic effect. How are we supposed to return to a bird's eye view of players maneuvering on a field in real time after we've been up close and personal watching the sweat slash away as a player is tackled to the ground in slow motion? With music, increased sound effects and editing, we are completely immersed in a constant moving highlight reel obscuring the flow of an actual complete game. These are all elements that lead viewers to want everything bigger, harder and faster. Films can also impress upon us what we are presumed to want in life. The glory of the game is not simply encapsulated in winning the game, but also winning the guy or girl, winning the respect from your parents and winning appreciation from the world. Films actively contribute to the ways in which people are understood and experienced in the "real world." This is why films have the capacity to change the way we view female athletes in reality. If we can cinematically imagine that a female athlete can have equal access to explore her skills in a predominantly male sport, without having to fit into a patriarchal definition, we can then apply this mentality in our everyday lives.

The bottom line is that sports are underestimated as a tool for equality between men and women. As Eileen McDonagh and Laura Pappano write in their book *Playing with the Boys: Why Separate Is Not Equal in Sports,* "If women cannot compete fairly on the field, they cannot compete fairly off it, either. As long as the phrase 'you play like a girl' remains an insult, female abilities are undervalued—for all women, whatever their race, class, or other birth characteristics."[1] They conclude, "The next frontier in the long history of achieving equal rights for women in the United States is *sports*."[2] Harry Edwards agrees in his article "Desegregating Sexist Sport": "No matter how vociferous women become in their quest for human rights, until they have succeeded in overthrowing male domination of sport, they might as well be running on a treadmill."[3] Sports are more than just a game on the field; they connect to both social and political realms of our society. We sing the national anthem before we engage in a game. The president of the United States personally invites the winners of our professional leagues to the White House. Even the Olympics have been utilized in political protest. Sports are one of the most influential institutions in our world. We must be aware of the implications when this much influence is present and there isn't an equal gender representation.

While I agree that the presence of females playing sports and exuding aggression has the ability to change social conditions and the status of women, not enough of the sports films I've discussed broadcast the full measure of social changes necessary to end sexism in sports. These female athletes (with the exception of Diana, Haley and Andrea) are still controlled and restricted by gender definitions. Their stories' non-sports conclusions (i.e., entering into relationship, being a mother, dying) overshadow their athletic actions. Sports and competition involve competitiveness and aggression that women have not previously been allowed to take part in. With that in mind, we must let aggression be a part of who these cinematic female athletes are and not a characteristic confined to their athletic identity.[4] Sports films cannot continue to send messages that aggression is the male domain. We must avoid associating the attributes of sports, such as competitiveness, strength and aggression, with maleness and instead see them as a part of human nature. Dottie from *A League of Their Own* should not have to sacrifice being athletic in order to care. Molly from *Wildcats* shouldn't be assumed to be less of a good mother while coaching football. Stories need to follow through with the image of Becky in *Little Giants,* standing at the end of the tunnel dressed as half cheerleader, half football player, as a space of possibility—deconstruction and reconstruction—in gender discourse.

It's important that I don't conclude this book without noting an important conversation of intersectionality, most specifically, a conversation about race. Of the 30 films discussed in this book, only five have non-white lead female characters: *Girlfight, Bend It Like Beckham, Love & Basketball, Juwanna Mann* and *Eddie.* Of those five films, four of them exhibit empowered portrayals of cinematic sports heroines. Feminist interpretation necessarily takes into account an Intersectional method, as explained by Patricia Hill Collins to mean that gender, race, ethnicity, class, religion, sexuality and nation always must be analyzed together, as these intersecting social statuses qualitatively influence the kinds of gender oppression an individual or group experiences.[5] For example, white women in white supremacist patriarchal cultures are considered the epitome of beauty and their femininity has long been linked with grace and passivity. But African American women, as a consequence of racism and a history of enslavement, have long been understood to be hypersexual and "savage," in these senses, of being more body than mind. With this in mind, one cannot deny critical thought about why Diana continues a life as a boxer whereas Maggie does not. These racially inflected stereotypes continue to influence popular representations.

To put it plainly, there needs to be a degendering of sports. As Mariah Burton Nelson writes in *The Stronger Women Get, the More Men Love Football:*

> When a woman steps out of the bleachers or slips off her cheerleader's costume and becomes an athlete herself, she implicitly challenges the association between masculinity and sports. She refutes the traditional feminine role (primarily for white women) of passivity, frailty and subservience. If a woman can play a sport—especially if she can play it better than many men—then that sport can no longer be used as a yardstick of masculinity.[6]

This can begin with our cinematic portrayals. Movies are the one place where anything can happen. Let the female athlete's skill speak for itself.

Let the best, not the biggest, team win. Let these cinematic sports heroines be represented as what they are: athletes, coaches and owners. There is no ultimate man, woman, ethnicity or class status; there are just people who differ in their talents and abilities. Sports are simply another avenue to celebrate these skills.

I dare you to search the Internet for the history of women's sports and not be astounded at how far back it goes and how grand it truly is. Women have been involved in sports since the late 1800s. Long before the AAGPBL, women were playing baseball. The first women's boxing match was held in 1876. The first international women's ice hockey tournament was played in 1916. Joan Payson became the first woman to buy a major league sports franchise when she co-founded and became majority owner of the New York Mets in 1961. And women have been playing and coaching rugby, the sport that American football originated from, since the 1970s. This is just a taste of the rich history of real female athletes, coaches and owners defying dated female constructions. It's about time their cinematic portrayals catch up.

Chapter Notes

Introduction

1. Using content analysis as a research method in her article "Bodies in Action: Female Athleticism on the Cinema Screen," Katharina Lindner observed that between the years of 1990 and 2006 (restricted to films produced within Western socio-cultural context) there had been "thirty-nine sports films with athletic *female* protagonists, while 164 films feature athletic *male* protagonists." Lindner continues, "Overall, 80 percent of all sports films depict male athletic characters only, while 14 percent depict female characters only, and 6 percent depict both male and female characters." Katherine Lindner, "Bodies in Action," *Feminist Media Studies* 11, no. 3 (2011): 325.

2. See also Harry M. Benshoff and Sean Griffin, *America on Film: Representing Race, Class, Gender, and Sexuality at the Movies* (West Sussex: Wiley-Blackwell, 2009).

3. Mariah Burton Nelson, *The Stronger Women Get, the More Men Love Football: Sexism and the American Culture of Sports* (New York: Harcourt Brace, 1994), 16.

4. Ernestine Miller, *Making Her Mark: Firsts and Milestones in Women's Sports* (Chicago: Contemporary Books, 2002), xiii.

5. See also Marita Digney, "No One Wins: The Miss America Pageant and Sports Contests as Failed Initiations" in *The Soul of Popular Culture: Looking at Contemporary Heroes, Myths and Monsters*, edited by Mary Lynn Kittelson (Chicago: Open Court, 1998), 268.

6. See also Lois Bryson, "Sport and the Maintenance of Masculine Hegemony" in *Women, Sport and Culture*, edited by Susan Birrell and Cheryl L. Cole (Champaign: Human Kinetics, 1994).

7. Abigail M. Feder, "'A Radiant Smile from a Lovely Lady': Overdetermined femininity in 'Ladies' Figure Skating," *Women on Ice: Feminist Essays on the Tonya Harding/Nancy Kerrigan Spectacle*, edited by Cynthia Baughman (New York: Routledge, 1995), 22.

8. In her article "Nancy and Tonya and Sonja: The Figure of the Figure Skater in American Entertainment," Jane Feuer writes, "Tonya Harding could never have made a career in the traditional figure skating image. Tonya was never 'artistic.' Her skating reputation was made on the basis of her triple jumps and power. Her image prior to the attack was one of an 'athlete,' so that when she became newsworthy, it was easy to add on 'working class' and 'slut.' Then Tonya could be opposed to Nancy, who was artistry/middle class/princess." Jane Feuer, "Nancy and Tonya and Sonja: The Figure of the Figure Skater in American Entertainment," in *Women on Ice: Feminist Essays on the Tonya Harding/Nancy Kerrigan Spectacle*, edited by Cynthia Baughman (New York: Routledge, 1995), 16–17.

9. See also Laura Mulvey, "Visual Pleasure and Narrative Cinema" in *Film Theory and Criticism*, edited by Leo Braudy and Marshall Cohen (New York: Oxford University Press, 2004) and Ann E. Kaplan, *Women and Film: Both Sides of the Camera* (New York: Methuen, 1993).

10. Harry Edwards, *Sociology of Sport* (Homewood: The Dorsey Press, 1973), 102.

11. Nelson argues that "the lesbian label used against female athletes (and against politicians, pilots, and other women who enter traditionally male domains) becomes clearer in this context: it names male fears of female empowerment." Nelson, *The Stronger Women Get, the More Men Love Football*, 40.

12. Jackie Byars found a common pattern in melodramas which she refers to as the "intruder-redeemer" theme: a male will enter the story, identify the problem (a heroine in need for one reason or another) and will offer a solution, most often, himself as the love interest. Jackie Byars, "Feminism, Psychoanalysis, and Female-Oriented Melodramas of the 1950s" in *Multiple Voices in Feminist Film Criticism*, edited by Diane Carson, Linda Dittmar and Janice R. Welsch (Minneapolis: University of Minnesota Press, 1994), 117.

Chapter 1

1. In *American Women and World War II,* Doris Weatherford writes, "Magazine ads showed starving prisoners of war clinging to barbed wire under tropical sun, looking desperately for help from beyond the seas. 'Womenpower Days' were declared with special stories and photographs of women at work. Posters proclaimed, 'Victory is in Your Hands,' 'Shopgirl Attacks Nazis,' and (trying to allay nagging doubt) 'War Workers Stay Womanly.'" This stood as a push for women to work but the start of a controlled effort to keep them "womanly." From the start of the war, "worry began over whether or not women would relinquish the gains they were making. At the same time that headlines pleaded for women to join the war industries, they also warned women not to take this call too seriously. The invitation was intended, it should be understood, for the duration only." Doris Weatherford, *Amer-ican Woman and World War II* (Edison: Castle Books, 2008), 117, 306.

2. Establishing this first female athlete in a younger age profile "feeds into heteronormative perceptions of acceptable female athleticism as a pre-adult phase to be ultimately outgrown as girls develop into women and acknowledge the duties and responsibilities of womanhood." Lindner, "Bodies in Action," 322.

3. In *Women in Baseball: The Forgotten History,* Gai Berlage shares, "The 1950s also brought major changes in the social definition of women's roles. Again there was strict sex-role segregation. The war was over, and women were expected to relinquish their jobs to the men. The ideal female role became that of full-time housewife and mother. Women's magazines such as *Good Housekeeping* glorified that role, and Americans seemed happy to embrace traditional roles once again. After the war's disruptions, family togetherness and stability were particularly appealing." This adds to the unique empowering quality of *Pat and Mike*. Gai Ingham Berlage, *Women in Baseball: The Forgotten History* (Westport: Praeger, 1994), 153.

4. Carlos Clarens, *George Cukor* (London: Secker & Warburg, 1976), 10.

5. Ibid.

6. Ibid., 71.

7. As Jay Coakley writes in *Sports in Society: Issues & Controversies,* "Both men and women are capable of violence on and off the playing field. However, women may not connect violent actions to their identities in the same way that some men do. Prevailing definitions of *masculinity* lead many people to feel that violence is more 'natural' for men than for women, and it may lead men to feel comfortable with violence in their sports." Jay Coakley, *Sports in Society: Issues & Controversies* (New York: McGraw-Hill, 2004), 209.

8. William Beard, *Persistence of Double Vision* (Edmonton: University of Alberta Press, 2000), ix.

9. Ibid.

10. Robert E. Kapsis and Kathie Coblentz, *Clint Eastwood: Interviews* (Jackson: University Press of Mississippi, 1999), viii.

11. Nat Hentoff, "Flight of Fancy," *Clint Eastwood: Interviews*, edited Robert E. Kapsis and Kathie Coblentz (Jackson: University Press of Mississippi, 1999), 156.

12. Henri Béhar. "Portrait of the Gunslinger as a Wise Old Man: Encounter with Clint Eastwood." *Clint Eastwood: Interviews*. Ed. Robert E. Kapsis, and Kathie Coblentz (Jackson: University Press of Mississippi, 1999), 190.

13. Leslie Heywood and Shari L. Dworkin, *Built to Win: The Female Athlete as Cultural Icon* (Minneapolis: University of Minnesota Press, 2003), 119.

14. Ibid., 121.

15. As Heywood and Dworkin write, "Though the movie can be read as reassurance to heterosexual viewers, it can also be read as an argument for a new heterosexual femininity that includes power of the female athlete as icon, as a challenge to assumptions about innate male superiority based on physical strength, a challenge that helps to establish a kind of flexible power differential that laws and claims for women's innate 'differences' often cannot." Heywood and Dworkin, *Built to Win,* 123.

16. "If observing the social roles of femininity leads women to hopelessness, sexual exploitation, and suicide as it does in *Girlfight,* observing the social roles of masculinity has for women the power to redress those wrongs and to make people see women as something rather than nothing, as beings-in-themselves rather than as solely beings-for-others." Ibid., 121.

17. As Maud Lavin writes, "With more women spending more of their adult lives in the workplace and living without a man, there is an increased awareness by many women of the necessity to be aggressive at times just to survive—for example, arguing, strategizing, and pushing for a raise." Maud Lavin, *Push Comes to*

Shove: New Images of Aggressive Women (Cambridge: MIT Press, 2010), 237.

Chapter 2

1. As Leora Tanenbaum writes, "like the suffragists of yore, girls and women involved in sports today, particularly team sports, represent a massive effort of female collaboration: To win a game, they must work together with members of the team." For women, "sports go against the grain of what is expected, since girls and women are not 'supposed' to be competitive and not 'supposed' to get down and dirty" (283). Leora Tanenbaum, *Catfight: Women and Competition* (New York: Seven Stories Press, 2002), 283, 284.

2. The league "promoted its players as good-looking, feminine, 'All-American' women who were teachers, secretaries, models clerks, and the like." Barbara Gregorich, *Women at Play: The Story of Women in Baseball* (Orlando: Harcourt Brace, 1993), 86.

3. The film was a commercial success even though most critics were not fans; they accused the film of carrying a condescending attitude toward women, "the absence of any real baseball being played" and Marshall "playing to easy laughs rather than taking a risk and elevating the film to more than just entertainment." Mary G. Hurd, *Women Directors and Their Films* (Westport: Praeger, 2007), 145.

4. "For these few hundred fortunate women, playing baseball instilled courage and confidence beyond measure, so that when the game was over a large number of them went on to become doctors, lawyers, teachers—professions beyond their means and expectations before their baseball careers." Gregorich, *Women at Play,* 88.

5. In *The Beauty Myth,* Naomi Wolf explains that "the quality called 'beauty' objectively and universally exists. Women must want to embody it and men must want to possess women who embody it. This embodiment is an imperative for

women and not for men, which situation is necessary and natural because it is biological, sexual, and evolutionary.... "Beauty" is a currency system like the gold standard. Like any economy it is determined by politics and in the modern age in the West it is the last, best belief system that keeps male dominance intact." Naomi Wolf, *The Beauty Myth: How Images of Beauty Are Used Against Women* (Lanham: Scarecrow, 2009), 12.

6. Alexander Doty argues, "The intense tensions and pleasures generated by the woman-woman and man-man aspects within the narratives of [traditional films addressed to straight audiences] create a space of sexual instability that already queerly positioned viewers can connect with in various ways, and within which straights might be likely to recognize and express their queer impulses." Alexander Doty, "There's Something Queer Here," *Out in Culture: Gay, Lesbian, and Queer Essays on Popular Culture*, edited by Corey K. Creekmur and Alexander Doty (Durham: Duke University Press, 1995), 77.

7. Sports embrace a "particular form of masculinity: toughness, aggression, denial of emotion, and a persistent denigration of all that's considered female." Nelson, *The Stronger Women Get, the More Men Love Football*, 6.

8. Derrick Henry, "Dorothy Kamenshek, 'League of Their Own' Figure, Dies at 84," *The New York Times*, 23 May 2010, New York ed.: A22.

9. Women are thought to naturally operate with more sympathy, easily connecting with others. As Tanenbaum astutely writes, "habitually jumping up to serve your husband coffee while he lounges on the sofa is the result of a power imbalance and social conditioning, not hormones. Empathy, in other words, is about power, not gender." Tanenbaum, *Catfight*, 60.

10. Gregorich, *Women at Play*, 88.

11. Shelley Calton, *Hard Knocks: Rolling with the Derby Girls* (Heidelberg: Kehrer Verlag, 2009), 11.

12. Ibid.

13. Mary Celeste Kearney writes, "Derby Skaters display their sexual agency in an ironic fashion *during* athletic competition, thereby confounding attempts of patriarchal, heteronormative recuperation.... While an increasing number of professional sports figures are 'sexing up' to supplement their paltry individual incomes, derby skaters exploit one of the new forms of power available to young females in order to keep their league afloat." Mary Celeste Kearney, "Tough Girls in a Rough Game: Televising the Unruly Female Athletes of Contemporary Roller Derby," *Feminist Media Studies* 11, no. 3, 286–287.

14. Michael Messner argues that violence is not an innate masculine skill of combat sports, the "tendency to utilize violence against others to achieve a goal in the sports context is learned behavior." Michael Messner, *Out of Play: Critical Essays on Gender and Sport* (Albany: State University of New York Press, 2007), 96.

Chapter 3

1. See also Eileen McDonagh and Laura Pappano, *Playing with the Boys: Why Separate Is Not Equal in Sports* (New York: Oxford University Press, 2008) x, 8.

2. David Zang writes, "The Bears offered the first film portrait of a new culture that no longer believed sport and good character were synonymous terms." Zang argues against the notion that *The Bad News Bears* is a direct predecessor to films such as the *Mighty Ducks* and *Little Giants*. These new Disney films may carry a connection in that they rely on the underdog triumphant format, but they also "rely heavily on good character and victory as the only real equalizers for one's lack of talent, wrong gender, or timorous bearing." David W. Zang, *Sports Wars: Athletes in the Age of Aquarius* (Fayetteville: University of Arkansas Press, 2001), 143, 153.

3. As Mulvey writes, "The man con-

trols the film phantasy and also emerges as the representative of power in a further sense: as the bearer of the look of the spectator, transferring it behind the screen to neutralize the extra-diegetic tendencies represented by woman as spectacle." Mulvey, "Visual Pleasure and Narrative Cinema," 842.

4. Jessica Gavora argues, "Whereas in every other area of life, from the military to the boardroom to the bedroom, women's rights activists have insisted that women be allowed to compete in the same arena with men, Title IX activists have worked in athletics to protect women's special status. They implicitly acknowledge that if women were forced to compete with men for positions on the playing field, very few would make the cut. On this narrow score, difference is accepted. But on every other count, sameness is insisted upon, and it is from this dubious premise that Title IX has come to have such an unsettling impact on athletes." Jessica Gavora, *Tilting the Playing Field: Schools, Sports, Sex and Title IX* (San Francisco: Encounter Books, 2002), 6.

5. Eleanor Byrne and Martin McQuillan, *Deconstructing Disney* (London: Pluto Press, 1999), 1–2.

6. Lavin refers to the action of introducing a female athlete in disguise as a "gender tease." These sequences involve a disguised female athlete "whose body language and aggressive risk taking means her playmates/competitors mistake her for a boy." Lavin writes, "I take these gender teases to be historically specific: for all the girls playing sports out there, we're still at a moment when unbridled and uninhibited athleticism is normally gendered as masculine—and it has to be demonstrated (still) that a girl can do this, too—even and especially a femme one. More than that, though, is the pleasure of mixing gender signs in the realm of aggression, and the creativity and deployment this implies for the subgroup, here women, formerly (and still in part) denied expression." Lavin, *Push Comes to Shove,* 66.

7. Nelson, *The Stronger Women Get, the More Men Love Football,* 25.

8. Remembering Jacky Byars "intruder/redeemer" theory we discussed with *National Velvet.* We are watching the same pattern develop in both *Bad News Bears* and *Little Giants.*

9. Mulvey, "Visual Pleasure and Narrative Cinema," 847.

10. As Nelson writes, "girls learn that female strength is unattractive to men, and that being attractive to men is paramount." Nelson, *The Stronger Women Get, the More Men Love Football,* 45.

Chapter 4

1. Edwards, *Sociology of Sport,* 231. See also Lindner, "Bodies in Action," 322.

2. *The Cutting Edge* grossed $25,105,517 domestically. http://www.imdb.com (accessed July 15, 2013).

3. *The Cutting Edge: Going for the Gold* (2006), *The Cutting Edge 3: Chasing the Dream* (2008) and *The Cutting Edge: Fire & Ice* (2010).

4. They were Victoria Azarenka, Serena Williams and Samantha Stosur. http://espn.go.com (accessed July 15, 2013). Furthermore, according to Forbes, Serena Williams' "$45 million in career prize money is the most of any female athlete and is fourth among all tennis players, male or female." http://forbes.com (accessed July 15, 2013).

5. In 1970, Patrice Donnelly set the college record in women's 100-meter hurdle at 13.5 seconds. She was once the fourth ranked hurdler in the world.

6. Roger Ebert wrote that *Personal Best* was "one of the healthiest and sweatiest celebrations of physical exertion I can remember." He continues, "It is filled with uncertainties, risks, cares, and rewards of real life, and it considers its characters' hearts and minds, and sees their sexuality as an expression of their true feelings for each other." Roger Ebert, *Move Home Companion: 400 Films on Cassette, 1980–*

1985 (Kansas City: Andrews & McMeel, 1986), 245.

7. See also Linda Williams, "Personal Best Women in Love" in *Women, Sport, and Culture,* edited by Susan Birrell and Cheryl L. Cole (Champaign: Human Kinetics, 1994).

Chapter 5

1. RuPaul, *Lettin' It All Hang Out: An Autobiography* (New York: Hyperion, 1996), viii.

2. As Judith Butler introduces her concept of performativity, she writes, "When the constructed status of gender is theorized as radically independent of sex, gender itself becomes a free-floating artifice, with the consequence that *man* and *masculine* might just as easily signify a female body as a male one, and *woman* and *feminine* a male body as easily as a female one." She continues, "As much as drag creates a unified picture of 'woman' (what its critics often oppose), it also reveals the distinctness of those aspects of gendered experience which are falsely naturalized as a unity through the regulatory fiction of heterosexual coherence." Judith Butler, *Gender Trouble* (New York: Routledge Classics, 1990), 8, 187.

3. Nelson reveals, "Men's strength advantage is actually marginal, meaning that there is more variation among individual men than between the average man and the average woman." There is also a misnomer that sports gender indifference is based on the nature of women and men's bodies. As she writes, "few professional athletes have 'natural' bodies; otherwise we'd bump into pro football–sized men in the supermarkets." The training and diet of athletes change their bodies tremendously. Perhaps the most common argument against an equal playing field is brute strength and body size, an argument that has been manipulated by sports media. As Nelson writes, "But because sports seem natural, and because in the sports media we so often see men who are bigger and stronger than the biggest, strongest women, these men make a convincing subliminal case: not only are men better athletes, men are superior physical specimens. And because the men engaged in sporting events are so often enacting some form of mock combat, we receive the message: Men are inherently, naturally aggressive and, as a gender dominant." Nelson, *The Stronger Women Get, the More Men Love Football,* 57, 61.

4. See also Wolf, *The Beauty Myth,* 12.

5. See also Kathleen Rowe, *The Unruly Woman* (Austin: University of Texas Press, 1995).

6. *Juwanna Mann*'s domestic total gross was $13,670,733. http://boxofficemojo.com (accessed July 17, 2013).

7. Although dunking is less common in women's basketball, it is allowed. Only six dunks total have been scored in the WNBA and one in the Olympics. In "Below the Rim: Why Are There So Few Dunks in Women's Basketball?" Brian Palmer blames a difference in height and vertical leap between women and men. He also shared that many coaches advise against dunking due to risk of injury and throwing away the opportunity for an easy two points. http://www.slate.com (accessed July 17, 2013).

Chapter 6

1. According to D. Stanley's Eitzen's book *Fair and Foul: Beyond the Myths and Paradoxes of Sport,* as of 2009, women ran only 18.6 percent of women's intercollegiate programs. Astonishingly, as a whole, only 17.7 percent of head coaches of men's and women's teams were women. Also take into account that fewer than two percent of women's positions in men's programs were in combined men's and women's sports such as track, swimming and tennis. D. Stanley Eitzen, *Fair and Foul: Beyond the Myths and Paradoxes of Sport* (Lanham, MD: Rowman & Littlefield, 2009), 151. The International Olympic Committee, one of the most powerful administrations

in sports, had no women involved until the 1980s. As of 2013, only 16 of the 107 members of the IOC are female. Coakley, *Sports in Society,* 255.

2. Women coached 90 percent of women's teams when Title IX was passed. Once Title IX had been put into action in 1978, that number dropped to 58 percent. By 2002, it dropped even further to 44 percent. Coakley, *Sports in Society,* 254.

3. Coakley writes, "coaching and other forms of leadership in sports often are seen in terms that are consistent with traditional ideas about masculinity: if you 'coach like a girl,' you are doing it wrong; if you 'coach like a man,' you are doing it right. Under these conditions, women get jobs only when they present compelling objective evidence of their qualifications, combined with other evidence that they can do things the way successful men have done them in the past." Coakley, *Sports in Society,* 256.

4. See also Nelson, *The Stronger Women Get, the More Men Love Football,* 165–194.

5. In traditional societal context, male coaches have a "two-person single career" meaning they coach while their wives take care of the kids. It's also still true that some wives take on another aspect of supporting their husbands by hosting events and dinners for the team and recruits. Female coaches can be seen to have a "one-person dual career." They must coach and care for the team *and* their children. This is represented quite clearly in *Wildcats.* Whereas we watch Molly try to balance her attention to her kids and her attention to coaching, there is no male character who is even revealed to have a family that requires any of their attention. Annelies Knoppers, "Gender and the Coaching Profession" in *Women, Sport, and Culture,* edited by Susan Birrell and Cheryl L. Cole, (Champaign: Human Kinetics, 1994), 124, 125.

Chapter 7

1. James Gilligan, author of *Preventing Violence,* a book that argues shame as the leading cause of violence, asserts that "violence for men is successful as a strategy. Women, however, are shamed for being too active and aggressive (called bitches or unfeminine) and honored for being passive and submissive." We watch these cinematic female owners have to match their male counterpart's aggression in order to be effective. Unfortunately, when these heroines enact this aggression, they are punished for it. James Gilligan, *Preventing Violence* (New York: Thames & Hudson, 2001), 39.

2. See also Judith A. Cramer, "Conversations with Women Sports Journalists" in *Women, Media and Sport: Challenging Gender Values,* edited by Pamela J. Creedon (Thousand Oaks: Sage, 1994).

3. The sports world doesn't just reflect masculinity, as Michael Messner argues; it amplifies it. He goes on to explain that the common aspects of boys' and men's sports are "dominance bonding in the male peer group; a suppression of empathy toward self and others; and a 'culture of silence' in the peer group—which together tend to enable some men's sexual violence against women." The core of "dominance bonding" can be found in the locker room. This is where a man's only rival in his quest to prove himself is other men. The education and competition in words and actions breed hegemonic masculinity. An athlete must have empathy for his opponent to succeed. That empathy crosses over into the treatment of women. If a player does not follow in the mental trend of toughness or keep silent of judging his teammates, he is emasculated and assumed the worst, a homosexual. Michael A. Messner, *Out of Play: Critical Essays on Gender and Sport* (Albany: State University of New York, 2007), 107, 109. Furthermore, Gilligan notes that "in patriarchal societies men are assigned the role of 'violence-objects,' and women are assigned the role of 'sex-objects.' *Major League* is a movie about men. Men cannot be dominated or else they are shamed. So Rachel must be

defeated in the only way properly supporting masculinity: violence." Gilligan, *Preventing Violence,* 59.

Conclusion

1. McDonagh and Pappano, *Playing with the Boys,* 6.

2. Ibid., 7.

3. Harry Edwards, "Desegregating Sexist Sport," in *Out of the Bleachers: Writings on Women and Sport,* edited by Stephanie L. Twin (New York: Feminist Press, 1979), 118.

4. As Lavin writes, "if there's a widening of the range of women's ability to express, articulate, and represent their own aggression, this would mean an expansion in the identity 'woman.'" Lavin, *Push Comes to Shove,* 5.

5. Patricia Hill Collins, *Black Feminist Thought: Knowledge, Consciousness, and the Politics of Empowerment* (New York: Routledge, 2000).

6. Nelson, *The Stronger Women Get, the More Men Love Football,* 27.

Bibliography

Any Given Sunday. Dir. Oliver Stone. Warner Bros. Pictures, 1999. Film.

The Bad News Bears. Dir. Michael Ritchie. Paramount Pictures , 1976. Film.

Bad News Bears . Dir. Richard Linklater. Paramount Pictures, 2005. Film.

Baughman, Cynthia. *Women on Ice: Feminist Essays on the Tonya Harding/Nancy Kerrigan Spectacle.* New York: Routledge, 1995. Print.

Beard, William. *Persistence of Double Vision.* Edmonton: University of Alberta Press, 2000. Print.

Béhar, Henri. "Portrait of the Gunslinger as a Wise Old Man: Encounter with Clint Eastwood." *Clint Eastwood: Interviews.* Edited by Robert E. Kapsis and Kathie Coblentz. Jackson: University Press of Mississippi, 1999. Print.

Bend It Like Beckham. Dir. Gurinder Chadha. 20th Century–Fox, 2002. Film.

Benshoff, Harry M., and Sean Griffin. *America on Film: Representing Race, Class, Gender, and Sexuality at the Movies.* West Sussex: Wiley-Blackwell, 2009. Print.

Berlage, Gai Ingham. *Women in Baseball: The Forgotten History.* Westport: Praeger, 1994. Print.

Blue Crush. Dir. John Stockwell. Universal Studios, 2002. Film.

Bryson, Lois. "Sport and the Maintenance of Masculine Hegemony." *Women, Sport and Culture.* Edited by Susan Birrell and Cheryl L. Cole. Champaign: Human Kinetics, 1994. Print.

Butler, Judith. *Gender Trouble: Feminism and the Subversion of Identity.* New York: Routledge, 1990. Print.

Byars, Jackie. "Feminism, Psychoanalysis, and Female-Oriented Melodramas of the 1950s." *Multiple Voices in Feminist Film Criticism.* Edited by Diane Carson, Linda Dittmar, and Janice R. Welsch. Minneapolis: University of Minnesota Press, 1994. Print.

_____. "Gaze/Voices/Power: Expanding Psychoanalysis for Feminist Film and Television Theory." *Female Spectators: Looking at Film and Television.* Edited by E. Deidre Pibram. London: Verso, 1988.

Byrne, Eleanor, and Martin McQuillan. *Deconstructing Disney.* London: Pluto Press, 1999. Print.

Cahn, Susan. "No Freaks, No Amazons, No Boyish Babes." *Chicago History Magazine* (Spring 1989): 30. Print.

Calton, Shelley. *Hard Knocks: Rolling with the Derby Girls.* Heidelberg: Kehrer Verlag, 2009. Print.

Clarens, Carlos. *George Cukor.* London: Secker & Warburg, 1976. Print.

Coach. Dir. Bud Townsend. Marimark Productions, 1978. Film.

Coakley, Jay. *Sports in Society: Issues & Controversies.* New York: McGraw-Hill, 2004. Print.

Collins, Patricia Hill. *Black Feminist Thought: Knowledge, Consciousness, and the Politics of Empowerment.* New York: Routledge, 2000. Print.

Cramer, Judith A. "Conversations with Women Sports Journalists." *Women,*

Media and Sport: Challenging Gender Values. Edited by Pamela J. Creedon. Thousand Oaks: Sage, 1994. Print.

The Cutting Edge. Dir. Paul Michael Glaser. Metro-Goldwyn-Mayer, 1992. Film.

D2: The Mighty Ducks. Dir. Sam Weisman. Buena Vista International, 1994. Film.

Digney, Marita. "No One Wins: The Miss America Pageant and SportsContests as Failed Initiations." *The Soul of Popular Culture: Looking at Contemporary Heroes, Myths and Monsters.* Edited by Mary Lynn Kittelson. Chicago: Open Court, 1998. Print.

Doty, Alexander. "There's Something Queer Here." *Out in Culture: Gay, Lesbian, and Queer Essays on Popular Culture.* Edited by Corey K Creekmur and Alexander Doty. Durham: Duke University Press, 1995. Print.

Ebert, Roger. *Movie Home Companion: 400 Films on Cassette, 1980–85.* Kansas City: Andrews & McMeel, 1986. Print.

Eddie. Dir. Steve Rash. Hollywood Pictures, 1996. Film.

Edwards, Harry. "Desegregating Sexist Sport." *Out of the Bleachers: Writings on Women and Sport.* Edited by Stephanie L. Twin. New York: Feminist Press, 1979. Print.

_____. *Sociology of Sport.* Homewood: The Dorsey Press, 1973. Print.

Eitzen, Stanley D. *Fair and Foul: Beyond the Myths and Paradoxes of Sport.* Lanham, MD: Rowman & Littlefield, 2009. Print.

Feder, Abigail M. "'A Radiant Smile from a Lovely Lady': Overdetermined Femininity in 'Ladies' Figure Skating." *Women on Ice: Feminist Essays on the Tonya Harding/Nancy Kerrigan Spectacle.* Edited by Cynthia Baughman. New York: Routledge, 1995. Print.

Feuer, Jane. "Nancy and Tonya and Sonja: The Figure of the Figure Skater in American Entertainment." *Women on Ice: Feminist Essays on the Tonya Harding/Nancy Kerrigan Spectacle.* Edited by Cynthia Baughman. New York: Routledge, 1995. Print.

Fuller, Linda K. *Sport, Rhetoric, and Gender: Historical Perspectives and Media Representations.* New York: Palgrave Macmillan, 2006. Print.

Gavora, Jessica. *Tilting the Playing Field: School, Sports, Sex and Title IX.* San Francisco: Encounter Books, 2002. Print.

Gilligan, James. *Preventing Violence.* New York: Thames & Hudson, 2001. Print.

Girlfight. Dir. Karyn Kusama. 20th Century–Fox, 2000. Film.

Gourlie, John M. "*Million Dollar Baby:* The Deep Heart's Core." *Clint Eastwood: Actor and Director.* Edited by Leonard Engel. Salt Lake City: University of Utah Press, 2007. Print.

Gregorich, Barbara. *Women at Play: The Story of Women in Baseball.* Orlando: Harcourt Brace, 1993. Print.

Halberstam, Judith. *Female Masculinity.* Durham: Duke University Press, 1998. Print.

Henry, Derrick. "Dorothy Kamenshek, 'League of Their Own' Figure, Dies at 84." *The New York Times*, 23 May 2010. New York ed., A22. Print.

Hentoff, Nat. "Flight of Fancy." *Clint Eastwood: Interviews.* Edited by Robert E. Kapsis and Kathie Coblentz. Jackson: University Press of Mississippi, 1999. Print.

Heywood, Leslie, and Shari L. Dworkin. *Built to Win: The Female Athlete as Cultural Icon.* Minneapolis: University of Minnesota Press, 2003. Print.

Hurd, Mary G. *Women Directors and Their Films.* Westport: Praeger, 2007. Print.

Juwanna Mann. Dir. Jesse Vaughan. Warner Bros., 2002. Film.

Kaplan, Ann E. *Women and Film: Both Sides of the Camera.* New York: Methuen, 1983. Print.

Kapsis, Robert E., and Kathie Coblentz. *Clint Eastwood: Interviews.* Jackson:

University Press of Mississippi, 1999. Print.

Kearney, Mary Celeste. "Tough Girls in a Rough Game." *Feminist Media Studies* 11, no. 3, 283–301. Print.

Knoppers, Annelies. "Gender and the Coaching Profession." *Women, Sport and Culture*. Edited by Susan Birrell and Cheryl L. Cole. Champaign: Human Kinetics, 1994. Print.

Ladybugs. Dir. Sidney J Furie. Paramount Pictures, 1992. Film.

Lavin, Maud. *Push Comes to Shove: New Images of Aggressive Women*. Cambridge: MIT Press, 2010. Print.

A League of Their Own. Dir. Penny Marshall. Columbia Pictures, 1992. Film.

A League of Their Own: The Documentary. Dir. Mary Wallace. Columbia Tristar , 1994. Film.

Lindner, Katharina. "Bodies 'in Action': Female Athleticism on the Cinema Screen." *Feminist Media Studies* 11, no. 3 (2011): 321–345. Print.

Little Giants. Dir. Duwayne Dunham. Warner Bros., 1994. Film.

The Longshots. Dir. Fred Durst. Dimension Films, 2008. Film.

Lorber, Judith. *The Politics of Women's Bodies: Sexuality, Appearance, and Behavior*. New York: Oxford University Press, 2010. Print.

Love & Basketball. Dir. Gina Prince-Bythewood. New Line Cinema, 2000. Film.

Major League. Dir. David S. Ward. Paramount Pictures, 1989. Film.

McDonagh, Eileen, and Laura Pappano. *Playing with the Boys: Why Separate Is Not Equal in Sports*. New York: Oxford University Press, 2008. Print.

Messner, Michael A. *Out of Play: Critical Essays on Gender and Sport*. Albany: State University of New York Press, 2007. Print.

The Mighty Ducks. Dir. Stephen Herek. Buena Vista International, 1992. Film.

The Mighty Macs. Dir. Tim Chambers. Quaker Media, 2009. Film.

Miller, Ernestine. *Making Her Mark: Firsts and Milestones in Women's Sports*. Chicago: Contemporary Books, 2002. Print.

Million Dollar Baby. Dir. Clint Eastwood. Warner Bros., 2004. Film.

Motocrossed. Dir. Steve Boyum. Disney Channel, 2001. Film.

Mulvey, Laura. "Visual Pleasure and Narrative Cinema." *Film Theory and Criticism*. Edited by Leo Braudy and Marshall Cohen. New York: Oxford University Press, 2004. Print.

National Velvet. Dir. Clarence Brown. Metro-Goldwyn-Mayer (MGM), 1944. Film.

Nelson, Mariah Burton. *The Stronger Women Get, the More Men Love Football: Sexism and the American Culture of Sports*. New York: Harcourt Brace, 1994. Print.

Pat and Mike. Dir. George Cukor. Metro-Goldwyn-Mayer (MGM), 1952. Film.

Personal Best. Dir. Robert Towne. The Geffen Company, 1982. Film.

Rowe, Kathleen. *The Unruly Woman*. Austin: University of Texas Press, 1995. Print.

RuPaul. *Lettin' it All Hang Out: An Autobiography*. New York: Hyperion, 1996. Print.

Scraton, Sheila, and Anne Flintoff. *Gender and Sport: A Reader*. London: Routledge, 2002. Print.

Secretariat. Dir. Randall Wallace. Walt Disney Pictures, 2010. Film.

She's the Man. Dir. Andy Fickman. Dreamworks SKG, 2006. Film.

Slap Shot. Dir. George Roy Hill. Universal Pictures, 1977. Film.

Stick It. Dir. Jessica Bendinger. Buena Vista Pictures, 2006. Film.

Tanenbaum, Leora. *Catfight: Women and Competition*. New York: Seven Stories Press, 2002. Print.

Wasko, Janet. *Understanding Disney: The Manufacture of Fantasy*. Malden: Blackwell Publishers , 2001. Print.

Weatherford, Doris. *American Woman*

and World War II. Edison: Castle Books, 2008. Print.

Whip It. Dir. Drew Barrymore. Fox Searchlight Pictures, 2009. Film.

Wildcats. Dir. Michael Ritchie. Warner Bros., 1986. Film.

Williams, Linda. "Personal Best: Women in Love." *Women, Sport, and Culture.* Edited by Susan Birrell and Cheryl L. Cole. Champaign: Human Kinetics, 1994. Print.

Wimbledon. Dir. Richard Loncraine. Universal Studios, 2004. Film.

Wolf, Naomi. *The Beauty Myth: How Images of Beauty Are Used Against Women.* New York: Harper Perennial, 2002. Print.

Zang, David W. *Sports Wars: Athletes in the Age of Aquarius.* Fayetteville: University of Arkansas Press, 2001. Print.

Index